Home in the Islands

HOME IN THE ISLANDS

Housing and Social Change in the Pacific

EDITED BY

Jan Rensel and Margaret Rodman

UNIVERSITY OF HAWAI'I PRESS, HONOLULU

HD
7387.55
A3
H65
1997

97 98 99 00 01 02   5 4 3 2 1

Library of Congress Cataloging-in-Publication Data
Home in the islands : housing and social change in the Pacific /
edited by Jan Rensel and Margaret Rodman.
p.   cm.
Includes bibliographical references and index.
ISBN 0–8248–1682–X (cloth : alk. paper). — ISBN 0–8248–1934–9
(paper : alk. paper)
1. Housing—Pacific Area—Case studies.   2. Pacific Area—Social
conditions—Case studies.   I. Rensel, Jan, 1951–   . II. Rodman,
Margaret, 1947–   .
HD7387.55.A3H65   1997
363.5'099—dc21   97–789
CIP

Book design by Kenneth Miyamoto

To our parents,
*the first to teach us the meaning
of home*

Contents

Prologue

∩

MARGARET RODMAN

THE HOUSES that caught my eye were the ones that moved.[1] They were almost where I remembered them, where as an anthropologist I had mapped them—but not quite. The village in the hills of Ambae, Vanuatu, looked the same as I remembered it from an earlier field trip. In our own bamboo house nothing seemed to have changed. A Canadian flag and fly-specked photos from a Minolta calendar still decorated the walls. My husband, Bill, who had not smoked a pipe in the three years since we had left Ambae, found a handful of pipe cleaners in a jar on the table. Our son at age six had made a paper airplane of which he had been very proud; spider webs reinforced the thread by which it now hung from the ceiling. In our house, if you ignored the mildew, everything looked the same.

The rest of the village had an equally timeless quality. I doubt I would have noticed the changes in houses and what they said about changing social relationships if I had not remapped the village. One house had turned its back on its neighbor. Another had pivoted a quarter turn. Other houses seemed not to have moved, but, as if splashed by fragments from the moving houses, their walls bore the paint and distinctive woven bamboo panels of dwellings I remembered from years past, which, when I looked for them, were gone. The moving houses were both unknown and yet remembered places through which I could now see processes of change that had been going on all along. I had not seen them before, both because they were subtle, and because I had not looked for them.

The maps of a portion of the village (figures 1 and 2) show what I mean. The map in figure 1 was drawn when I first saw the moving houses. It shows changes that occurred between 1978[2] when I first

1

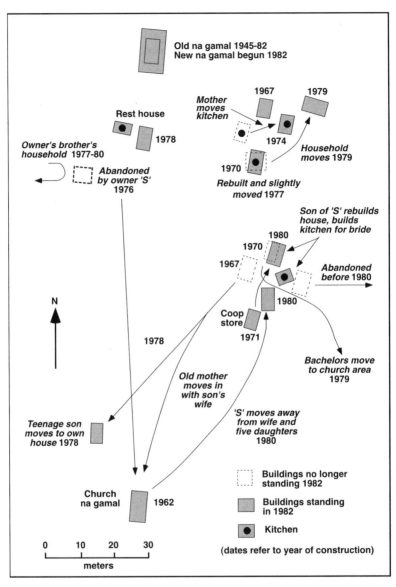

Old na gamal 1945-82
New na gamal begun 1982

Rest house

Owner's brother's
household 1977-80

1978

Mother
moves
kitchen

1967   1979

1974

1970

Household
moves 1979

Rebuilt and slightly
moved 1977

Abandoned
by owner 'S'
1976

Son of 'S' rebuilds
house, builds
kitchen for bride

1980

1970

1967

Abandoned
before 1980

N

1980

Coop
store

1971

Bachelors move
to church area
1979

1978

Old mother
moves in
with son's
wife

'S' moves away
from wife and
five daughters
1980

Teenage son
moves to own
house 1978

Buildings no longer
standing 1982

Buildings standing
in 1982

Church
na gamal

1962

Kitchen

0   10   20   30

(dates refer to year of construction)

meters

1 Movement of houses and people, Lovatuweliweli hamlet (Vanuatu),
1982

mapped the village and 1982 when we returned. We occupied the
building labeled "rest house." Local people had built the house for us
in 1978. The final account on a sheet torn from a school exercise
book was headed "How we used up all your money." To us, a thousand dollars for a house of bamboo with an iron roof and woven

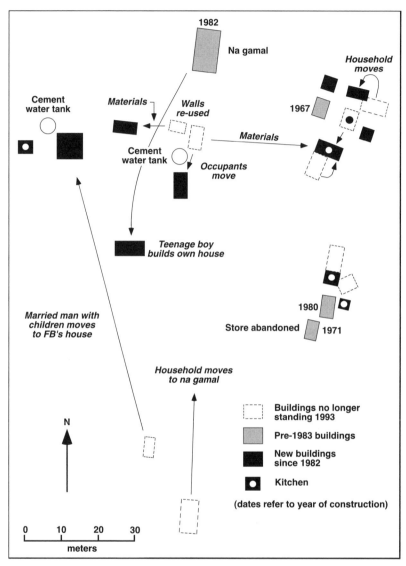

2 Movement of houses and people, Lovatuweliweli hamlet (Vanuatu), 1993

split-bamboo floor, plus detached kitchen, seemed good value. It was the first house we had owned. (When we returned to Canada and bought our second home, it was much better at using up all our money.)

The name "rest house" was wishful thinking on our part. We intended our bamboo house to be a gift to the community, a way of

reciprocating people's hospitality to us anthropologists, and hope-
fully an opportunity for local people to attract some tourist dollars
from adventurous travelers who wanted to experience life in an
"authentic" Vanuatu village. But almost no one came, and when we
returned it seemed that the house could never become a community
house, because it was ours. However, because it was ours, it could be
occupied by our relatives, and after we left in 1982, it was. The son
of the old chief who adopted Bill moved into his Canadian brother's
house for a while. The chief's sister's son ("S" on the maps), driven
out of the house to the south of ours because he thought the place
was "poisoned" and was making him sick, moved with his wife and
children to the church hall (church *na gamal*) and later to the chief's
new *na gamal,* rebuilt on the site of the old one.[3] A few years later,
this ill-fated man dropped dead while leading a traditional dance at a
saint's day celebration. His widow moved into our house and the
chief's son moved back to the compound in the northeast of the map.
Not all these moves are shown on the maps, which capture between
them only three points in time (1979, 1982, and 1993). I recount
them to suggest the extent to which people move between houses.

Not only the people, but the houses were moving, as the rotated
buildings on the right side of both maps suggest. In the best of
circumstances houses of bamboo do not last long, often no more
than ten years. The necessity of periodic repair and reconstruction
provides frequent opportunities for change. The domestic cycle
places demands on housing in Vanuatu, as anywhere, but houses
can change easily in response to changing household needs. When
the family size increases or decreases, instead of buying another
house or building an addition, people can build another house, say,
for teenage boys, using natural materials that are freely available or
inexpensive.

Frequent cyclones speed the process of destruction and make the
need to rebuild tediously frequent. In 1985, for example, 90 percent
of the housing on Ambae was destroyed in a single storm.[4] Thatched
roofs and bamboo walls are constructed in prefabricated panels; in
most cases, some panels from walls and roofs that had blown off
could be salvaged. Often they did not end up on the original house,
which might have been rebuilt on the same site, moved slightly, moved
a lot, or rebuilt as a smaller dwelling or a kitchen. Social relationships in the village could be read in the built form by noting whose
walls ended up on whose house, which way the houses faced, and
who lived in them.

In the end, our house moved, too. When we visited in 1985, its floor and walls had been repaired, but the house posts were weak. Still, the house was remarkably well-built and lasted, with further repairs, until 1992. When we received word that our house had finally fallen down in a cyclone, we sent money to have it rebuilt. We knew that S's widow and her daughters had been living in the house and that they would make room for us when we came back. When we arrived in August 1993, we found that part of the old walls had made their way down to Bill's brother's place, while other bits were used to build a dwelling to our west, where the widow and daughters were sleeping.

We were surprised and somewhat disoriented to find that *the house was not even where we had left it.* It had moved about ten meters; it faced no longer north, but east; and the layout had changed completely. To local people, our house was still our house, complete with the Canadian flag, although the Minolta photos, the pipe cleaners, and paper airplane from 1978 were finally gone. To us, the house was at once hauntingly familiar, yet strange.

Our house in Vanuatu, like many of those discussed in this book, gives material expression to processes of social change so subtle and gradual that to casual observers nothing seems to have altered. Such ordinary modifications in domestic space seem cyclical, but they do not end quite where they started. Other changes in housing considered here—from remote islands to urban environments in the Pacific —are more extraordinary, and their causes and consequences more dramatic. Our home in the islands offers a beginning and an ending to the chapters that follow.

Notes

Figures 1 and 2 originally appeared as figures 3.5 and 3.6 on pp. 100 and 101, respectively, in a chapter by Margaret Rodman in *Land, Custom and Practice in the South Pacific,* edited by Prof. R. G. Ward and Elizabeth Kingdon (Cambridge, 1995). The figures are reproduced here with the permission of Professor Ward and Ms. Kingdon and of Cambridge University Press, Australian Branch.

1. A more academic version of the 1982 portion of this research experience appeared in *American Anthropologist* (Rodman 1985).

2. This was our second field trip but the first time that I had lived in or mapped this village. My husband, William Rodman, and I have made five visits to Vanuatu between 1969 and 1993. I am grateful to the Social Sciences and Humanities Research Council of Canada for its frequent support

in the form of doctoral and postdoctoral fellowships, research grants, and a research time stipend, and to the Wenner Gren Foundation and York University for funding the 1993 research.

3. The term *"na gamal"* is used widely in Vanuatu for a men's gathering place where kava is consumed. In the south of the group, these are often clearings in the bush, but in the north they tend to be buildings facing a cleared area suitable for kava consumption. On Ambae, a *na gamal* has a rectangular floor plan with a thatched roof that, ideally, reaches the ground on the long sides of the building. In the past, women were not allowed in a *na gamal,* but even a *na gamal* in traditional style is no longer off-limits to women. Today, while the traditional style is admired and leaders aspire to build such a *na gamal,* the term is used generically for many kinds of meeting houses. One finds a church *na gamal* (see south of map in figure l) in many villages, serving as a parish hall and kitchen. The *na gamal* shown in the north of the village on both maps belonged to the local leader who adopted Bill. The *na gamal* on the site in 1978 was rectangular but walled rather than roofed to the ground. In l982, the leader organized the rebuilding of the *na gamal* so that it was larger and more traditional in appearance.

4. We present the narratives people told about the storm and its aftermath in Rodman and Rodman (1992).

1
Introduction

JAN RENSEL

ORDINARY HOUSES have extraordinary stories to tell. Grand, monumental, and ceremonial structures frequently inspire awe and analysis, but mundane, domestic arenas we most often take for granted. It is true that unusual events—such as having to move, coping with damage or loss, or embarking on fieldwork in a strange place—will focus our attention on housing for a time. But as the crisis passes, housing generally recedes to the background of our consciousness. As a result, much of what we could learn from it "goes without saying" (Carsten and Hugh-Jones 1995, 3–4; see also Bloch 1992).

Yet anthropological studies have been providing insights into humanity's relationships with housing for more than a century. Some of the earliest ethnographers (e.g., Morgan 1965 [1881], Durkheim and Mauss 1963 [1903]) explored a reciprocal dynamic that is fundamental to the interaction of people and housing: People shape their living spaces, which in turn influence how they live their lives and help to perpetuate the cultural structures that produced them.[1] This is not a homeostatic process, however; people not only house themselves but modify their houses, and even redefine their purposes and meanings. Housing may function as shelter, container, status symbol, home; it may provide a basis of belonging, represent membership in or dominance by an encompassing macro-society, or assert cultural uniqueness or resurgence.

Architects, along with anthropologists, geographers, folklorists, and historians continue to be fascinated with describing the multiple factors that help to explain variability in, and distribution of, built forms (especially those identified as vernacular or traditional; see below). In their review article, Lawrence and Low (1990) canvass the

7

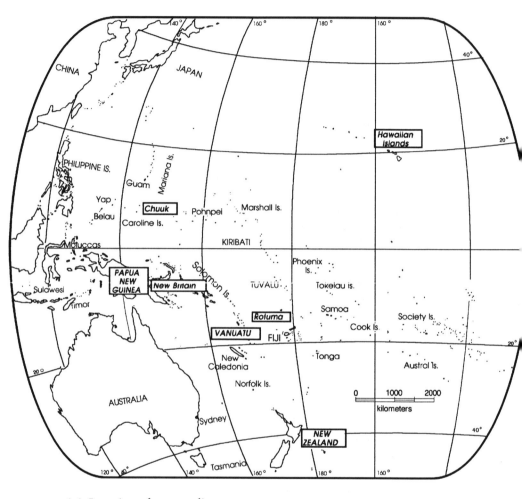

1.1 Location of case studies

broad array of perspectives on built environments that have developed over the past several decades. These include, among others, relatively straightforward accounts of ecological and social structural functions of housing in different societies; psychological approaches emphasizing spatial perception and proxemics and exploring issues of privacy and territoriality; and complex symbolic analyses that examine the ways built environments nonverbally express culturally shared meanings, reaffirming conceptions of social, political, and cosmological order.

While many of these issues are incorporated in the case studies in this volume, here the focus is on *change*. Just as in the prologue the houses that moved were the ones that caught Margaret Rodman's eye, in the remaining chapters the stories of the houses that changed are highlighted. The changes in these stories are social, political, and economic as well as physical, personal, and regional—histories writ small and large. Here are stories of colonized peoples incorporating introduced materials and responding to imposed ideas about order, "good houses," and proper living. Here migrant families seek opportunities and solutions to the physical limits of their housing in a range of new settings. Here families carve out their livelihoods in remote homesteads over generations, where their houses reflect the evolving circumstances they faced, the personal choices they made. These are tales of imperialism and resistance, identity and resilience, transformation and persistence. And all these dramas are played out and recorded in changes in housing over time.

Housing change is inextricably tied to changes in the social relationships that housing embodies and represents and from which it emerges. Further, housing, in its physical forms, uses, and meanings, is impacted by and responds to changes in global political economy. Houses can be seen as a nexus where sociocultural, economic, and political forces interact, transcending disciplinary boundaries. Ordinary housing provides a focal point for discovery and exploration of the stories embodied therein.

Housing as Product and Process

In this volume we use the term housing to connote the dynamic nature of human interaction with domestic space. Housing is both noun—an object, something people have, make, live in—and verb—an activity, something people do. Other scholars have noted a similar noun/verb duality in the term "dwelling": In his pioneering global survey of vernacular domestic habitation, Oliver (1987, 7) discusses

dwelling as both process—the activity of residing—and artifact—
the place or structure that is the physical expression and focus of
residence. In the North American context, Saegert (1985) also prefers
the active, relational connotations of the term "dwelling." But in
contrast, she limits "housing" to its noun-sense as object, identifying "units of housing" as "commodities . . . we search for rather
than produce" (Saegert 1985, 287; in the same vein, see Lawrence
1987, 3–5).

The buildings considered in this volume span a range from kin-
group-built thatched houses in remote Pacific Islands villages to
government-subsidized cement-and-steel high rises in densely populated capital cities. Given this scope, we have chosen to use the term
"housing" reinvested with the fuller range of its meanings. Fore-
grounded here are the processes through which people create and re-
create their living spaces, as well as the values and meanings those
constructions represent and perpetuate. But also appropriate here is
the added connotation of the noun "housing"—as living spaces provided by the state. A number of authors explore the varying social
impacts of and responses to such environments (see chapters by
Macpherson, Modell, and Franco and Aga).

Vernacular, Traditional, and Changing Architecture

Most studies of housing in other than metropolitan settings focus on
either "vernacular" or "traditional" housing. Although these and
other descriptors are sometimes used interchangeably, their connotations and emphases differ to some extent.[2] In his ground-breaking
study, Rapoport (1969, 4–5) suggested that a satisfactory definition
of vernacular was difficult, but elected to focus on the process of its
design and construction. Expanding on this, scholars today emphasize a number of characteristics in explaining their uses of the term.
According to Brunskill (1981, 24), for instance, vernacular architecture is built with an intention of permanence; is traditionally rather
than academically inspired; provides support for the daily activities
of ordinary people; reflects an attachment to place, especially through
the use of local building materials; and serves not only utilitarian but
affective functions.[3] In a more general sense, Oliver (1987, 9) reminds
us of the linguistic contrast from which the term is drawn: Vernacular speech is the language of the common people, as opposed to the
language of the court or college; vernacular architecture is built by
people themselves without professional help.

In the introduction to their edited collection, *Common Places,* Upton and Vlach (1986, xv) note that people tend to define vernacular by what it is *not*—not high style, sophisticated, monumental, or designed by professionals—and that people frequently use the term as though it referred solely to old, rural, domestic buildings. (In keeping with this emphasis, their 1986 volume *does* concern mostly old, rural, domestic architecture, in the eastern United States.) But in fact vernacular architecture has become much more amorphous in its object, now encompassing not only dwellings but commercial buildings and churches, public spaces and landscapes—even whole settlements—in settings throughout the world. Rather than a specific type of building (process or product), vernacular architecture has grown to represent a range of scholarly approaches and key questions. While some studies trace the expression of ethnic identities in the diffusion of particular features of architecture and space, others document and bring to life construction procedures and materials from different times and places, or seek to interpret the models vernacular builders drew on, how they passed them on, and what they intended to accomplish. Functional approaches examine how spaces are provided, defined, and transformed into "places" by their use, as well as how space and furnishings shape perceptions and frame social relationships (similarly, in this volume, see especially the chapters by Dominy, Flinn, and Macpherson). And despite connotations of pristine timelessness, "vernacular buildings and vernacular landscapes are always changing" (Upton and Vlach 1986, xx). Most pertinent to the focus of the present volume, some students of vernacular architecture identify in built form and uses of space the impacts of changes in populations, their socially defined needs, and the importation of new ideas, resources, and styles, as well as reflections of larger political and social movements.

Change can also have a place in the studies of those whose focus is labeled "traditional" architecture. Defining and locating "traditional" is a central concern of a cross-cultural, interdisciplinary volume entitled *Dwellings, Settlements and Tradition* (Bourdier and AlSayyad 1989). In determining whether something is traditional, Bourdier and AlSayyad emphasize cultural origins with common people and the process of transmission. These criteria do not preclude change, and indeed a number of the studies in their collection specifically address the impact of forces such as colonialism, migration, and government-supported housing schemes.

Although vernacular and traditional architectural studies do not necessarily ignore changing forms, both specialties focus on common elements, those that clearly represent group-accepted norms. As Upton and Vlach (1986, xvi) note with regard to vernacular architecture, "The more self-sufficient and socially secure a community is, the more definite is its sense of identity and the more fixed are its architectural conventions.... Scholars are usually most confident about their definitions of the vernacular when they study structures with a more pronounced ethnic character." This may help to explain why vernacular studies have tended to focus on traditional architecture.

Tradition and Change in the Pacific

Studies that deal with housing in Pacific Islands also have focused on traditional or vernacular forms that were common prior to Western contact; that is, buildings and spaces constructed by the people themselves, drawing on local technologies, concepts, and materials. In his study of traditional architecture in Vanuatu, Coiffier's definition resonates with Bourdier and AlSayyad's above: "A building is said to be 'traditional' when its design reflects knowledge exclusive to a local culture and when the economic relationships formed by the need for materials remain within one area" (Coiffier 1988, ix).

This focus is often a logical result of the nature of the researchers' questions. For instance, the few examples of Pacific Islands architecture included in surveys of vernacular architecture worldwide (such as Oliver 1987, Duly 1979) are understandably those most easily identifiable as indigenous, most clearly demonstrating local responses to natural environmental conditions, and incorporating design features supportive of cultural values and practices. A recent volume on housing (Fox 1993) developed by the Comparative Austronesian Project at the Research School of the Pacific, The Australian National University, seeks to document commonalities underlying the range of physical manifestations in domestic space in a number of Pacific Islands and island Southeast Asian settings. But while several of the contributors acknowledge significant recent shifts in housing form and practice, they leave unexplored commonalities traceable to government regulation and economic development (see Rensel 1995).

Pacific Islands societies, along with colonized peoples throughout the world, have faced a range of similar external forces—governmental, religious, economic, social—with far-reaching impacts on their lives, not least on the form and arrangement of their living spaces. Some authors of housing studies in the Pacific choose to limit their consideration to the period before contact or colonization, specifi-

cally to avoid the project of untangling the diversity of outside influences and complexity of impacts (see, e.g., Hockings 1989, xii).
Some, especially architecture and anthropology students in the region,
conceive their task as salvaging information and compiling as complete an ethnographic record as possible before traditional knowledge and house forms disappear entirely. In the preface to his *Traditional Architecture in the Gilbert Islands* (1989), Hockings notes that
his project was prompted in part because "the traditional forms
themselves, and the knowledge of their creation and use in the minds
of the Gilbertese, [are] in a state of decay" (1989, 15). Similarly,
Coiffier (1988) includes among his purposes the education of young
ni-Vanuatu in the quality of their own history of technological
achievements, aimed at helping them understand the choices made by
their ancestors in creating built and social environments appropriate
to local situations (Coiffier 1988, ix; see also Riwas 1985, 1).

Yet a number of researchers document housing changes prior to
Western contact in response to influences within the region. A history
of Enga housing by seven coauthors (six of them Enga) emphasizes
that "traditions must not be thought of as static: they change continually. They are enriched by new events and by additions from the
stories of neighbouring peoples" (Kembol et al. 1976). The authors
cite examples of some Enga groups borrowing features of men's
house forms, such as a circular floor plan and horizontal rather than
oblique ridgepole, from nearby Melpa territory. In his examination
of types of traditional buildings in Vanuatu, Coiffier (1988) specifies
that the Southern Islands type was influenced by Polynesian technology. Vea's 1985 study, *Changing Shape of Traditional House Forms
in Tonga,* ties different Tongan house forms to changing social and
hierarchical relations within Tonga from prehistory onward, including Samoan influences in the twelfth to fifteenth centuries.

Invading clans from Samoa (with ancestral ties to the Gilbert
Islands) dramatically affected architecture and settlement patterns in
the central and southern Gilberts (Hockings 1989). Legends recount
that the first act of the invaders in each island was to erect a meeting
house in their own style. Whereas before this there were no villages
per se, each meeting house *(maneaba)* and space around it *(te marae)*
became focal points for districts and the first "public" spaces for
meetings and hosting visitors. At the same time, the invaders reorganized the districts into clan estates, embodied in villages and physically symbolized by seating places within the meeting house. Thus
architecture and spatial arrangement were important tools used by

invaders to impose their social system on those they conquered
(Hockings 1989, 35–44, 244–245).

Similarly, postcontact sociopolitical history can be read in housing, its forms, arrangements, and uses. Colonial administrators, missionaries, planters, and others often required islanders to reorganize
their lives both temporally and spatially. As Thomas (1994, 140) has
observed for Fiji, the missionary enterprise "created an entire social
geography of stations and circuits, which in some cases reflected
indigenous political divisions or trade routes but gave even these new
functions; it sought to impose a new temporal regime of work, leisure, celebration and worship; through education it offered a new
global and local history [focused on mission activity]." As well, government legislation reflected "a paradigm of order that privileged
openness, visibility, ventilation, boundaries and a particular spatial
differentiation of activities. A house was perceived as being 'crowded'
if occupied by any sort of larger extended family; 'crowding' itself
seemed to be necessarily unhealthy" (Thomas 1994, 119).

In his history of the colonization of Australia, Carter (1987)
emphasizes that the first task of the colonial project was to produce
empty space. Once space was considered devoid of indigenous inhabitants and even of indigenously named features, then "places" could
be created, through naming, mapping, and, eventually, settlement.
The places that colonial governments and missionaries tried to create
in the process of converting and "civilizing" islanders involved extensive changes to settlement patterns, houses, and households. Such
changes are explored by Shaw, Chowning, and Rensel in this volume.

The transformations of domestic space that occurred in the parts
of the Pacific addressed by our contributors resonate with the changes
to the shape, furnishings, and occupancy of Tswana housing in
southern Africa analyzed by Jean and John Comaroff (1992). In
much of the Pacific, British colonial hegemony was as "homemade"
as it was in Africa (Comaroff and Comaroff 1992, 265–294). While
Pacific Islands (with the possible exception of New Caledonia) did
not attract the attention of larger-scale urban planners from Europe
attempting to find in the more densely settled colonies experimental
solutions to problems plaguing cities back home (Wright 1991, 53–
84; see also Rabinow 1989 and King 1976), the islanders shared colonial housing experiences with indigenous peoples elsewhere in the
world.

Yet few studies of Pacific Islands housing[4] give more than passing
attention to such relatively recent and powerful socioeconomic, reli-

gious, and political influences. Because our primary concern in this volume is not so much whether housing is traditional or vernacular, but how it affects and reflects people's lives, we focus especially on housing *change*, its causes, and implications.

Rather than conceptual, our boundaries are geographic and temporal: people and housing in the Pacific Islands from Hawai'i to New Zealand, Papua New Guinea to the Federated States of Micronesia, over the past two centuries, but especially in recent decades. Our overall intent has been to address the following questions: What has changed over time in Pacific Islands housing, broadly defined? What political, economic, demographic, social, religious, and natural forces have contributed to transformations—and continuities? How have changes in housing in Pacific Islands impacted social interaction and relationships?

The issues that emerge from consideration of these questions are of relevance to studies of socioeconomic change and development, particularly those having to do with the impacts of demographic shifts, changing household composition and size, gender roles and relations, reliance on imports and remittances, and migration. In addition, the contributors to this volume address many issues of interest to students of housing generally. These include consideration of boundaries between public and private, inside and outside; implications of changes in gendered spaces; and alteration in status relations and their expressions. Also of concern here are social and moral agendas over time and under different political and religious regimes; and issues of identity and attachment to place, notions of community, and meanings of "home" (see Rodman's conclusion). Exploring these issues within the framework of change, the authors highlight their dynamic nature.

The contributors trace not only decades of change in physical structures and arrangements, but the tangled roots of those changes, whether sociopolitical, religious, environmental, or economic. Local populations' experiences of housing change are documented through changes in social practices, attitudes, and meanings.

The first few case studies concern small Pacific Islands communities where, despite their remoteness, a variety of local and externally based factors have affected built environments. Colonial governments and Christian missionaries promoted housing styles and materials, settlement locations, and household compositions that differed from indigenous patterns. Economic involvement with outsiders, as well as migration and remittances, increasingly allow access to new

construction materials and styles. Innovations in housing are both
cause and consequence of changes in social organization and relations. Yet cases of resistance to external pressures, a resurgence of
interest in traditional house forms, and even a community's response
to homelessness among Hawaiians, demonstrate the persistence of
distinctive cultural values.

The remaining chapters deal with housing and social change in
more urban Pacific Islands settings. Migration to urban centers, even
small ones like Weno in Chuuk, involves dramatic changes in housing and creates new tensions for social relationships.[5] In some cases
people have options to create buildings to support and perpetuate
cultural values and practices; in others they are faced with having to
develop novel solutions to cope with structures that exacerbate
adjustments to new environments.

Forces for change vary from place to place in their combinations,
intensity, and timing; indigenous responses also differ, according to
people's cultural and personal agendas and priorities. So although
there are similarities, a close examination reveals that no two trajec-
tories in housing and social change are alike. Whatever the circumstances, the evidence reveals that histories are encoded in housing
change—not only personal and family histories, but those of wider
social, cultural, economic, religious, and political processes as well.

Housing Change in Remote Locations

External forces combine with local concerns to produce a particular
history of change, not only in house styles and materials, but in the
meaning of houses and the social relationships they represent. In the
case of Rotuma (Rensel, chapter 2), houses have been central to the
social reproduction of Rotuman kin groups for centuries. Rotumans
reckon blood ties on the basis of common ancestors' claims to named
house sites. They actively affirm their kinship by engaging in reciprocal sharing, for which house building and maintenance provide many
opportunities. Rotuman houses thus stand as tangible reminders of
the relationships and responsibilities of all who participate in their
construction, repair, and use.

Jan Rensel draws on written descriptions of Rotuman houses dat-
ing from the early nineteenth century, as well as missionary and colonial records documenting changes in housing materials, styles, and
construction techniques. Walls of plaited sago or coconut palm
fronds were gradually replaced by lime and stone around the turn of
the century, then by wood or cement in the mid-1900s. Thatched
roofs similarly have given way to corrugated iron over time. Various

factors contributed to the shift in materials. Through early trade and sailing on European ships, Rotumans observed different house styles and obtained new types of furnishings. Catholic and Methodist missionaries, who began conversion efforts on Rotuma in the mid-nineteenth century, introduced new construction techniques involving lime and stone, and propagated new attitudes about what constituted "good" housing. Periodic hurricanes that destroyed thatched houses while depleting the supply of sago and coconut palm gave impetus to Rotumans' interest in alternatives.

The disaster relief program that followed one such hurricane in 1972 led to the near disappearance of thatched houses on Rotuma, replaced by structures of cement and iron. Since that time, money and goods remitted by migrant Rotumans have played a major role in promoting the construction and renovation of houses with imported materials. In the same period, piped water and water-sealed toilets became available through government projects. Individual houses and communities increasingly depend on generators for lights and electricity, and on appliances such as gas stoves and kerosene refrigerators.

Housing changes have far-reaching implications for social relations on Rotuma. Thatch and wooden poles for basic structures are available to Rotumans from their own land and that of relatives. Extended family members, including men, women, and children, can assist in the construction process, and are thanked with feasts and gifts of food. In contrast, access to imported materials requires sufficient earned income, or off-island relatives willing and able to contribute. To the extent that remitted cash and materials are substituted for local materials, ties with migrant supporters gain prominence over local relationships. Opportunities for sustaining reciprocal involvement with on-island kin are also eroded by the emerging practice of arranging for skilled (primarily adult male) laborers to build houses, and compensating them with cash.

Changes in housing also have implications for authority and status relations on the island. Houses of Rotuman chiefs formerly were distinguished by their size, reflecting both chiefly responsibility for hosting visitors and community support in providing materials and labor. Chiefs today who desire cement structures must have access to cash through earnings or remittances, like everyone else. Thus their homes may be neither the largest nor the most elaborate in their districts, nor do they represent as clearly their people's loyalty and commitment.

Rotuman considerations of social merit may be implicated by

changing house styles. Hard work and generosity are core values by which one is evaluated socially. Recent evidence suggests that the provision of a Western-style house for one's family is superseding garden productivity and community sharing in importance. It appears, however, that the transition from thatch to cement is not totally unidirectional. Some returning migrants have chosen to build Rotuman-style, thatched-roof dwellings, with the help of their kin groups. Although the new houses usually incorporate modern furnishings, plumbing, and electricity, the use of thatch in the traditional style suggests the persistence of powerful cultural symbolism.

The involvement of colonial governments and Christian missionaries spurred significant changes in housing styles throughout the Pacific Islands. In areas where warfare had been endemic, colonial pacification allowed different construction styles and settlement patterns to develop. Colonial governments established housing regulations for public welfare purposes, especially health and sanitation, but promoted other changes, such as clustered settlement, for administrative convenience. In the case of the Samo of Papua New Guinea, R. Daniel Shaw (chapter 3) reports that government administrative procedures initially prompted a shift in the location of longhouses, from dispersed forest sites to aggregated villages. Changes in building form, from group longhouse to smaller family dwellings, developed later as practical responses to changing social and local environmental circumstances.

Precontact Samo lifestyles were dominated by subsistence activities and the need for protection against raids by other groups. These priorities were reflected in the location and form of longhouses, which also served as centers of social and ceremonial activity. Construction, using ironwood poles, sago palm roofs, rattan, and vines, required months of cooperative labor on the part of longhouse members. But as local soils and food resources diminished, a longhouse group would seek another site in the forest and begin the cycle of construction and gardening anew. Thus they ranged through the region over time, eventually returning to a longhouse/garden site when the forest had replenished the soil naturally.

Australian colonial administration led to cessation of intergroup warfare, thus eliminating the need for defensive structures. At the same time, the government designated village sites for administrative purposes. People were drawn in from outlying sites when rebuilding their longhouses, but the concentration of residents in one location put increased pressure on the surrounding land and resources. People found they had to spend more and more time away from the village, sometimes building small bush houses at distant garden sites as temporary shelters. In addition, they had to work one day a week for the government as a form of taxation, and young people began attending school. When longhouses in the village required replacement, competing demands on materials and time eventually resulted in construction of smaller houses as residences for nuclear family groups.

Besides effecting changes in Samo kinship terms and social structure, which Shaw details in his chapter, living in aggregated villages has led to a redefinition of the Samo house, now primarily a sleeping space rather than a social, ceremonial, or defensive site. As Shaw points out, however, when the members of one Samo village decided to build a community meeting house in 1990, they did so in the form of a traditional longhouse. Although it serves as a ceremonial center and guest house rather than as a primary dwelling for village members, this building reflects community identity and pride much as former longhouses did.

In the Cape Hoskins region of West New Britain, the colonial government, reinforced by Methodist missionaries, also affected residence patterns and housing styles. Ann Chowning (chapter 4) traces such changes over more than seventy years in the Lakalai village of Galilo, where, until the end of World War I, people lived in small hamlets. Each hamlet included a men's house and gathering place, and several houses for women and children. Houses were ground based, constructed of wood, bark, and sometimes palm-leaf thatch. Interaction between men and women was limited by a number of taboos, important for success in battle. Hamlet residents considered one another kin and shared food and numerous daily activities. Hamlets typically were grouped into larger villages. Members of a village gardened together and cooperated in large-scale enterprises such as major ceremonies and warfare with neighboring groups, but trust was tenuous. Quarrels and rivalries often led to splits and the establishment of new hamlets.

The arrival of Methodist missionaries in 1918 and Australian rule the following year combined to initiate far-reaching changes. The colonial government forbade segments of villages to split or move. By establishing a single school and church for each village, the missionaries reinforced the government's administrative emphasis. The church also preached against the taboos that kept men and women apart, and because the abolition of warfare removed a reason for avoidance, men began to spend much more time with their wives.

Gradually men's houses were abandoned. As a result of these changes and growing individualism, hamlet unity has all but disappeared.

Government regulations concerning health and sanitation also affected house construction, although practices changed less quickly than structures. For instance, in Galilo the government required that houses be built on piles, but older people often chose surreptitiously to sleep in ground-based cook houses. Attempts to introduce privies were similarly resisted; although a few were constructed, men rarely used them, and some women not at all.[6]

Such incidents illustrate the point that changes in housing in the Pacific have not been merely a matter of passive acceptance of externally imposed conditions. Although power differentials were great, local people adapted to colonial demands and missionary teachings while persisting with their own preferences when they could. They also exercised choice in selecting among new building techniques and materials as they became available, striving to meet their own needs and goals.

Where people are able to make choices in shaping their built environments, particularly where structures are modified and added to over time, it is possible to undertake a kind of "archaeology" of housing change. Physical evidence accompanied by photographs, written diaries, and oral histories, as provided by Michèle Dominy (chapter 5) in her study of homesteads in the high country of New Zealand's South Island, demonstrate how houses record the interaction of changing personal, cultural, environmental, and socioeconomic circumstances.

Dominy's study describes changes in the built environment in the New Zealand high country over three generations, during which time a shift has occurred from the sheep station homestead of the past, with a large hired staff, to the contemporary station as a family farm unit. Her analysis of transformations in the use and design of domestic physical space reveals generational transformations in conceptual and social systems, including attitudes toward the natural environment and changing definitions of gender roles.

Evolving attitudes to the environment are apparent in the placement and design of contemporary homesteads and the opening up of older homesteads. For example, expanded verandahs, bigger windows, natural colors, gardens, and windbreaks with curvaceous rather than straight lines have replaced the cold, dark, sheltered homesteads and formal gardens of the past. Changing patterns of location and design suggest growing control over the landscape and reflect a perceptual shift in which high country people have integrated the vastness and ruggedness of the high country into their lives.

Changes in women's roles interweave with changes in the structures of the houses, and reflect broader economic developments. Altered cooking spaces and eating arrangements reflect a downturn in the farming economy with consequent changes in social relationships. Shrinking staff and the elimination of station cooks shifted the job of meal preparation to the women in the family. Social distance also lessened between owners and workers, as the latter, fewer in number, came to take their meals with the family rather than eat in separate areas.

The continuing evolution of high country homesteads through accretion and reconfiguration also reflects the stages of the family's developmental cycle. As Dominy phrases it, "walls stretch and contract" (page 129) with the birth and departure of children, rooms are transformed continually through use, aging parents move aside as their married children take over the farm. Finally, changes represent personal choices, as members of each generation leave their mark in the buildings and grounds they are passing through, and passing on to their children. Thus the built environment is a "cumulative identity marker denoting continuity of family habitation" (page 130), even as it represents changing historical circumstances.

Housing Change in Urban Centers

Some of the same issues of housing and social change, along with new tensions, face Pacific Islanders in more densely populated and urban settings.[7] For the Micronesians of Pollap atoll who migrate to the Chuuk state capital on Weno, adjustment problems may be mitigated because the Pollapese have been able to purchase several contiguous land plots that have come to form the basis of their community. But, as Juliana Flinn (chapter 6) reports, there are strong contrasts with the home island. On Pollap some houses are constructed of imported, purchased materials, but many are still made of thatch in the traditional style. These thatched houses represent self-sufficiency, close connections with the land, and cooperative kin relations. On Weno, all Pollapese houses use imported materials, but they range from tiny, rough shacks to much larger, well-appointed houses. The social differentiation represented by this range is related to employment rather than traditional principles of kinship, gender, and age. It is the younger, formally educated islanders who are finding jobs and, with direct access to money, enjoying the prestige of more elaborate homes.

Flinn notes that increasing differentiation in housing is raising conflicts with Pollapese values of reciprocity and generosity. The newer buildings, built with purchased materials and paid labor, and requiring less regular maintenance and repair, reduce opportunities for mutual aid among kin. In addition, the new house types provide more privacy, allowing people to hoard food and hide goods from public view. People regularly lock their houses in Weno, and sometimes lock interior rooms as well. Struggling both to take advantage of new economic opportunities and to retain important values and traditions, Pollapese migrants have developed a practice of public sharing through group preparation and distribution of food on a weekly basis.

Migrants to other areas, particularly those with limited incomes, often have to cope with available housing rather than have the option of building their own homes and communities. This causes difficulties when buildings are designed for households with different characteristics and social priorities than those of the immigrant families. Samoan households, for instance, are frequently larger and typically more fluid than European nuclear families. Cluny Macpherson (chapter 7) describes the case of Samoan migrants to New Zealand in the 1960s. The migrants were often persuaded by financial incentives to buy new homes in low-cost subdivisions. These homes, however, were not well suited to their needs, since household compositions were constantly changing as new migrants arrived and then moved on. Built for two adults and two children, the living space and facilities were not only inadequate for Samoan families, but were further stressed when households needed to host guests and entertain large numbers of people for important cultural gatherings.

The solution in this case has been to add garages, and use them in novel ways. Less expensive and not subject to the stringent regulations regarding house extensions, garages have been adapted by Samoan migrants in New Zealand as temporary living quarters for unmarried men, meeting places for migrant village councils of chiefs, homes for newly formed church congregations, venues for fund-raising activities, sites for language retention classes, and recording studios for a new genre of Samoan migrant music. The convenience of such flexible space made garages an ideal solution, allowing the perpetuation of cultural traditions in a new setting.

Samoan migrants in Honolulu face other problems, exacerbated by inappropriate housing, according to Robert Franco and Simeamativa Mageo Aga (chapter 8). While many Samoan migrants live in rural areas of Oʻahu (the Waiʻanae coast or Lāʻie–Hauʻula on the north shore), approximately 28 percent of those on the island live in the Kalihi valley area of metropolitan Honolulu, and many of those in public housing. Like the Samoans in New Zealand, Kalihi residents have problems hosting large groups of visiting kin. But they have more serious problems. In their chapter, Franco and Aga describe the stark contrast between houses and village layouts in Samoa, and the "vertical villages" of Kūhiō Park Terrace (KPT), two sixteen-story high-rise towers. Whereas the openness of the village arrangement and the wall-less Samoan *fale* 'houses' allow for continual community observation of behavior, and support shared responsibility for socialization through collaborative work and service, the small, closed units of KPT's high rises limit supervision of children to parents, often single mothers, who are poorly prepared for child rearing without the support of other adults.

Samoans link the closed, private character of housing at KPT to social problems such as child abuse and neglect, drug use, and gang violence. Recently a community policing effort has contributed to a greater sense of security and safety at KPT. At another Kalihi public housing site, Samoan residents built a traditional *fale* that temporarily provided a gathering space for group conversation, play, and work. But until more permanent solutions are found, the challenge for Samoans in Honolulu is to develop parenting education focusing on socialization and disciplinary practices that both draw on Samoan cultural values, and work in the confines of American public housing.

Perhaps the most dramatic case of housing change is considered in the contribution by Judith Modell (chapter 9), who writes about Hawaiians facing the bitter irony of being homeless in their own land. Focusing on the work of a task force in Waimānalo, who in 1991 proposed their own solutions to the housing crisis, Modell argues that such local responses to homelessness reflect Hawaiian cultural values, demonstrate the links between the concept of "home" and notions of family, kinship, and the person, and become part of the negotiation crucial to housing policy anywhere.

Rejecting temporary shelters on land set apart from the rest of the community ("cluster villages"), the Waimānalo Task Force plan stressed incorporation: providing people with respectable bases from which to resume their social place in the community. The solutions ranged from moving people in with families who already had homes in the area, into spare rooms, tents, or garages, or building houses on selected sites within, not separated from, the rest of Waimānalo. Moreover, they recommended that houses in each site be few in number and sturdy in construction, thereby having the potential to blend into the community rather than remain separate and stigmatized.

Despite community resistance, a "barracks-like" cluster village has been built in Waimānalo. The task force process, however, contributed to a broader discussion of houses as places of social interaction and individual dignity. At another cluster village, Māʻili Land, improvements toward this end came in the form of replacing communal kitchens with unit kitchens. The task force helped give clear voice to local conceptions of "home" for Hawaiians; the particular form of housing is not so important as following the guiding principle of incorporation and acceptance in the broader community.

The Stories Houses Tell

In recent years, calls have increased for work that integrates multiple perspectives in the study of housing. Kent (1990, 2–3) urges anthropologists to notice and document uses of space and built environment, while recommending that architects study aspects of culture likely to influence the use of space. Carsten and Hugh-Jones (1995, 4) point out that architectural works typically focus "on the more material aspects of dwellings, including environmental conditions, resources, technology, techniques of construction and types of building," and may deal with "spatial organization, symbolism and aesthetic values of buildings, but they often say relatively little about the social organization of the people who live inside."[8] Among anthropologists, they see a tendency to focus on ritual rather than ordinary aspects of life:

> But the house has another side. It is an ordinary group of people concerned with their day-to-day affairs, sharing consumption and living in the shared space of a domestic dwelling. It is out of these everyday activities, carried on without ritual, reflection or fuss and significantly, often by women, that the house is built. This house, all too easily taken for granted, is one that anthropologists have tended to ignore. One conclusion we would emphasize is the need for further research on an anthropology of everyday life which might both balance, and eventually be incorporated into, studies of ritual and ideology. (Carsten and Hugh-Jones 1995, 45)

In this volume we present the stories of everyday life embodied in, influencing, and being influenced by housing in the Pacific Islands. While for most cases the luxury of detailed written and photographic documentation is not available, for those who learn to read the evidence, the stories are there. As Rodman discovered in the hills of Ambae, Vanuatu, houses, and parts of houses, move. Buildings may be reoriented or relocated. The current state of social relationships thus can be read from the built form by noting whose walls end up on whose house, which way dwellings face, and who lives in them.

Similarly, the houses in Rotuma and Weno and Lakalai, the abandoned longhouses and new meeting halls in the Samo villages, the garages in New Zealand, and the high rises in Honolulu, even the lack of homes for some Hawaiians—each have stories to tell. These are stories about colonial and missionary agendas, local and global economies, environmental disasters, cultural identities, social connections, family continuity, personal choices. The people who shape these houses both tell these stories, and reading them, know more of and continue to create their own history.

Notes

Margaret Rodman joins me in expressing our appreciation to Alan Howard for countless hours of redrafting all the maps and other figures on the computer; to Pam Kelley and Cheri Dunn at University of Hawai'i Press for patience, good humor, and helpful suggestions throughout the publication process; and to two anonymous reviewers for their constructive and encouraging comments on an earlier version of this volume. We would also like to acknowledge the Association for Social Anthropology in Oceania for providing a meeting format and atmosphere conducive to the thoughtful development and exchange of ideas over time. Finally, we are grateful for the support of our respective institutions, York University and University of Hawai'i, especially for access to electronic mail, which immensely facilitated communication between us and our contributors.

1. In his study of the Kabyle house, Bourdieu (1990 [1970]) explores one aspect of this fundamental relationship—house as mnemonic for socialization —prefiguring the development of his notion of *habitus*.

2. Other descriptors include indigenous, folk, popular, primitive, tribal, and anonymous, depending on disciplinary basis (and bias). Aside from the pejorative implications of some of the latter terms, there are limits to their applicability and accuracy; for instance, can housing be considered indigenous if local people build it with imported materials (Bourdier and AlSayyad 1989, 6)? And, furthermore, who is to say?

3. In his discussion of vernacular building, Lawrence (1987, 16–17) cites

Brunskill's list of characteristics. Bourdier and AlSayyad (1989, 6) use Brunskill's criteria to define their focus on the traditional.

4. Notable exceptions include Vea 1985, Kembol et al. 1976, and Rutz 1984.

5. In his review of the study of urbanization in the Pacific Islands, Mayo (1987) notes that absolute size is not an adequate criterion for designating a place as urban; more appropriate is the *relative* concentration of population. People are drawn from outlying areas to more densely settled port towns and government centers in pursuit of education, employment, novelty and excitement, etc. Thus the urban centers in this volume include Weno as well as metropolitan Auckland and Honolulu.

6. In his book, *Longhouse to Village*, Shaw (1996, 27) reports a tale from Samo that has been told, with variations, for other locales: Under government supervision the villagers dutifully built latrines, and used them as instructed. After a year, however, a government inspector found the outhouses maggot infested, and ordered them burned. Happy to comply, the Samo villagers returned to their traditional practice of using the forest. The following year another official arrived and, finding no latrines, demanded that the regulation be followed. By this time the Samo had learned how to please the administration: They built new outhouses, but used the forest. Thereafter they passed the annual government inspection.

7. Self-constructed "squatter" houses in Pacific port towns are an important but understudied form of vernacular architecture. Whereas some unauthorized settlements pose serious problems for safety and sanitation, Plocki (1975, 4) notes that squatter houses in Port Moresby "are usually much larger than the government's standard [low-income houses], usually have bigger verandahs [and] individually lockable rooms, are cooler and generally more comfortable, especially now that the government has accepted these areas, and the Housing Commission is bringing in services and roads." Plocki (1975, 13) also suggests that government housing developments provide less security than squatter areas, "where people are at least protected by being part of the group."

8. An important exception is the work of Waterson, whose 1990 volume, *The Living House,* explores the architecture of Southeast Asia. This book illustrates the range of perspectives for studying houses and what they can tell us about spatial organization, construction, cosmology, ritual, kinship groups, historical power relations, and daily social relations.

2
From Thatch to Cement
Social Implications of Housing
Change on Rotuma

Jan Rensel

For centuries, houses—their construction, maintenance, use, and even their location—have been central to the social reproduction of kin groups *(kạinaga)* on the island of Rotuma.[1] *Kạinaga* membership is a matter of both blood relationship and active demonstrations of commitment. Blood ties are reckoned on the basis of a common ancestor who lived on or had claim in a named house site. And commitment to a kin group is demonstrated by giving materials and labor to building, maintaining, and furnishing a house, as well as by being a part of activities that take place in and around it. By attending gatherings, contributing resources, helping prepare food, and eating together with those who dwell in a given house, Rotumans repeatedly proclaim their connectedness. Rotuman houses stand as tangible reminders and powerful symbols, embodying the responsibilities and relationships of all who participate in their construction, repair, and use.

Rotuma, like other Pacific Islands, has undergone significant social, economic and demographic change, especially during the past few decades. Studies elsewhere have pointed to the far-reaching effects of outmigration and remittances, for instance (see, e.g., Bertram and Watters 1985, 1986; Hooper and Huntsman 1973; Severance 1976; Shankman 1976, 1992; O'Meara 1986). Economic problems associated with these processes include declines in agricultural productivity, weakened potential for development, maintenance of high living standards by external subsidies, and consequent vulnerability to external economic fluctuations. Social impacts range from the erosion of traditional authority patterns and status structures, and incipient class formation based on material wealth, to the devaluation of collective work, community fragmentation, the spread of individualism, jealousy, and dissatisfaction. Many of the effects of population movement, shifting economic bases, and increased access to cash and imported materials are represented tangibly in Pacific Islands houses. Changes in house materials, construction, and use can provide a focal point for examining wider patterns of transformation.

Since the earliest recorded descriptions of Rotuman houses in the nineteenth century, there have been many documented changes in house styles, materials, and construction processes. Contributing factors range from missionary influence and increasing external trade, to hurricanes, relief programs, and migrant involvement. Changes in structures, and processes surrounding their construction, maintenance, and use, are affecting social relationships in some important ways. This chapter is concerned with tracing changes in housing on Rotuma, identifying significant factors producing those changes, and exploring the implications for Rotuman social relationships.

Background

The island of Rotuma is relatively remote, located 465 kilometers north of the northernmost island in the Fiji group, and only slightly closer to Futuna, its nearest neighbor (see map; figure 2.1). Rotuma has been politically affiliated with Fiji for more than a century, first as a British colony and since 1970 as part of the independent nation. Rotuma's people are, however, culturally and linguistically distinct, having strong ties with Tonga, Samoa, and other Polynesian islands to the east.

The island is composed of seven districts, each of which has its own paramount chief and a number of subchiefs. A chief is selected from and by a special group of kin called a *mosega* (literally, 'bed'), who claim descent from a particular house site with which the chiefly title is associated. Although Rotumans cooperate on communal projects under the direction of their subchiefs and chiefs, and frequently engage in interhousehold exchange of food and labor, households are largely self-sufficient. Rotuma is a fertile volcanic island of forty-three square kilometers, surrounded by a fringing coral reef of varying width and productivity. The land supports the cultivation of a range of starchy staple crops as well as other vegetables, fruits, and coconuts. Most Rotuman households keep chickens and pigs, and some raise a few goats or cows as well. Local protein sources include

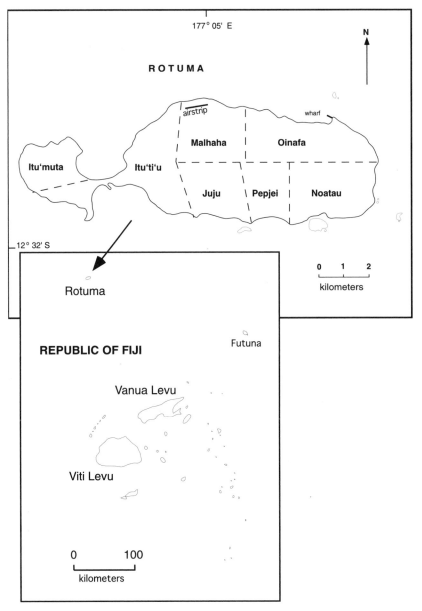

177° 05' E

N

ROTUMA

airstrip

wharf

Malhaha

Oinafa

Itu'muta

Itu'ti'u

Juju

Pepjei

Noatau

12° 32' S

0   1   2

kilometers

Rotuma

Futuna

REPUBLIC OF FIJI

Vanua Levu

Viti Levu

0   100

kilometers

2.1 Rotuma

meat from these animals, and fish, shellfish, and seaweed from surrounding waters.

In addition to subsistence production Rotumans have engaged in external trade for at least two centuries. Locally produced food formed the basis for commerce with whalers and other European ships from the time of first recorded contact with Europeans (HMS *Pandora*) in 1791. In addition, Rotumans eagerly signed aboard passing ships as crew and earned money as sailors and pearl divers. Trading in copra was established by the 1870s, and copra has remained Rotuma's chief export, despite fluctuations in production and declining profits in recent decades. After incorporation as a British colony in 1881, Rotuma was closed as a port of entry, so most opportunities for trade, employment, and education were pursued in and through Fiji. Although the population on Rotuma has remained relatively stable, the proportion of Rotumans away from the home island has grown steadily, such that in 1986, 70 percent of Rotumans were living in Fiji rather than in Rotuma (see table 2.1).

Employment opportunities on Rotuma more than doubled from 1960 to 1989. According to an island-wide survey conducted in 1960 by Alan Howard, 71 Rotumans held wage positions; a similar survey in 1989 recorded 174 Rotumans earning wages. The primary employers were the Fiji government (e.g., school teachers, medical staff, laborers) and two Rotuman cooperatives that handled copra sales and imported food and other supplies.[2] Of 414 households on Rotuma surveyed in 1989 (85 percent of all households on the island), 167 households (40 percent of those surveyed) included wage, pension, or self-employed earners. Household members also earn money from a variety of sources, including casual labor, sporadic exports of crops and animals, and on-island trade—for in-

Table 2.1
Rotumans on Rotuma and in Fiji, 1956–1986

	1956	1966	1976	1986
Rotuma	2,993 (68%)	3,235 (56%)	2,707 (37%)	2,588 (30%)
Fiji	1,429 (32%)	2,562 (44%)	4,584 (63%)	6,064 (70%)
Total	4,422	5,797	7,291	8,652

Source: Fiji Census Reports, Government Press, Suva, Fiji

stance, selling garden produce to government workers. In addition, nearly half (48 percent) of the households surveyed reported receiving cash remittances from relatives in Fiji or abroad. Many households benefit as well from other forms of continuing involvement of Rotuman migrants, such as help obtaining material goods from Fiji, and assistance with small entrepreneurial projects, including handicraft sales and tourist visits (see Rensel 1993 regarding the importance of migrant involvement to the material well-being of Rotuma).

A mounting reliance on imported rather than local food is suggested in records of Rotuman chiefs, who monitor garden production in their respective districts. Between 1966 and 1981, production of most staple starch crops fell, in some cases dramatically. Crop plant counts for that fifteen-year period show, for instance, that taro *(Colocasia)* declined from 326,000 to 289,000 plants; yams *(Dioscorea)* from 101,000 to 69,000; and cassava *(Manihot)* from 332,000 to only 99,000. These drops cannot be attributed to a shortage of manpower. Not only has the island population remained fairly constant from 1956–1986, but the numbers of Rotuman men between the ages of fifteen and fifty, who do most of the gardening, have also held steady at around 500–600 (approximately 20 percent of Rotuma's population).

More revealing of possible causes for drops in local food production are the records of the Rotuma Cooperative Association (RCA), which handled most of the island's trade from the late 1950s until recently. RCA turnover figures from 1957 to 1986 clearly display a "jaws effect" as purchases of imported goods diverge from copra sales (see Bertram and Watters 1985, 510). Whereas consumer spending initially was closely tied to copra income, by 1986 RCA store purchases (F$1,022,790) outstripped copra sales (F$323,120) more than three to one.[3] Growing income from wages, remittances, and sources other than copra has served to fuel import consumption.

Although households use much of their income to purchase tinned or packaged foods, a more obvious result of increasing cash affluence can be found in changes in housing on the island. Rotumans have a long history of seeking to improve housing and make construction and maintenance processes less labor intensive. In the following section I begin with some of the earliest available descriptions of Rotuman houses, before turning to the changes recorded over ensuing decades.

Early Descriptions

Building Materials and Styles

An idea of housing styles on Rotuma from the early 1800s can be gleaned from the accounts of some of the first European visitors (Bennett 1831; Eagleston 1832; Osborn 1834–1835; Cheever 1834–1835; Lesson 1838–1839; Lucatt 1851; Haley [1851] 1948). Houses were constructed of poles and logs, with thatched sago palm roofs and plaited sago or coconut palm walls. Most dwellings were described as "small," enclosing a space perhaps 15 to 20 feet wide (Eagleston 1832, 409). Chiefs' houses were noted as being larger, for instance 40 by 16 feet (Haley 1948, 259) and 25 feet high (Lesson 1838–1839, 433). These early written accounts describe Rotuman houses as rounded at the ends (see figure 2.2), but according to Elisapeti Inia, a retired Rotuman schoolteacher and recognized authority on Rotuman custom,[4] the rounding was due to Samoan or Tongan influence; the ends of Rotuman houses were originally flat *(tarut fạri)*.

2.2 Thatched Rotuman meeting house showing many elements common to traditional dwellings, though the plaited walls of the latter would be full rather than half height. The rounded ends of the thatched roof, recorded by early nineteenth-century observers, are attributed by Rotumans to Samoan or Tongan influence. Alan Howard, 1960.

Low doors, which admitted little wind as a protection against hurricanes, required people to enter on hands and knees. Floors were composed of earth, dry grass, and pebbles or small pieces of coral, covered with rough mats of plaited coconut leaves *(farao)*, sometimes with a pandanus mat *('epa)* overlay.

Cooking and eating took place outside or in a separate outbuilding *(kohea* 'kitchen'), also made of poles and thatch. In practice, these spaces were more accessible to members of other households than were the interiors of dwellings. This facilitated the Rotuman custom of assisting others with cooking in *koua* 'earth ovens' as well as that of sharing meals.

Young unmarried men ordinarily slept away from their parents and siblings. It was considered improper for them to sleep inside the house, in close proximity to their sisters. Groups of young men sometimes built their own thatched sleeping houses, sometimes on high poles *(rī sipạkit)*. By staying together, as well as by participating in other joint activities such as preparing *koua* and gardening, youths strengthened not only their relationships with each other but ties between their respective households.

Rotumans customarily built their houses on a foundation, or *fūag rī*, of raised earth, surrounded by stone walls (Osborn 1834–1835; Cheever 1834–1835; Lucatt 1851, 167). Most reports indicate that foundations were from two to four feet high, but descriptions range from one foot (Allardyce 1885–1886, 134) to six feet high (Allen 1895). Foundations up to twelve feet high, presumed to have been used for chiefly dwellings, were discovered inland by Gardiner (1898, 433). Some writers suggested these raised house sites were useful in keeping the floors dry during periods of heavy rains (Osborn 1834–1835; Lucatt 1851, 167; Boddam-Whetham 1876, 266). For Rotumans, however, *fūag rī* were and are significant in notions of kinship. It is the house foundation to which Rotumans generally refer when they describe how they are related to someone, for example: "My mother's mother is from the *fūag rī* where he stays," or "He is related to that *fūag rī*." *Fūag rī* are also reference points for eligibility to stewardship of associated *kạinaga* garden lands, and some foundations carry with them chiefly titles.

Home Furnishings and Housekeeping

Early visitors to Rotuma reported but little in the way of house furnishings: "mats, carved bare wood pillows, a few clubs, spears and drinking vessels of coconut shells" (Osborn 1834–1835). Lesson

(1838–1839, 434) mentioned low tables for eating. Coconut shells strung on sinnet for carrying water could be hung up in the house (Eagleston 1832), and "in the centre of the house is generally slung a little koop net on which are deposited their provisions etc." (Cheever 1835). A more elaborate description of a storage device is given by W. L. Allardyce, who was acting resident commissioner in 1881:

> There is scarcely a house which does not possess, suspended from the ridgepole, a kind of large four-sided swinging basket, called kokona, which serves as a larder and cupboard, and general receptacle for things which are intended to be out of the way of the children and rats. To guard against the latter a piece of circular wood, a foot or more in diameter, is obtained, and a hole bored in the centre, through which the main string of the kokona passes. Underneath this piece of wood, when a suitable height, a knot is made, not large enough to pass through the hole in the wood, which is thus kept stationary. However, the slightest weight on any part of it, at once gives the wood a sudden tilt downwards, and the rat is dropped on to the floor, clear of the kokona, and alongside of the cat. (Allardyce 1885–1886, 134)

Given the importance of mats as primary furnishings as well as items in ceremonial exchange, one could assume that plaiting them took up much of women's time. Mat making is often a cooperative activity, with women helping each other process pandanus and taking turns working on each other's mats. Cleaning a Rotuman-style house includes sweeping the floor, sunning the mats, and picking up leaves and other rubbish in the compound. Although some nineteenth-century European visitors found Rotuman houses "small, dark and dirty" (Forbes 1875, 227), others were impressed with how neat and "scrupulously clean" they were (see, e.g., Lesson 1838–1839, 434; Bennett 1831, 201; Haley 1948, 258). Timing may have affected observers' impressions: For instance, according to Rotuman custom, when men go out deep-sea fishing, women are not to clean the house. Similarly, for five days after a burial, houses of families in mourning remain unswept.

House Construction and Repairs

Customarily, Rotuman house building is a group process, although it may be guided by one who is particularly skilled (*majau* 'expert, carpenter'). Members of the *kainaga* assist, along with neighbors and friends. With thatched structures, women as well as men contribute materials and labor, helping to collect and prepare the poles and sago or coconut palm fronds. Host household members may also work on the building, but more of their efforts go toward providing food for the other workers. As noted in 1913 by A. M. Hocart, the host household prepares a feast for the *majau* both before and after the house is built, and provides meals for the workers every day on which they work (Hocart 1913, field note 4846). In addition, members of the household remain indebted to those who help them. They should be ready to reciprocate with their labor when needed. In his 1940 autobiography, Rotuman Methodist minister Rev. Fuata Taito describes the process:

> If I had a big job to do, which would take a long time to do by my-self, I would announce it in our village meeting. The chief always asks the question, "Has anyone a job to do which needs help?" Then he calls our names individually, and when he comes to my name, I reply, "Yes, sir, I want to build a hut, and would like ten men to help me if possible." He then appoints a suitable date for it, and calls on whoever can to put their own jobs aside for the day, and go and help Fuata to build his hut.
>
> On the appointed day, those who could come would be there. Although I said ten helpers, I might get fifteen or only five. It all depends on myself. If I have been always ready to help others I shall be sure to have more than I requested, but if I always make excuses and stay home to do my own work, I will be disappointed at the number who come to work that morning. All I have to do is to provide a meal for the workers before they start to work, and another before they go home after the day's toil, and nothing else beyond thanking them for their help. If the hut is not quite finished, they will come back on another day to finish the job. (Taito 1940, 11)

In addition to expectations of future reciprocal assistance, relatives who help with building projects may reap other benefits. A house on a *fūag rī,* or on *kạinaga* land, is subject to use rights by members of the *kạinaga,* and these claims can be strengthened by contributing labor toward construction.

Thatched buildings need periodic upkeep, providing further opportunities for demonstrating kin commitments. Rotumans valued sago palm as more durable than coconut palm for roofing thatch (Bennett 1831, 201; Evans 1951, note 25). According to the report of a Methodist minister who stayed on the island for several years in the 1880s, a sago palm roof "put on nicely is said to last without rethatching for twelve or sixteen years" (Allen 1895). To protect thatched roofs during strong winds, pairs of coconut palm fronds were (and are) laid over the roof vertically, tied together at the top. Still, thatched roofs and plaited walls must be periodically replaced. As with the process of building a new thatched structure, rethatching is an activity that typically involves a group of relatives and neighbors contributing materials and labor on a reciprocal basis and being thanked with food.

In their location on named *fūag rī* 'foundations', and in the processes of their construction and maintenance, Rotuman-style thatched houses served as constant reminders to their inhabitants of the network of kin relations that supported them. Over the past century, however, several influences combined to effect wide-reaching changes in house materials, styles, construction and repair practices. In the next section I consider how a range of social, environmental, demographic, and economic variables have affected Rotuman housing standards, and in turn, the place of houses in the enactment of social relations.

Factors Affecting Housing Change

Missionary Influences

Christian missionaries, who arrived on Rotuma in the mid-nineteenth century, affected housing on Rotuma both intentionally, as an explicit agenda, and indirectly, by introducing new building materials and techniques. The British Methodists in particular associated material lifestyle with spiritual orientation, and consciously tried to provide models of dress, cleanliness, and housing for Rotumans to emulate. Brother Osborne, writing from Sydney after leaving Rotuma in 1873, praised the work of his predecessors, Rev. and Mrs. William Fletcher and other Methodist teachers, and credited changes in housing on Rotuma to their efforts:

> Before Wm. Fletcher's last appointment to the island, there was a comparatively large number of Christians, but they were necessarily very ignorant . . . their houses were the meanest hovels imaginable, and they themselves were unutterably filthy. . . . Through the instrumentality of Mr. & Mrs. Fletcher, and several really superior Fijian teachers, the most gratifying changes were effected. Hundreds *lotu'd* [entered the church] . . . then they purchased soap . . . then they grew dissatisfied with their hovels, and commenced the erection of substantial and neat houses. So rapidly did they advance, that when I was appointed to take Mr. Fletcher's place, nearly four

years ago, I found that there was a membership of upwards of 450, & a large attendance at the schools. There were also scores of well-constructed wattle and lime houses neatly whitewashed, having doors and glazed windows. (Methodist Church of Australasia, Letters Received, March 1, 1873)

Reverend Fletcher recognized and continued to use the power of example and intergroup competition to effect changes in construction practices when he returned to the island after Brother Osborne's departure. Following a severe hurricane that devastated crops and destroyed buildings in 1874, he wrote from Rotuma:

> The people see the need of better houses, and will gradually I think use stone instead of the plaited cocoa-nut leaves, or even lime. I have just completed a stone room for myself, which will be invaluable as a refuge, should my family need one in another storm, and meanwhile I have a capital study. It serves too for the weekly meetings of my teachers. The building is about twenty one feet by fourteen feet inside. The walls are seven feet high from the floor and twenty inches thick. It is my first attempt as a mason—& may it be my last! It is the first building entirely of stone on the island. I was induced to undertake it partly to encourage the people to let the roofs of their chapels rest directly on the walls. Doubting the security of this arrangement, they preferred to erect the whole framework of the building, and then fill in between the posts with stone and mortar. I have prevailed on the Noatau people, amongst whom I reside, to leave the posts they had prepared, and they are now putting up a new chapel of stone fifty feet by thirty. The height will be about eleven feet. . . . And as the power of rivalry is strong amongst the chiefs, the erection of one good stone place of worship may result in the erection of many more. (Methodist Church of Australasia, Diary of Reverend Fletcher, October 27, 1874)

Brother Osborne was caustic in his assessment of the effects of the work of the two French Catholic priests on the island, in part because the Catholics did not put the same emphasis on changing the domestic conditions of the Rotumans:

> It is painful to be compelled to state that Roman Catholicism in Rotumah is really no better than heathenism. It does not raise the people socially or morally; their houses and their persons are nearly as filthy as ever they were. (Methodist Church of Australasia, Letters Received, March 1, 1873)

The Catholic priests, rather, focused on building two huge churches and school complexes on the island. Virtually all the materials for the churches—including wood, stained glass windows, altar, statuary, bells, and even gargoyles for the clock tower—were imported from France. The building process took decades. The priests involved the local people in the construction and decoration of these buildings, thereby teaching them new skills. By 1938 the British resident commissioner, A. E. Cornish, reported:

> The new school and dormitory at the Rotuman Catholic Mission, Sumi Station, is now nearing completion and a very worthy and solid building it will be. When completed this will be the best building in Rotuma, even the churches, as buildings, cannot be compared with it. The Sumi Mission school offers more opportunities to boys than ordinary school lessons. Most of the boys turned out by this school are good carpenters and have a good knowledge of cement work, engines etc. The girls at these mission schools do excellent needle-work, frequently gaining prizes at the Suva Show. (Rotuma District Office, Outward Letters: Annual Report of 1938, 9)

In the following year's report Cornish noted the completion of electrical wiring, painting, and building of cupboards at the school, commenting with pride, "Any visitor would be amazed to find such a building in an isolated island such as this" (Rotuma District Office, Outward Letters: Annual Report of 1939, 7).

Environmental, Social, and Economic Impetus to Change

The work of the missions—both through inculcating their values about appropriate housing and through teaching construction skills—undoubtedly influenced Rotuman aspirations for European-style housing. But the preference Rotumans demonstrated for new housing styles may have its roots less in ideology than in practical response to opportunity. A number of factors combined in the late 1800s to make a switch to new house styles both possible and desirable.

Rotuma is periodically subject to hurricanes, often necessitating the reconstruction of buildings islandwide. Unfortunately, the supply of thatch is frequently depleted at the very time it is most in demand. A hurricane in 1874 destroyed virtually all the houses on the island (Boddam-Whetham 1876, 262), and replacement thatch was scarce (Rotuma District Office, Outward Letters: November 24, 1884). The resulting housing crisis may have been aggravated by the behavior of the victors in one of a series of religious wars about the same time. The Methodists reportedly burned houses belonging to Catholic and "heathen" Rotumans (Forbes 1875, 242), although such behavior is specifically denied in the accounts given to Gardiner (1898, 470) some twenty years later.

When Europeans introduced the use of lime *(soroi)*, made from burnt coral, as a building material in the 1870s, Rotumans greeted the innovation enthusiastically. At first they plastered it over their thatched walls, then began to build new stone houses *(rī hạfu)*, plastered inside and out with lime (Gardiner 1898, 435). By 1884, Resident Commissioner W. M. Gordon reported that "stone-and-lime houses which are well built and accurate in dimensions, are rapidly taking the place of the present thatch houses" (Rotuma District Office, Outward Letters: November 24, 1884).

To the extent that the new style houses were built of local resources, obtaining and preparing materials and erecting structures remained processes dependent on *kạinaga* assistance. Like Rotuman thatched houses, limestone houses were built on named foundations and embodied in tangible form the caring support of the relatives who contributed to their existence. However, they also set a new standard for what constituted a good house. According to Allen (1895), the Rotumans building stone houses used "wooden doors, and windows of European manufacture." They began to incorporate other imported materials as well, such as cloth curtains and corrugated iron roofs. Acquired through barter or purchase, these materials reflected the increasing participation of Rotumans in the market economy through sailing and copra trade as well as widening exposure to alternatives for house styles and furnishings.[5]

The proportion of *rī hạfu* on the island gradually increased over the next several decades. In a 1948 report commissioned by the colonial government, J. W. Sykes wrote that "most of the houses are built of stone cemented with a mixture of coral lime and sand and covered with a roof of sago palm leaf thatch" (Sykes 1948). He noted that there were also many European-style houses with wooden walls and iron roofs, although these were not well maintained. One would gather from his report that there were few, if any, houses with thatched walls on the island. But just a few years later, District Officer H. S. Evans (1951, note 25) provided a numerical assessment of housing types that indicates thatched structures had persisted to some extent. He reported, "Rather over one third of the houses are attractive cottages of coral lime concrete, brilliantly white with lime wash; rather less than one third are Rotuman houses with sago leaf

Table 2.2
Rotuma House Styles, 1951–1989

	1951[a]	1966[b]	1981[b]	1989[c]
Walls of:				
Limestone or cement	(35%)	240 (51%)	269 (83%)	361 (82%)
Wood	(32%)	60 (13%)	31 (10%)	24 (5%)
Iron	(9%)	84 (18%)	25 (8%)	46 (10%)
Thatch	(24%)	89 (19%)	0 (0%)	8 (2%)
Total houses	(100%)	473 (101%)	325 (101%)	439 (99%)

[a] Reported by H. S. Evans, resident commissioner of Rotuma. Percentages only.
[b] Records of Rotuma Council, compiled and reported by district chiefs.
[c] Survey of 414 households (85% of all households on Rotuma) conducted by Jan Rensel and Alan Howard.

walls; twenty-four percent are timber houses and the remaining nine per cent of corrugated iron." Most roofs were still thatched, with no more than 12 percent of the houses having iron roofs.

By 1966, according to a report prepared by the Rotuma Council of district chiefs and representatives (see table 2.2), more than half the houses had stone or cement walls (both called *rī hafu*). Thatched houses *(rī ota)* had decreased to less than one-fifth, houses with iron walls *(rī pota)* had increased to 18 percent, and only 13 percent were timber houses *(rī 'ai)*. Fifteen years later, in 1981, the Rotuma Council reported that 83 percent of houses had stone or cement walls. Wooden and iron-walled houses constituted 10 percent and 8 percent of island houses, respectively. These changes, and especially the fact that there were virtually no Rotuman-style thatch houses standing, were due in large part to the 1972 hurricane named Bebe and the relief program that followed.

Hurricane Bebe

Hurricane Bebe destroyed or damaged most buildings on Rotuma. Afterward, under the provisions of a government disaster relief program, Rotumans were given small loans (averaging about F$274) in the form of materials, typically including six bags of cement for a house foundation, eight galvanized iron pipes for supports, timber for rafters, roofing iron, and nails. The New Zealand Army came to

Rotuma to assist with the rebuilding effort, and brought the materials. The rafters were cut and assembled at one site, then loaded
onto a truck with the other materials and delivered to sites around
the island. A model house was built in one district, with two or three
men from each district assisting. These men then worked along with
one soldier, assigned as foreman, to direct construction by eight-
person teams in their own district. After pouring the foundations, the
teams placed iron posts upright in the cement to act as roof supports,
then erected the rafters. People were left to choose and build their
own walls out of whatever material they could afford and obtain.[6]

The construction teams competed to see how fast they could build
the basic structures. The work of the New Zealand Army and their
Rotuman assistants has now assumed legendary status on the island:
During a period of twenty-one days, I was told, they built 302 new
housing units. As can be seen from the house counts in table 2.2, this
represented a significant proportion of the dwellings on the island.

Besides the obvious physical differences, this massive reconstruction effort provided opportunities for other kinds of change. Some
families chose not to rebuild their houses on kingroup house foundations.[7] According to the 1989 survey, only 58 percent of island households were located on *fūag rī*. Although the majority of Rotuman
homes are still built on *kạinaga* land,[8] those located away from *fūag
rī* may be less subject to claims by other *kạinaga* members. Those
investing time and materials in a more permanent structure may have
been hoping to ensure its being passed on to their own offspring.

Hurricane Bebe and subsequent government aid provided significant impetus to housing changes on Rotuma. However, the overall
trend toward more elaborate, individually owned housing is sustained
to a great extent by the outmigration of Rotumans to paid positions
abroad, and the cash and imported materials these migrants send
back to the island.

Migrant Involvement

As mentioned above, there has been a dramatic increase in the proportion of Rotumans living in Fiji over recent decades. Although the
population residing on the island remained fairly stable from 1956–
1986, average household size decreased from 7.4 to 5.8 persons.
Much of this can be attributed to a marked increase in the number of
households with one to three persons. While in 1960 Howard found
that such small households made up only 11 percent of Rotuman
households, in 1989 almost 30 percent of households fell into this

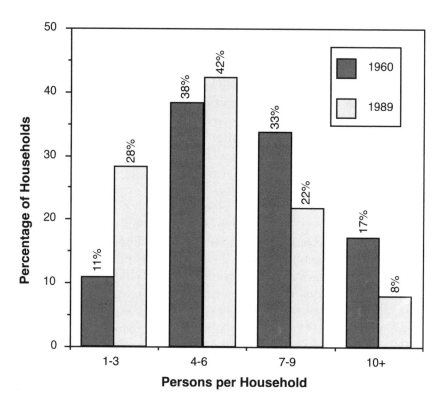

1960 data from unpublished survey by Alan Howard
1989 data from survey conducted by Jan Rensel and Alan Howard

2.3 Household size on Rotuma, 1960 and 1989

category. At the same time, the percentage of households on the
island composed of ten or more people dropped from 17 percent in
1960 to only 8 percent in 1989 (figure 2.3).

The increase in small households may be attributed in part to
return migration by individuals who choose to establish separate
households rather than join existing ones. In addition, some formerly
larger households now are represented by a single individual, who
has been designated caretaker for the family home. He or she maintains the house with the financial support of family members abroad.
Small and large households alike benefit from remitted cash and
materials for house construction, improvement, and expansion.

The transformation in housing materials implicates a corresponding shift in relationships that supply them. Thatch, stone, and lime can be obtained locally on land belonging to *kạinaga* and with the help of relatives near at hand. The use of imported materials requires access to money or to people with money, generally migrant relatives. Relationships with *kạinaga* off island who provide such support thus assume a higher value. Besides nurturing these ties with periodic gifts of produce or other island specialties, Rotuma residents try to provide their kin with comfortable accommodations when they visit. Comfort is defined increasingly in terms of the urban settings from which the visitors come, that is, a European-style house and furnishings.

Rotuman Houses 1989

Building Materials and Styles

In an islandwide survey in 1989, Alan Howard and I found that the typical household compound included one or more cement dwellings *(rī noho)* with separate outbuildings for cooking *(kohea)*, shower, and toilet (see figure 2.4).[9] The 401 households providing information on structures included a total of 439 dwellings, 352 of which had cement walls (80 percent); most had corrugated iron roofs. Only 9 stone-and-lime houses were in use as dwellings, although a number of such buildings were standing empty. There were 24 houses with walls of wood. *Rī noho* with thatched walls numbered 8, representing a slight comeback from 1981 (refer to table 2.2). In addition, 30 of the 46 iron-walled houses had thatched roofs. Thatch was much more commonly used for constructing shelters for cooking and eating; 72 percent of such structures were thatch roofed, with walls of iron, wood, thatch, or simply no walls at all.[10]

Many dwellings surveyed in 1989 consisted primarily of one large room divided by curtains, reproducing in cement the layout of thatched houses. But in newer buildings it was more common for interior walls of wood or cement to separate sitting rooms from bedrooms. Interior walls have been found to provide superior structural support in the face of hurricanes.[11] They also add privacy; as one result, it is now acceptable for young men to sleep at home rather than elsewhere.[12]

Piped water from the underground freshwater lens has been available on Rotuma beginning in the late 1970s. It has taken several years to establish the islandwide system of reservoirs and pipelines, and the job is not yet complete. A recent government aid program

2.4 Contemporary Rotuman dwelling of cement, wood, and corrugated iron with louvered glass windows, showing new cement-block addition at rear. The house is on an elevated foundation surrounded by rocks; a border of croton plants decorates the front. Note also the thatched kitchen in the back, and the iron wash house. Jan Rensel, 1990.

also provided water-sealed toilets, although most of these were installed in outbuildings. In recent years some houses have been constructed with kitchen, washroom, and toilet facilities under the same roof with dwelling spaces. Although many prefer the outdoor *koua* for cooking local foods, with greater use of imports like rice, noodles, and tinned meat it is more convenient to prepare meals inside. Participation in cooking and eating are correspondingly more restricted to members of the household.

Construction Processes

Despite changes in materials and styles, reciprocal labor arrangements for building projects have persisted. Nearly all households surveyed in 1989 indicated their houses had been built by family members, neighbors, and friends; only nine households islandwide reported having hired labor for house construction.[13] Reciprocal assistance is particularly prevalent in building thatch or corrugated iron dwellings, *kohea*, or other shelters. But for wooden and cement buildings the different requirements for strength and skill limit participation, particularly of women, although there are a number of capable female carpenters on the island.

Further, there are indications of a growing tendency to pay laborers for house construction and renovation. In 1989, I conducted a thirteen-week survey of the activities of seventeen households in one village. Of the ten households that engaged in construction projects during the survey, eight gave money to nonhousehold members who assisted. I have heard from others on the island that Rotumans are increasingly reluctant to help build houses, especially modern cement and wooden structures, without being given money. Some of the trend toward paying workers can be explained in terms of a need for skilled labor to install windows, ceramic tile, and other imported features.[14] Other reasons may be grounded in a perception that those who are building more elaborate homes have access to money and therefore should share this resource, not just the conventional meals and implicit promises of in-kind reciprocation.

The matter of relative wealth is especially prominent in the case of migrants building homes on the island—returning retirees, or Rotumans who live abroad but want a place of their own to stay when they come on holiday. In the late 1980s, for example, a migrant in London sent money to a relative in her home district to hire and supervise laborers in constructing a home her family could live in when visiting the island. Two medical doctors (one a Rotuman, one an Australian married to a Rotuman man) were each paying workers to build elaborate, architecturally designed homes on the island. In contrast, some returnees build traditional thatch houses; recently two men who came back to Rotuma from Fiji to take chiefly titles chose to construct rī ota, assisted without financial compensation by their people.

House Repairs and Improvements

Types of housing repairs, and the processes for accomplishing them, have changed along with materials. Rotumans were receptive to a longer-lasting alternative when lime was introduced as a building material in the late 1800s. Lime-and-stone houses, however, require periodic white-washing with additional lime (Evans 1951, note 25). Likewise, wooden houses need paint and are subject to termites, and iron roofs eventually rust and must be repaired or replaced (Sykes 1948). One advantage of cement houses is that they require little maintenance, especially if left unpainted. Increasingly, however, householders on Rotuma are choosing to paint their cement structures, and to add features such as indoor plumbing, electrical wiring, and bathroom tile. As noted above, individuals with special skills are sought for the renovation work, and are compensated in cash. In 1989, 145 households islandwide reported having made renovations to their dwellings in the preceding year. The projects, such as reroofing, painting, and adding extensions, cost from a few hundred to several thousand dollars, and were paid for by employed household members or remittances.

Furnishings and Housekeeping

In 1960, Howard conducted an islandwide household survey that included an assessment of dwellings as "European" or "Rotuman" style. Howard's Rotuman research assistants classified the houses based on their own criteria. They characterized Rotuman style as houses with mats on the floor and very little furniture. European style referred to houses with enough furniture (tables, chairs, sofas, beds, cabinets, etc.) to accommodate a European guest comfortably. By these criteria, 33 percent of houses were assessed as European style (Howard field notes 1960).

According to Howard, in 1960 the only status distinction Rotumans made on the basis of external construction was between the dwellings of ordinary Rotumans and those of government officers and managers of the trading firms, whose houses were much more elaborate. The research assistants' decision to distinguish among *Rotuman* houses on the basis of internal furnishings rather than wall materials suggests that external appearance made little social difference, while furniture and appliances signified a different style of living (Howard, personal communication). Indeed, our subsequent research supports the view that household goods have important implications for daily activities and social relations.

In our 1989 survey, Howard and I included detailed inventories of household furnishings and appliances. These revealed increasing purchases of imported durables over the past thirty years, illustrated by a tally of selected consumer items by years obtained (see table 2.3). The majority of households reported some European furnishings: For instance, 65 percent had chairs, 79 percent tables, and 87 percent beds. Although some furniture was and is built by household members or occasionally by a carpenter on the island, building materials are usually imported; and virtually all other furniture is purchased and shipped to the island.[15]

With more and more Rotuman houses equipped with Western-

Table 2.3
Selected Consumer Goods on Rotuma by Years Obtained

Items	no date	pre-1970	1970–1974	1975–1979	1980–1984	1984–1989	Total owned
Sewing machines	38	68	55	51	79	59	350
Refrigerators	6	8	8	18	43	38	121
Motorbikes	9	2	9	28	53	75	176
Lawnmowers	4	1	6	9	29	43	92
Bicycles	2	1	5	8	26	38	80
Freezers	3	1	0	5	8	20	37
Generators	1	1	2	1	8	26	39
Cars & trucks	4	0	0	4	5	18	31
Videotape players	0	0	0	0	4	22	26
Washing machines	0	0	0	0	1	9	10

Data obtained from 1989 survey of 414 houses conducted by Jan Rensel and Alan Howard style furniture, mat making assumes a smaller portion of women's responsibilities. Although mats remain highly important for ceremonial exchange, and commonly are used as floor coverings or beds, women reportedly spend less time plaiting mats than they used to, and young women often do not learn how to plait mats at all. When I asked what women are doing instead, people suggested they were spending more time looking after their houses. Respondents to a 1989 survey reported activities such as sewing curtains and bed sheets, making doormats, and crocheting doilies, not to mention washing and ironing household linens. Much attention went into the appearance of houses, with borders of colorful bougainvillea and croton bushes planted outside and containers of fresh or plastic flowers, pictures, and other ornaments decorating indoor spaces. The care of houses seems to have assumed greater importance in Rotuman perceptions than in 1960 (Howard, personal communication). Although some activities, such as needlework, are pursued in social settings such as women's groups, more of the house-related work done by women today is done individually.

Social Implications of Housing Change

Valuation and Support of Relationships

Changes in housing on Rotuma obviously go far beyond physical structures. The decision to invest in a new house has significant implications for a household's relationships in the Rotuman community. In choosing to build or extend with imported materials, one is frequently emphasizing ties with migrants over those with local *kạinaga*. Participation in the work process is limited, including fewer women and only men with particular skills. While a house built of local materials by a large cooperating group stands as a constant reminder of their care and support, one constructed by few, paid workers embodies correspondingly less social meaning.

Subsequent activities are also affected. With the increasing practice of giving money for help and materials, reciprocal assistance is downplayed. With changes in the form and furnishing of dwellings, opportunities for shared activities between nearby households are diminished. For households with fewer members, correspondingly greater attention may be devoted to supporting relationships with off-island relatives by sending produce and hosting visits.

Location and Permanence

Since Rotumans reckon rights to house sites rather than to specific structures, a house built on family land not on a traditional foundation may be reserved for one's children without contention. The construction of permanent houses on *füag rī* will necessitate some renegotiation of criteria for claims to the site. It appears that capital investment in a house is being recognized as sufficient justification for a lineal family group to remain on a *füag rī*. This has the added implication of strengthening the claims of immediate descendants, by their continuing presence, to not only the site but associated garden lands and title, if any.

The shift to permanent buildings itself has implications for Rotuman dispute management. Avoidance is one of the major strategies for dealing with conflict. A serious falling-out may result in one party's relocating to avoid contact with the other. One such instance arose in 1989, when a household tore down their thatched dwelling and rebuilt it at another location because of a disagreement over claims to the first site. This option is practicable for people with iron or wood houses, but out of the question for those with cement buildings. People may be able to get away temporarily by visiting relatives elsewhere on the island, in Fiji, or abroad, but eventually they must return or face having to give up a sizable investment of cash, labor, and materials. Even more difficult are disputes over land claims in which someone else attempts to force a household to leave. Bad feelings are exacerbated by the specter of losing not only the land but a permanent house and the work and relationships it represents.

Wealth, Rank, and Social Merit

Rotuman concepts of what constitutes a good house have been shaped by missionary teaching and example, experiences with other outsiders, and concerns for practicality and convenience. Whatever its genesis, the predominance of European-style housing bears witness to a valuing of imported over indigenous models. The switch to concrete structures after Hurricane Bebe was impelled not only by practical concerns and a desire for stronger materials, but also by a pursuit of European goods for status purposes. By embracing Western-style goods as status markers, Rotumans perhaps inadvertently have contributed to changes in social relationships.

Over the past few decades, according to some observers, a Rotuman's house has become the "measuring-stick whereby one gauges people's wealth and status" (Plant 1991, 205). Prior to cession in 1881 there was little material difference among Rotuman houses in style and furnishings. Chiefs' houses were distinguished primarily by their larger size, which reflected chiefly responsibility for hosting visitors. In the past chiefs could call on community labor to build their houses, but today if they want something other than a thatched dwelling they are in the same position as everyone else: Materials, and to some extent labor, cost money. A related change is an apparent decline in the custom of claiming the particular house site that goes with a title when a person is made a chief. When a man appointed to a certain subchiefly title moved back to Rotuma from Fiji in 1988, the household head staying in a cement house on the site affiliated with that title adamantly refused to allow the returnee to move there. The new subchief subsequently built a thatched house on other *kạinaga* land.

At the same time, for some, Western-style houses may be becoming increasingly important for establishing claims to chiefly titles. In 1988, during a discussion of qualities to look for in a candidate for chieftainship, one Rotuman suggested to me the following criteria, in this order (emphasis added):

1. A handyman who works hard and can do a lot of things well
2. Someone who participates in the community—not a loner
3. A Christian who is active in church affairs
4. Someone who looks like a chief and *has a good house and therefore can be looked up to*
5. Someone who speaks well
6. One who is educated and can speak English well
7. One who loves the people, that is, takes care of them

The inclusion of housing in such formulations was not noted during previous anthropological research on the island in 1960 (see Howard 1970). A negative example is the case of one district chief who in 1990 was subject to criticism for having a humble thatched dwelling rather than a "proper house" in which to entertain visitors. At present, the houses of most district chiefs are cement structures, but neither the largest nor the most imposing in their districts.[16] Rather, people with higher earned incomes, or financial support from off island, command the resources to develop elaborate housing.

A Good House—and A Good Provider

Evaluation of social merit aside from rank considerations seems also to have been affected by increased access to Western-style housing. Customarily, a Rotuman's ability to provide an abundance of food, primarily garden produce, has been of central importance in evaluating social merit. Recently, however, there is some suggestion this measure has been eclipsed by one's ability to provide a Western-style house. Wilson Inia, Rotuma's first senator to the Fiji legislature, said in a 1974 speech in support of the savings and house loans programs of the Fiji National Provident Fund:

> One of the great responsibilities of a father to a family is to provide a house while he is alive, or if he has passed away, to leave behind sufficient funds for the mother or the children to build a house. That is good advice to a Rotuman whether he be in Suva or in Rotuma. Any father who cannot provide that is a bad father. (Parliamentary Debates, October 14, 1974)

I was told in 1988 that there is a Rotuman saying: *"Nōnō ka rī lelei, ma 'inea ne huạ' lelei."* 'When the house is good, you know the occupants [those who look after it] are good.' But this may not represent as much a disjunction from former bases for attributing merit as it may first appear. The term *huạ'i* (shortened to *huạ'* in this context) connotes the *work* of caretaking. Rotumans who are long-term residents on the island, and are aware of the social histories of buildings, are more likely to distinguish between merely *having* a nice house and *having done the work* to procure the materials and build one. Not taken in by appearances, those who know whose work is represented can judge houses much as they evaluate food production and contributions.

Social pressure does not deter Rotumans from trying their best to build and furnish their preferred house in whatever ways are open to them. But not all Rotumans make the same choices. Over the past decade, the advent of two-story houses on the island represents one extreme. The man who built the first such house was subject to criticism from others for his ostentatious display, but others have since begun to follow his example: The 1989 survey turned up six houses with two stories. These have been built with migrant or returnee money and represent a valuing of comfort and status (defined in urban wage-earner terms) over fitting into the community. In fact, for people with less urban experience, such elaborate houses have a distancing and intimidating effect. At the other end of the spectrum are the examples, mentioned above, of the two migrant Rotumans who built thatched houses when they returned to the island to accept chiefly titles. Their decision to do so may reflect other considerations, such as a desire to limit monetary investment in imported materials until they could see how the new positions would work out. But by electing to build traditional Rotuman houses with the help of the people they came to lead (and serve), these new chiefs also gave priority to reconnecting with the community through the familiar and time-honored practice of reciprocal labor.

Notes

This chapter is based on a review of historical documents, including the field notes of previous ethnographers, and on research I conducted with Alan Howard on Rotuma during six field trips, ranging from a few weeks to six months, between 1987 and 1994. My research was sponsored in part by a Fulbright Grant administered by the Institute for International Education. Oral versions of this paper were presented at the University of Hawai'i and the University of the South Pacific. I am grateful to those who responded with comments and suggestions, especially Dr. Vilsoni Hereniko, Paul Vaurasi, Mrs. Elisapeti Inia, and Prof. Asesela Ravuvu. This chapter is a reorganized and expanded version of an article entitled "Housing and Social Relationships on Rotuma" that appeared in *Rotuma: Hanua Pumue (Precious Land)* (Fatiaki et al. 1991).

1. For a guide to Rotuman pronunciation, see Churchward 1940, 13.

2. By the end of 1995 both cooperatives had ceased doing business. While this sizably reduced the number of wage positions on the island, opportunities for entrepreneurs have increased, and a number of individual trading enterprises have sprung up.

3. One Fiji dollar is worth approximately sixty-seven cents in U.S. currency.

4. Elisapeti Inia instigated the development of curriculum materials for teaching Rotuman language, oral traditions, and custom in schools in Rotuma and Fiji. Her materials were recently adopted and expanded under the auspices of the Curriculum Development Unit of the Fiji Department of Education, with Mrs. Inia's guidance and involvement.

5. Through their own experiences abroad as sailors, and the example of visiting Europeans, Rotumans were exposed to and adopted a number of innovations in furnishing their houses. For instance, a Mr. Emery, former mate of an English whaleship who left that position for health reasons, settled in Rotuma around 1829 and built a wooden house on the offshore

islet of Uea. He had English furniture, cooking utensils, and pictures on the walls. Emery married a Rotuman woman, and lived on Uea with about sixty other Rotumans who reportedly treated him as their chief (Cheever 1834–1835). Another sailor from a whaling ship, visiting in the early 1850s, noted that brightly colored curtains were used to screen the sleeping areas of a large house he and his mates visited. He surmised these had been traded by some whaling captain for hogs and other provisions (Haley 1948, 258).

6. Due to lack of funds, and competing demands for what money some families did have available, many houses took years to complete.

7. Paul Vaurasi, a Rotuman who worked for many years in the Fiji government's Department of Public Works, noted that new *fūag rī* are sometimes constructed in order to create level ground on which to build.

8. Of the 414 households responding to the 1989 survey, 306 (74 percent) said their houses were located on *kainaga* land. Other possibilities were *hanua togi*, land owned outright as a result of purchase from other Rotumans (9 percent); *hanua nā*, land owned outright as a gift (2 percent); *hanua pau*, land owned outright by those residing there, the only claimants as a result of attrition (3 percent); *hanua haisasigi*, land belonging to siblings (3 percent); lands belonging to government (2 percent) and church (3 percent); and no information given (4 percent).

9. As in English usage, there are several euphemisms for the toilet in Rotuman, including *rī mea'me'a* 'little house', *rī la'oaga* 'house for going', and *fa'u* 'out back', as in *ia la' se fa'* 'he went out back'. When Howard conducted his fieldwork on the island in 1960, outhouses were located either inland (the back, according to Rotuman orientation) or at the end of a wooden pier leading from the beach to beyond the high tide mark (Howard 1970, 31).

10. When roofing iron is replaced on dwellings, the old iron is often reused for *kohea* or other outbuildings.

11. I am grateful to Paul Vaurasi for pointing this out.

12. Howard reports that in 1960 only in a few villages did the boys build their own sleeping house; more often they used a structure that was temporarily available, or went to the home of an older single or widowed man (Howard 1970, 66). During my fieldwork in the late 1980s, I observed that while some slept in the home of their parents, many of the young men in Oinafa village took their mats and mosquito nets to the community hall and slept there instead.

13. Responses to the survey may reflect rhetoric more than reality, especially in cases in which people did not know the details of their dwelling's history.

14. Some Rotumans pay skilled laborers cash for their work, recognizing that government and other organizations pay them for doing this type of work. In other cases, such as a flurry of house renovations in Oinafa

prompted by a large celebration in 1989, skilled assistance is in great demand and short supply; people essentially competed for the workers' time by offering F$10 to F$12/day.

15. Interestingly, I observed that when a Rotuman household hosted a large group inside the dwelling, for instance for a small ceremony or a prayer meeting, they often pushed aside chairs and sofas or removed them from the area, spreading mats on which people sat. Although household members used their furniture on an everyday basis, with the arrival of even casual visitors everyone frequently ended up sitting on the floor.

16. An exception is the case of the chief in the highest ranking district on the island. A large guest house with a high roof and commanding aspect was constructed to house visiting VIPs during the 1981 celebration of the centennial of the cession of Rotuma to Great Britain. After a new district chief was installed in 1983, he claimed the guest house as his residence.

3
Samo House Styles and Social Change

∩

R. DANIEL SHAW

IN AUGUST 1963, Patrol Officer I. M. Douglas grew weary of searching out isolated longhouses in the dense rain forest of the Strickland Plain in the Western Province of what is now Papua New Guinea (see map; figure 3.1). To assuage his frustration he decided to establish administrative rest house sites that could easily be found. The people living in longhouses in the vicinity of these sites would, he reasoned, eventually grow weary of answering the government's call and turn these sites into villages (see map; figure 3.2). He recorded his long range intentions in his patrol report:

> In due course these rest houses may well act as magnets, drawing in the various outlying houses as their current dwellings become uninhabitable. In this way the area would be eventually reduced to eight or nine villages worthy of that name, thus greatly easing the job of administering the area. (Douglas 1963)

Over the next several years, other officers continued this approach throughout the Strickland Plain, a rest house often being built at an existing house site or a particularly picturesque spot in the forest where an officer enjoyed "resting." As Douglas predicted, the Samo eventually tired of repeatedly traveling to these sites for census, government information, and other dealings with the colonial administration. As their dwellings fell into disrepair, rather than building on land associated with their respective habitation cycle, they built at the *gaboo monsoon*[1] 'white man said house'.

Today seven hundred Samo live between the Nomad and Domami Rivers, which empty into the Strickland River over six hundred river miles from the Gulf of Papua. The undulating terrain is watered by

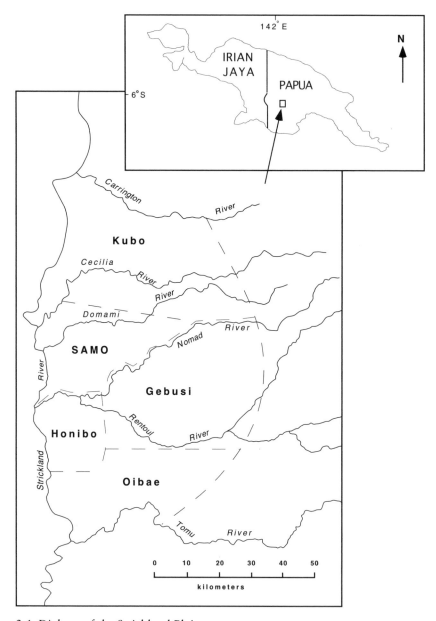

3.1 Dialects of the Strickland Plain

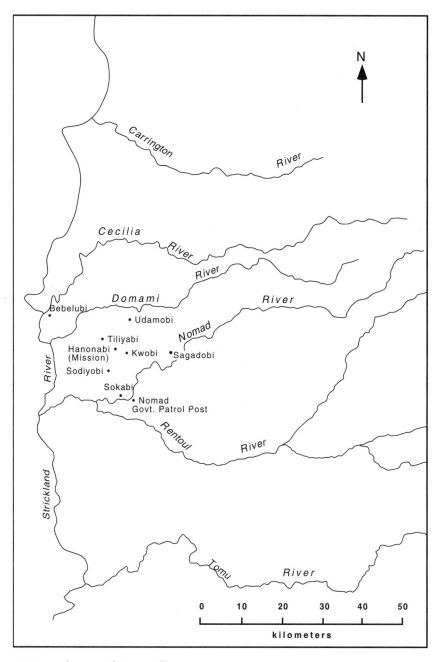

3.2 Distribution of Samo village sites

over two hundred inches of rain per year, ensuring a dense tropical rain forest that supports a moderate supply of wildlife. The Samo depend on the forest for their livelihood of plantains and sago supplemented by hunting and gathering (Shaw 1996, 77ff).

This chapter documents the process and effects of replacing an established rhythm of longhouse living with life in a village where several households aggregated for administrative purposes. The pre-contact Samo longhouse cycle, with extended families living in scattered, cyclically relocated longhouses, was dominated by subsistence activities and concern for protection against raids. The colonial government enforced safety and stability, but their demands also led to a transition from the large, forest-based longhouses to small, village-based dwellings. This shift involved far-reaching changes, observable not only in house size and style but in relations among people living in the houses. The account of the evolution of house forms and the concomitant social and linguistic adjustments made by their inhabitants highlights the persistence of cultural values pertaining to personal relationships, group cohesion, and community alliance.

A Samo Longhouse

Standing proudly on a ridge top surrounded by a cleared garden site edged by virgin rain forest, a traditional Samo longhouse (figure 3.3) provided occupants with a focal point for communal activity and relationship, protection from weather and enemies (both human and supernatural), and a context for effective communication.

The Physical Environment

The position of a house on a ridge top permitted a view of the surrounding region. The porch of a house, high above the sloping ground below, offered an ideal position to rain arrows down on unwelcome visitors. The garden area around a house, with its cut trees, created a labyrinth of obstacles to outsiders who might try to traverse it, thereby allowing occupants time to protect themselves against intruders. It also put distance between a house and the surrounding forest populated by fearsome spirit beings. The denuded ground immediately in front of a house allowed communal activities associated with the habitation: entertaining guests, engaging in ceremony and ritual, caring for the dead, and other aspects of Samo culture (Shaw 1990, 1996).

3.3 A traditional Samo longhouse stood alone in the middle of a garden that provided a three- to five-year food supply. The house was built on a named ridge top for protection against enemy raids. The porch afforded an excellent view of the surrounding area. R. D. Shaw, 1970.

The sheltered space of a house overflowed to the living space of the immediate ridge top, sloping garden, and sago-lined stream. On an ideal site, short-term annual crops and often coconut trees were planted near the house at the top of the ridge. The main crop of plantain occupied the slope, and perennial trees bearing pandanus, breadfruit, and galip nut were planted near the base of the ridge. In total, such a site could provide a livelihood over several years. A garden could be extended along the slope of a ridge until it terminated, thereby prolonging habitation while the mature sago in the adjacent swamp provided a steady food supply (sago and plantain combine to provide the bulk of Samo diet). The stream cutting through the swamp served as a ready source of fresh water. A site such as this also provided a means of long-range subsistence, drawing people back to harvest the tree crops long after a house collapsed. Such visits perpetuated memories associated with the habitation: an initiation ceremony, a funeral, or even a raid.

As the supply of sago diminished, residents were forced to process sago and garden sites at an ever greater distance from the existing longhouse. Over time it became increasingly less efficient to continue

domicile at the old house site, and a new habitation cycle was initiated at a location where the proximity of sago and ridge maximized
corporate labor for effective food production. The main ironwood
house posts were generally salvaged to be used in the new house.
This in turn extended the history of a house, as the new abode not
only bore similarity of architectural style but actually used the ironwood skeleton of main supporting posts. Such utilization of existing
materials reduced construction time and maintained continuity of
structure despite the shift in location. People continued to live in the
old house as long as possible. At the point when they could take up
habitation at the new site (where small garden houses often provided
transitional housing), the remainder of the termite-ridden rubble of
the old house was burned. The ash-enriched soil provided an ideal
medium for growing tobacco.

A longhouse, then, was more than a sheltered space. It was a
place, a ridge top, that extended the living space to the edge of the
forest surrounding the cleared garden. It provided an ongoing source
of food, memories, and a promise of reoccupation when forest nutri-
ents replenished the thin top soil depleted by a garden, and the sago
stand matured. The structure itself, however, was carefully organized
to order human relationships and activities and provide protection.

The Structure

Figure 3.4 gives the detail of a forest longhouse with its various divisions based on activity and where people normally slept. The porch
was considered, first and foremost, a fighting platform, and those
most able—that is, virile, unmarried males—slept there and set a
nightly watch for the protection of others. Opposed to the porch was
the kitchen, dominated by females whose primary activity centered
around the production and preparation of food. Longitudinally, the
house was divided by a wall separating the female sleeping area
(including an area for menstrual confinement) and the large activity
area beside which married males slept. This large room was the main
activity area of the house and took its name from ceremonial activity
—male dancing. A longhouse, then, was a concatenation of activity
areas particular to a division of gender and labor denoting those who
occupied that portion of the house—protecting warriors, producing
women, and ceremonially equipped adult males. Where people slept
in the house reflected their primary responsibility and anticipated
relationships with others within the household. Sexual relations between married adults was not considered a household activity but
relegated to the privacy of the forest.

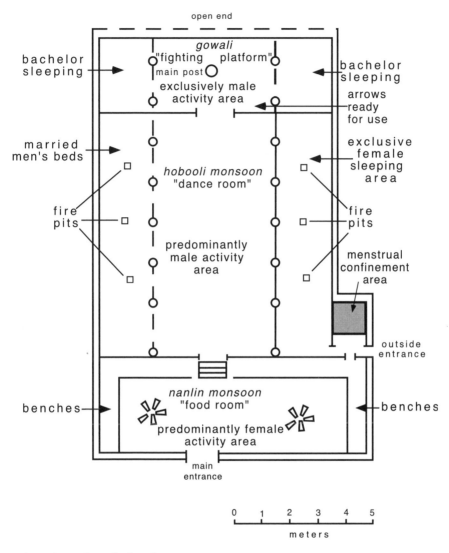

open end

bachelor sleeping

gowali
"fighting   platform"
main post

exclusively male
activity area

bachelor sleeping

arrows
ready
for use

married
men's beds

hobooli monsoon
"dance room"

exclusive
female
sleeping
area

fire
pits

predominantly
male activity
area

fire
pits

menstrual
confinement
area

outside
entrance

nanlin monsoon
"food room"

predominantly female
activity area

benches

benches

main
entrance

0   1   2   3   4   5

meters

3.4 Floor plan of a longhouse

The very construction of a longhouse made it a fortress against attack. The front doorway, entering the kitchen, was constructed to force entrants to step over logs stacked two feet high. Above the doorway, more logs were held in place by specially designed wooden pins or tied vines. In case of threat to the household the pins could be pulled (or vine cut), allowing the logs to block the doorway. Thus, intruders were "locked" out. The main portion of the house was built on a platform extending out over the sloping ground of the ridge. This made entry into the house very difficult, without using the side entrance to the women's area (something men, wary of men-strual pollution, would rarely do). Once barricaded inside, people were reasonably safe and the house more or less impenetrable. Serious raids were, therefore, carried out in great secret in hopes of finding the doorway unbarricaded and entrance to the house easy.

Interpersonal Relationships

A precontact household consisted of elderly males and their wives living together with their sons and their wives and children (what some may call an extended patrilocal family or, perhaps, a patri-clan). These twenty-five to fifty individuals interacted on the basis of relative age (reflecting initiation cycle rather than generation) and gender. When people were brought into the family, for example, a woman from another community was exchanged to become a wife to one of the young men, the terminology used for that individual was changed to reflect the nature of in-house relationship. Accordingly, sleeping space within the house was assigned commensurate with an individual's relative age, marital status, and gender. Such terminological and behavioral adjustments also served as a means of controlling behavior and ensuring cooperation within the household. Similar adjustments have been reported for many regions of Papua New Guinea (cf. Cook 1970, Kaberry 1967, and Watson 1970).

Due to a strict incest rule based on household exogamy, marriage alliances were always arranged with other households. To effect a marriage, females of the reciprocating communities were exchanged. More broadly, the male core of a household considered themselves allied to similar groups through sister exchange. This established a specific network of relationship and protection that later became central to adjusting terminology applied to coresidents at village sites. A longhouse, then, was occupied by a core of males who recognized siblingship based on common residence and when they were initiated with respect to each other.[2]

The other critical dimension affecting relationships within a longhouse community was gender. Same-sex relationships, characterized by shared sleeping quarters, identified the nature of close interaction with others within the household. Conversely, cross-sex interaction, indicated by separate sleeping quarters, produced gender-specific relationships epitomized by male protective activity and female productive activity. Maleness, for the Samo, emphasizes physical and spiritual survival, while femaleness implies productivity in sago swamp and garden as well as a means to maintain household viability through female sibling exchange and subsequent child bearing. This draws attention to interaction between allies scattered throughout the rain forest.

Alliance Relationships

Interaction patterns with other communities were established primarily through sister exchange arranged by the respective older brothers of the couple (Shaw 1974a). The male siblings of a newly married couple entered into a protective alliance that implied cooperation in a wide variety of activities, including extending the labor force for subsistence, assisting each other on ceremonial occasions, and military support in both protecting against raids and amassing the personnel necessary to launch a successful raid against mutual enemies (Shaw 1990, 83ff). As long as a marriage lasted, the resultant alliance held and relationship between communities was maintained. Hence, Samo marriages were carefully strategized events[3] designed to maximize community protection (Shaw 1974b, 239; 1990, 83ff) and provide an early-warning system against enemy raids. This network with a household at the center of its own self-determined social structure is presented in figure 3.5. Each successive level provided a community with a different set of relationships based on residence patterns and alliance through the exchange of women. Beyond this ever-widening (albeit ever-weakening) circle of trust were those with whom there was no exchange and little or no basis for trust—those who were considered enemies.

In short, a longhouse together with its surrounding space provided the Samo with a sense of belonging, both through relationships with others who identified the location as their *kiyali monsoon* 'sleep place', and to a site on which they depended for subsistence and protection. A forest longhouse served as the focus of the Samo concept of "place," epitomized by the word *sa*, a region within which people move about freely and beyond which they establish extended relationships in order to build a network of protection against enemies. In the cycle of longhouse movement, people eventually returned to sites occupied by "grandparents" approximately twenty-five years earlier.

The economic and social context of Samo life at the time of contact was shaped by the interaction of people living within a longhouse that, while site bound, enabled people to exploit an entire region of the forest. This natural cycle provided a reasonably predictable migration around a designated area of the forest based on the

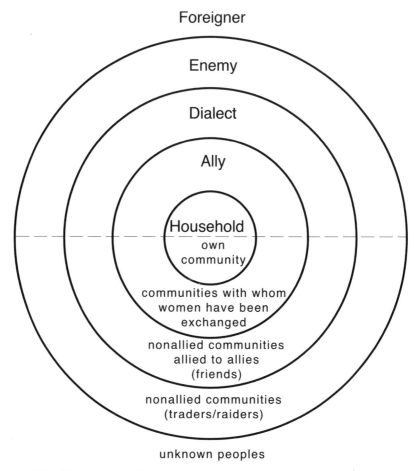

3.5 The alliance network

maturation of sago. Unfortunately, Patrol Officer Douglas knew nothing about this cycle that not only allowed an effective interaction with other households but also shaped language use.

The Linguistic Context

Each longhouse community not only served as the context for close interpersonal relationships and the center of an elaborate alliance structure, it was also the primary speech community for its members. Over time, each household, as it moved about its own relatively isolated territory, developed a microdialect. Women exchanged into a household maintained a degree of bilingualism and passed this on to their children. Thus, like many other societies in Papua New Guinea, the Samo are quick to recognize linguistic variation and maintain an incredible facility to learn and use other languages quickly. This diversity reflects a pattern extant throughout Melanesia (McElhanon and Voorhoeve 1970).

Seeking protection from enemies, household members were extremely wary of outsiders and did everything possible to maintain the integrity of each community. Since raiding was the primary means of compromised integrity, and allies, based on the mutual exchange of female siblings, were crucial for extending relationships, it was only natural that the alliance structure impact the formation of post-contact villages. It is to the process of community aggregation that I now turn.

A Samo Village

Douglas' rest houses did, in fact, serve as "magnets" to attract people to living sites. The rationale for aggregation to these sites, however, was based on the Samo concept of alliance, rather than Douglas' presumption of proximity. While it is true that those households that were geographically close to each other often interacted extensively, the relationship was viewed by the Samo as a product of alliance. Without alliance, interaction was guarded because there was no exchange on which to base trust. While it can be argued that proximity of longhouse communities precipitated relationships that led to exchange and mutual protection, the fact remains that without alliance there was no relationship.

Village Aggregation

When Douglas established a rest house at Kwobi, the people of Homamaku were in the process of building a new longhouse at the site. Because of their close alliance with the people living at Dogobi and Fifilobi, the latter two households eventually migrated to the Kwobi site. The accompanying map of Kwobi village in 1975 (figure 3.6) shows the longhouses and their geographical distribution on the ridge top.

The original houses built at Kwobi were in the traditional longhouse style. Fifilobi was the largest (approximately thirty feet wide and one hundred feet long) in order to accommodate its forty residents. The increased pressure of three households living at the same location produced considerable stress upon land and people alike. The land surrounding new villages was quickly planted, replanted,

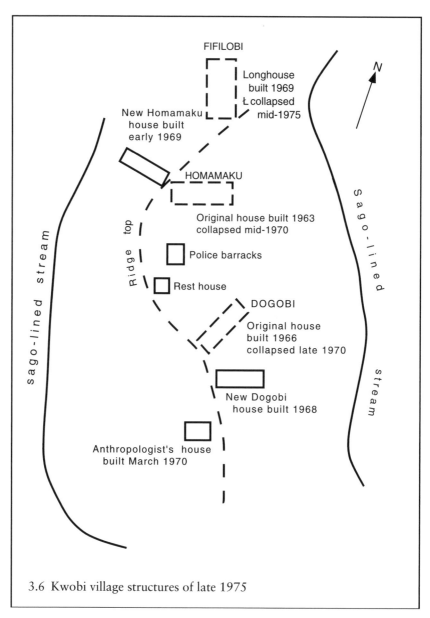

3.6 Kwobi village structures of late 1975

and exhausted. As the years passed people found themselves spending increasing amounts of time away from the village in subsistence
activity—often going back to their traditional regions of the forest.
Small bush houses on garden and sago sites were built with as little
effort as possible and considered only temporary housing for a particular need.

Another complication of village life involved working out the nature of new relationships as people shared a residential site. They had to determine the impact of previous alliance relationships as they now interacted daily in a context that more closely resembled family relationships at a particular location. (This problem will be further examined below in the section titled Alliance Relationships.) Occasional fights between members of different households, sorcery accusations, and friction over relationships with other allies characterized the transition period from longhouse to village (see Shaw 1996 for more details of this transition).

As the original house at Kwobi, the Homamaku house was the first to deteriorate and require replacement; Dogobi was not far behind. In each case the new house was smaller, but still built as a traditional longhouse. As in the context of migration around their land, there was overlap between old and new houses, as the old contributed materials to the new.

Change of House Style

By the time the Fifilobi house deteriorated to the point of collapse in mid-1975, circumstances had changed considerably. Household residents put forth three reasons for not building another longhouse. First, commensurate with lengthy habitation of a single site, there was a dearth of building materials in the vicinity of Kwobi. Second, people were required to spend one day a week in government labor as a form of taxation. This activity (primarily road building and maintenance) depleted the labor force necessary to build a longhouse and increased the amount of time construction would take. Third, over a decade of government protection resulted in little need for the fortress-like safety of a large longhouse. With the decision made, male siblings assisted each other in the work of building four smaller houses in close proximity to the deteriorating longhouse. Upon completion, these smaller dwellings were inhabited by key men of the household and their extended families.

In Kwobi, this pattern was subsequently followed by Homamaku and Dogobi households. As each communal house fell into disrepair, smaller family dwellings replaced them (figure 3.7). By 1980 there were no longhouse structures in Kwobi village (a pattern replicated in all seven Samo villages). As a result of this proliferation of small but clustered houses, a larger portion of the land area was occupied by houses. In addition, individual householders were kept busy in near-constant repair. Wood for building a dependable house was

3.7 The Homamaku cluster of family dwellings in Kwobi is typical of Samo villages today. The central plaza has been denuded of all vegetation, and constant habitation has pushed back the forest as occupants seek space for small garden plots. R. D. Shaw, 1984.

increasingly harder to find and had to be transported over a considerable distance. The labor force necessary to build a proper house was also more difficult to amass as government and oil company jobs and schools drew able-bodied men (who build and protect) away from the community for extended periods. The smaller dwellings, built relatively quickly with less substantial materials, had the disadvantage of deteriorating much more rapidly. As they disintegrated, new and often even smaller houses were built to replace them.

This pattern of building smaller houses in the vicinity of the origi-

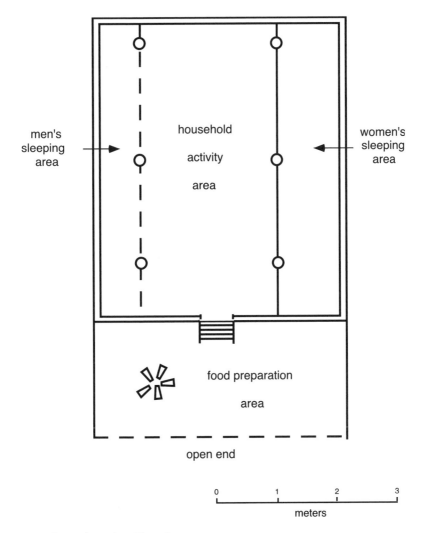

men's sleeping area

household activity area

women's sleeping area

food preparation area

open end

0   1   2   3
meters

3.8 Floor plan of a village house

nal longhouse site in an aggregated village underscores the importance of place within the aggregated community. Though not specifically assigned a portion of the village land area, the original site of
each longhouse appeared to establish usufructuary rights to that portion of the community; new houses built by family members were
always built in proximity to the original site. These individual houses
epitomize the change from a single communal longhouse to a series
of satellite family dwellings.

Each new house resembled a downsized longhouse, although most did not include the porch/fighting platform portion of the house (figure 3.8). Separate male and female sleeping quarters were strictly maintained, with the men's section doubling (as in the longhouse configuration) as the main activity area. In some cases the kitchen area was not completely enclosed; the roof of the main platformed section of the house was simply extended out over the ground immediately in front of it.

Relationships Within a Village

As the move from forest to village and subsequently to smaller, nuclear family dwellings has taken place, cultural ideals about the environment and appropriate gender separation in domestic spaces have influenced house design. Gender roles continue to impact activities in the general environment of forest subsistence. Thus, men continue to protect women engaged in productive activities in the forest and sago swamp. But although gender roles are still reflected by the main sections and separate sleeping quarters, within the confines of smaller houses the dividing wall has been figuratively broken down, as husbands and wives find increasing opportunity for sexual activity within the privacy of their house. Increasingly, a young man builds a new house soon after marriage, and children appear much sooner than in the precontact period. In the village context the protective responsibilities of unmarried warriors have been largely replaced by attending school, and the fighting platform is no longer necessary. Most unmarried adults who would previously have shared the sleeping space on the porch or in the women's section now attend school at the government station at Nomad or the mission at Hanonabi. Several have excelled in their studies and been promoted on to regional and even national high schools.

Alliance Relationships

The mutuality that existed between allies when villages aggregated contributed to a relatively smooth transition to communal interaction. At the same time it created a terminological dilemma. Inasmuch as all individuals living at a single site had traditionally used family terms and engaged in family activities within the community, how should allies now coinhabiting a village site refer to each other? Which took precedence for the Samo—location with its emphasis upon nondisruptive relationships within a community, or alliance with its focus on ceremonial and military protection? With added numbers of people inhabiting a village site and government protection ensured, the scales were tipped toward an emphasis on location. With terminology being, in large measure, a reflection of interaction between individuals, at a given site (be it a single longhouse or a multihouse village) it stood to reason that those interacting within a village would in due course adjust terminological references to reflect their interaction since their preaggregation alliances were no longer in focus. In fact, this is precisely what happened.

The incorporation process began as youngsters interacted as siblings within the community. Commonality of relationship and interaction within the location eventually led to their being initiated together at that site. A conversation with a group of boys at Mogwibi village, recorded in my fieldnotes, demonstrates the conscious adjustments people made:

> This afternoon I followed several boys in their play, listening to what they called each other and noting the reciprocal use of "sibling" terms. Finally, sitting on a log, I discussed this with them. I first asked about the terms they were using for each other and they confirmed the "sibling" usage. I then pointed out that their fathers had no relationship suggesting a basis for the boys to use such terms. The eldest, Wohonlen's son, responded with an incredulous look and answered: "We all live together and play here in Mogwibi. Living together here, I call them *manla*, 'younger brother', and they call me *onyon*, 'older brother'. Some day we will be initiated together."

The cooperation between village members interacting in common activities brought them into family-type relationships. Over a ten-year period terminology reflecting preaggregation alliance usage was gradually replaced by terms acknowledging postaggregation family-type involvement within the same village.

As potential exchanges leading to marriage were discussed among members of aggregated households co-occupying a village site, all adult males within the community were included and village exogamy assumed. Since self-alliance was viewed as counterproductive to their cultural need for protection, alliances with each other were set aside in favor of affiliating with other villages. In fact, the combined preaggregation alliances of Homamaku, Dogobi, and Fifilobi had reflected a wide distribution of women resulting in Kwobi being allied to every other Samo village except Bebelubi, the most distant Samo community (see figure 3.2). This was testimony to the genius of the Samo alliance structure and its emphasis on protecting isolated communities from enemy attack. With the government providing military protection for aggregated villages, ceremonial support became increasingly important, and the proximity of allies affected their ability to assist each other in ritual and ceremony (Shaw 1990, 123ff). Thus, between 1970 and 1980, the men of Kwobi established alliances predominantly with the two nearest villages, Sodiyobi and Tiliyabi.

More broadly, however, village aggregation reduced the field of available women. Where once there had been twenty-five longhouse communities within the dialect area, there were now only seven villages with whom to establish alliances. Hence, sibling exchanges with other dialects became increasingly frequent. Women from previously hostile groups could be exchanged and join a village without fear of raiding. Hence the extreme precontact multilingualism discussed earlier began to break down and dialect variation reduced.

Linguistic Adjustments

As men looked ever further afield for wives and established alliances that strengthened broader village ties, women of other dialects were increasingly incorporated into community life. With the reduced danger of overextending relationships with allies of enemies or even

Table 3.1
Percentage of Cognates across Dialects on the Strickland Plain

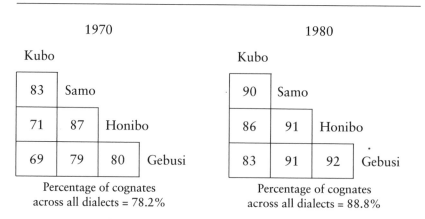

	1970				1980		
Kubo				Kubo			
83	Samo			90	Samo		
71	87	Honibo		86	91	Honibo	
69	79	80	Gebusi	83	91	92	Gebusi

Percentage of cognates across all dialects = 78.2%   Percentage of cognates across all dialects = 88.8%

Note: The percentage of cognates shared between each pair of dialects is indicated in the boxes. For instance, in 1970, Kubo and Samo shared 83 percent of their vocabularies, whereas in 1980 they shared 90 percent. Such an increase in cognates, found between every pair of dialects, indicates a reduction in dialect difference and a strengthening of linguistic identity as a single language (Shaw 1986).

Table 3.2
Changing Units of Samo Social Structure

Precontact groups		Aggregated grouping	
		unlabeled	'family'
monsoon	'household'		
		gaboo monsoon	'village'
oosoo buoman	'ally'		
		oosoo buoman	'ally'
ton	'dialect/language'		
		ton	'language'
hatooman	'enemy'		
		kooahage	'foreigner'

enemies themselves, over time most Samo villages established alliances with Kubo, Honibo, and Gebusi villages (see figure 3.1). The net effect of this broadening of the old alliance structure has been a 10 percent increase in lexical cognates shared by speakers of dialects on the Strickland Plain (table 3.1; see also Shaw 1986). Increasing linguistic homogeneity is, of course, not only a product of a broadened alliance structure. It also reflects the impact of pacification and mission activity throughout the region. Government patrols, with their need for carriers, provide excellent opportunities for individuals to engage peacefully in trade, and even discuss alliance possibilities.

The shift in terminology that designates the whole range of social groupings reflects the impact of village aggregation as well as linguistic adjustments that are continuing to make an impact throughout the entire region (table 3.2). The new structure is not a one-to-one shift from the precontact groupings. While a village is somewhat comparable to a grouping of precontact allies, it is not identical since they are now aggregated at one site. While the term for ally is the same, alliances are now made between villages, not individual households. Dialect differences have been somewhat blurred resulting in a broader, language-wide rather than dialect-specific identification. And foreigners with whom Samo interact, both other Papua New Guineans and expatriates, are quite different from enemies who raided and on whom alliance groups counterraided. Terminological usage, then, has been extended to ever-expanding groups, reflecting both outside intervention (primarily through a colonial approach to administration and mission influence) and local response. Some key shifts are shown in table 3.2, with the lines staggered to demonstrate the extension of terms and changes of meaning from the longhouse to the aggregated grouping context.

The New Order

Little did Douglas realize the incredible impact his rest houses would have on the lived environment within which Samo relationships are enacted, and corresponding terminological adjustments. With the shift to aggregated villages and the concomitant alterations in house style came changes in kinship terminology and social structure that impacted the entire region. With the longhouses gone and conditions at village sites negatively impacting the quality of Samo life, it was inevitable that the Samo would seek new ways to improve living conditions. Recent experiences characterize a desire to maintain cultural values in the context of a changing environment.

In June 1983 the inhabitants of Kwobi village went en masse to petition the government to allow them to relocate. Deteriorating houses, rapidly depleting supplies of building materials, and the distance to productive land had, in their minds, undermined the viability of Kwobi as a suitable village site. They reasoned that the community was nearly deserted for weeks at a time while people engaged in subsistence activities, and that inadequate housing was an increasing problem. In fact, the cycle of living in garden houses during peak periods of activity and returning to the village for government-related involvement closely resembled the precontact migration pattern that Douglas sought to alter. Hence they requested permission to move, as a village (all three original longhouse groups), to a site near the Adu River on land formerly part of Fifilobi's territory. The government denied their request on the grounds that a new road would have to be built to give administrative access to the site, and that the time and money necessary were neither available nor worth the government's effort. Disappointed, the Kwobi delegation returned to their dilapidated little houses and continued living on the overworked land that had by then seen continuous habitation for twenty years.

The Return of the Longhouse

In 1990 members of Kwobi village congregated on the central plaza of the ridge top. After considerable debate punctuated by numerous speeches castigating the government for the difficulty of their lives, they decided to build a community center that would provide amenities for group interaction not provided by family dwellings. Again, they approached the government and requested to allot their tax-work day to the building of the community center rather than road maintenance. This time their petition was granted, and work on a new building commenced. The product was a new longhouse that graced Kwobi village when I visited there in July 1991. The only building style they knew that would allow for the interaction of a large number of people was a traditional longhouse. Their stated purpose was to provide a place to engage in ceremony as well as to house guests. They also wanted a focal point for an initiation ceremony that was in the early planning stages. For them, the building of a longhouse met all these needs and more (it also served as a church for the Christian congregation).

Thus in the dynamics of culture change, the traditional Samo longhouse style has evolved into a meeting house for the entire village to use for communal activity and gatherings for a wide range of purposes. It is no longer primarily a living space for an extended family, but serves as a site for ceremony, traditional and Christian, as well as a guest house for visitors. It has become an all-purpose building ready to serve the needs of everyone as it stands proudly amid the clustered dwellings of the three communities that came to dwell at the site where Patrol Officer Douglas built a rest house in 1963. Douglas' influence lingers in village structures as well as in attitudes, since Kwobi residents felt compelled to request government permission based on the knowledge that their desires were contrary to established policy.

Further Implications of Village Aggregation

Another impact of aggregation and the shift in house style has been a distinct increase in the birth rate. During the decade from 1980 to 1990 the birth rate took a dramatic jump, and infant mortality was drastically reduced. Government statistics for the 1980s indicate a 9 percent growth rate compared to zero growth during the 1970s. Prenatal care has drastically increased the number of live births. Postnatal care, including immunization, has resulted in a much-reduced infant mortality—most deaths during the 1980s were elderly adults, not a preponderance of children as in the past. These changes can be attributed to two primary factors: first, the close proximity of married adults living in the relative privacy of a single family dwelling.

The relative infrequency of opportunities for a married couple to
have sexual intimacy in the forest during the precontact period has
been replaced with easy access in the comparative privacy of a home
in a postaggregation village.[4] The second factor contributing to a
higher birth rate is better medical attention through the Health
Center at Nomad and the residence of a medical orderly at the mission airstrip at Hanonabi two miles away.

Propinquity combined with outside contact has also altered maintenance of the traditional postpartum taboo (extending until a child's
spirit was well attached as evidenced by an ability to walk, talk, and
generally survive without the aid of breast milk—a period of approximately three years). A new generation of adults, impacted by extended contact with government and mission schools as well as increased medical care, no longer holds to the traditional rationale for
the postpartum taboo.[5] Approximately 50 percent of the present
adult population have been educated through at least third grade at
government and mission schools. Any stigma of having another child
within a three- to five-year span appears to have been buried with the
previous initiation cycle ('generation') of adults. Education and medical care, then, have combined with house nucleation to reduce the
cultural need for an extended postpartum taboo. Knowledge of basic
physical care now combines with traditional social care of children
to encourage the spirit to remain and continue energizing the body.
Modern knowledge combines with traditional beliefs to allow a more
productive lifestyle. The net effect is a much-reduced average age of
people living in present-day villages.

Conclusion

Douglas' rest houses, built over thirty years ago, precipitated a
sequence of events that had far-reaching effects for the Samo. Those
rest houses influenced house styles that changed due to lack of building materials and a reduced need for protection against enemies. The
shift in house style, however, is a prime manifestation (perhaps even
a cultural metaphor) of the overall social shifts that have impacted
the Samo since 1963. Within the resulting villages, terminology has
been adjusted to reflect the extended meaning necessary to define
relationships, while the nature of interaction between larger groupings has produced an expanded social structure.

Living in clusters of houses at a village site, people maintain relationships similar to interaction patterns associated with the old forest

longhouses. Interpersonal relationships have changed little, but have broadened to include the larger group of people who now live together in a village—a "gathering place." Within that context, the new, smaller, family-oriented houses, though derived from their forest predecessors, carry new meanings commensurate with outside contact and education. The documentation of this process (through data collected on all preaggregated households, census records, and village-based anthropological research) provided an opportunity to analyze Samo categories and their meaning.

While recognizable, the form of a house has been altered to fit the new context of village life rather than demands of forest living. A house is now primarily a sleeping space rather than an assemblage of social and ceremonial compartments. It no longer has significance for entertaining guests, for ceremony (purposes now maintained by the village through the availability of the new community center), or protecting from enemy raids.

Though life on the Strickland Plain has clearly altered from the precontact context, it is still very recognizable as Samo. For social anthropologists, this case study shows how an isolated forest society has creatively adjusted culture and language to accommodate an imposed administration and yet maintained aboriginal beliefs and values—a fascinating study of sociocultural cohesion in a colonial context.

Notes

This chapter draws on material gathered during extensive fieldwork from late 1969 through late 1981, a period during which my family lived half the time in the village of Kwobi. Patrol reports, village books, and interviews with patrol officers provide supplementary materials for the period from sustained contact in 1963 to derestriction in 1969. Frequent visits and correspondence since 1981 bring my records up to the present (see Shaw 1996). Partial funding for my fieldwork from the New Guinea Research Fund of the Summer Institute of Linguistics is hereby gratefully acknowledged.

1. The pronunciation of sounds in the Samo language is similar to that of corresponding English sounds, with some notable exceptions. /l/ has two allophones; [n] occurs word initial or when surrounded by nasalized vowels, and [l] occurs word medial. There are six phonemic vowels, including three back vowels: u, o, and <ɔ>. For ease of distinction orthographically, <ɔ> is represented by "o," and o by "oo." Nasalized vowels are orthographically symbolized with an "n" following the vowel. For ease of presentation the orthography used here coincides with the one in use among the Samo. See

Shaw and Shaw (1977) for a complete phonological description. Accompanying glosses are an approximation of Samo meaning in English.

2. Without going into a detailed description of Samo relationship terms (see Shaw 1976), readers should keep in mind that glosses reflect Samo usage that may imply information considerably in contrast to the meaning of terms in English. Thus Samo siblingship is not based on genealogy and generation, but on coresidence and time of initiation. Siblings, then, include a range of individuals extending from the initiation of individuals designated "parents" to the birth of "children" (Shaw 1974a). In view of the fact that those whom parents called "younger siblings" were designated "older siblings" by those of the next cycle, the sibling concept for the Samo is extended considerably beyond the normal bounds of the term "generation" in English (Shaw 1990, 59ff).

3. Cross-cousin preferential marriage was normative. Inasmuch as all community women in the previous initiation cycle were by cultural definition "mothers," and males sought to maintain previously advantageous alliances, one's "brothers" could remain loyal to cultural preference and the alliance structure by exchanging a "sister" with men of any community from whence women called "mother" came, e.g., incorporate a "mother's brother." This loose definition of "mother" allowed more latitude of choice than anthropologists often assume when discussing cross-cousin preferential marriage (see Shaw 1990, 83ff).

4. This was acknowledged by one man who responded to my amazement at the number of children by pointing to his house and sheepishly grinning while saying, "We live in the same house."

5. The Samo believe that each child receives the spirit of an ancestor at birth (Shaw 1990, 122ff). Anything that might take attention away from a child before its spirit is well attached (e.g., having another baby) was avoided.

4

Changes in Housing and Residence Patterns in Galilo, New Britain, 1918–1992

ANN CHOWNING

THE LAKALAI VILLAGE of Galilo in New Britain (Papua New Guinea) has undergone changes in housing and residence patterns that can be documented from the period when strong European influence began immediately after World War I. In addition to the presence of government and mission, economic changes combined with an increasing variety of new attitudes and values to allow more individual discretion in housing. Along with greater diversity in living arrangements, official policies limited some of the choices that had previously existed. The present built environment and spatial arrangements in Galilo emphasize village unity, encouraged by both government and church, rather than, as in the past, unitary, small, cohesive hamlets. Over a period of seventy-odd years, Galilo has altered both physically and socially so that although the names of the village and some of the hamlets remain, it looks and is very different from what the first missionaries found when they arrived to interrupt a major battle in 1918.

The Lakalai (West Nakanai) occupy the region around Cape Hoskins on the north coast of what is now West New Britain, a little over five degrees south of the equator (figure 4.1). Early in the century, when they first attracted the attention of outside observers and labor recruiters, the people of the Lakalai region had been badly affected by ashfalls from the local volcano, and many took refuge from the subsequent food shortages in other parts of West New Britain. Just as the old village pattern was being restored, the missionaries came, to be followed immediately by Australian patrol officers, and changes in residence were advocated by both parties. Fortunately we have available an account of the earlier situation, recorded by a German missionary from a few boys who attended his school on

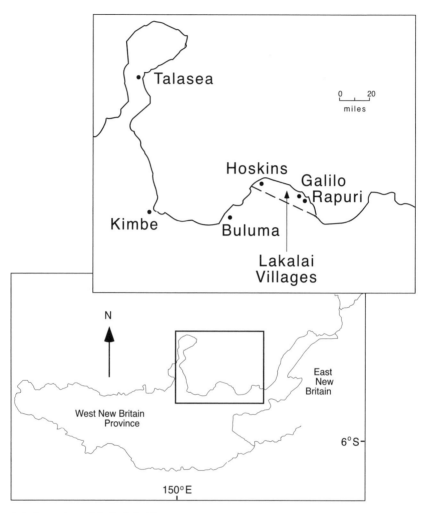

4.1 Location of Lakalai villages

the Toriu River (Hees 1915–1916). Their account was supplemented
by what elders told a team of anthropologists, of whom I was one, in
1954.[1] Since then a number of return visits, the most recent in 1992,
enabled me to observe a variety of changes in housing and social
relations, the most striking of which are described in this chapter.

The Situation in 1918

Galilo, like most Lakalai villages, was composed of several named
wards or hamlets. These split when members quarreled, and our

records show many shifts in village composition and layout over time (see Chowning and Goodenough 1971). In theory, however, and often in fact, the hamlet was the social center for its residents. Each hamlet contained a men's house; an adjacent grove of shade trees furnished with benches where men sat and often ate, called a *malilo*;[2] a tree providing a shady gathering place for women; a dance plaza; and several family houses.

Apart from deliberately planted shade, fruit, and areca (betel) nut trees, hamlets were kept clear of vegetation, particularly weeds and grass, which belonged to the domain of the spirit world. Though strips of vegetation separated the hamlets of a single village, clear paths ran between them and also connected the village with the joint garden area, the fresh water supply, and the beach. Galilo's water supply had been destroyed in one of the volcanic eruptions, and they shared that of another village, though not without acrimony. The village name, the single garden area (shared to reduce the labor of fencing against pigs),[3] and physical isolation from the next village were the main markers of village unity and identity. Neighboring villages that were normally on friendly terms were linked by paths, and visited freely, whereas it was highly dangerous to go through uncleared bush to other villages. Exceptionally small villages or those particularly threatened by warlike neighbors might be encircled by a palisade that could be closed off at night (Hees 1915–1916, 40). The Lakalai thought of themselves as surrounded by human enemies, including other Lakalai, as well as by supernatural hazards. As indicated below, the residence pattern helped protect from these and more mundane dangers.

Buildings: Construction, Functions, and Contents

The Lakalai built flimsy shelters outside the village to provide shade in the gardens or shelter for fishermen or families manufacturing sago in the swamps. In addition, during the yearly ceremonial season men constructed a place in which masks could be manufactured and stored, away from the view of women. (For a full account, see Valentine 1961.) All these were outside the village proper, as were canoe sheds on the beach. Here only village structures are described, omitting shelters for domestic pigs.

According to Hees, family houses and men's houses were built in exactly the same way, with two minor exceptions. First, some men's houses were very long so that the hull of a racing canoe could be stored in the rafters. Second, men's houses had two entrances, one facing the clearing and the other the bush, while family houses had only one. It seems likely that men going to the bush to defecate were trying to avoid the notice of women;[4] protection from shame was as important to Lakalai men as protection from physical danger. Nevertheless, except on special occasions such as the construction of masks, the boundary between areas used by men and by women was, by general Melanesian standards, not rigid, and Hees reports that sometimes a men's house and a family house would be under the same roof, separated only by an interior wall.

Both types of houses needed first to be weatherproof, providing shelter against rain, high winds, and cold at night. Annual rainfall is about 150 inches, and although it may occur at any time of year, it can be especially heavy during the several months of the northwest monsoon. The stone ovens on which the principal meal of the day was cooked were always inside, with one oven for each woman in the household. Beds were platforms, furnished with pandanus sleeping mats that could be rolled up during the day so that the same platforms served as seats. On cold nights small fires were kindled near the beds. Weather permitting, small cooking fires were also made outside the house, where people spent most of their time during daylight hours. Many houses had exterior benches built against the facades, and it was common to sit outside, often directly on the ground,[5] in order to carry out numerous activities, including cooking small meals over open fires and eating. At nightfall, however, most people retreated inside, shutting the door firmly to keep out a variety of spirits that were thought to enter the village area only after dark (see Valentine 1965). The interior of the house was also used to store family valuables, placed in bundles in the rafters where they would be secure from thieves. Goods likely to be damaged by insects, such as large nets for hunting pigs, would be hung where smoke from the stone ovens would protect them. The house also contained tall platforms on which food, coconut-shell water bottles, and utensils were kept, out of reach of dogs. A high threshold kept pigs from entering the house, which was built directly on the ground.

Houses were constructed of materials that were available locally and considered to be relatively long wearing, particularly the dried bark of the nettle tree used for the walls. A variety of leaves, sometimes supplemented with bark, was used for roofs. Everyone was familiar with the techniques of house construction.

Men's houses differed internally from family houses only in that they did not contain stone ovens, and the paraphernalia of love magic was typically stored inside, whereas other personal valuables were not. What the men's house offered was a chance for potential warriors to avoid the debilitating effect of too-close contact with women, especially those who were menstruating or had just given birth. A second, somewhat contradictory purpose of residential separation was to increase the sexual desirability of bachelors and young husbands, who lost appeal if women saw them eating. Such men ate inside the men's house while others normally ate out in the grove, where food was brought to them from the family houses. Even married men were expected to avoid spending too much time in family houses.

With rare exceptions, notably during sago manufacture and all-night ceremonies, women and children always spent the whole night within family houses, safe from both human and spirit attack. What houses did not guarantee was privacy; sexual intercourse between married couples usually occurred there, and some girls (and occasional married women) managed to receive lovers without awakening others. But the danger of observation always existed, since houses had no internal partitions.

The other feature that distinguished the family house was that the dead, of both sexes, were buried inside it. The widow and other female kin of the deceased were incarcerated for months in a small enclosure, but this might be in another house. Nevertheless, the house containing the corpse continued to be occupied, even during the period when the head was left protruding from the grave, though later, after foods for a mortuary feast had been accumulated, the house was dismantled or burned down. House sites were not inherited, as in some Melanesian societies, nor was any significance attached to the presence of the bones in the soil of the hamlet. Except for a short period after death, souls of the dead did not stay near their graves, and consequently old grave sites were not feared.

Hamlets and Village

Like the household, the hamlet was felt to be a secure place. Interclan feuds were not pursued among coresidents (Hees 1915–1916, 46), and women could enter the men's house of their own hamlet without fearing that love magic would be practiced against them. All members of a hamlet considered each other kin (Goodenough 1962), and they cooperated in various group enterprises, from seine fishing to house construction, though often with the assistance of the organizer's kin from other hamlets. All large catches of game and fish

were supposed to be shared among all constituent households, and
feast foods received from other hamlets would be similarly allocated.
Hamlet members acted together in putting on feasts and in contributing food and labor to a ceremony sponsored by any of the men. On a
small scale, each hamlet acted as a political unit under the general
guidance of the senior men, one of whom might be a Big Man
(Chowning and Goodenough 1971). Even if a hamlet did split after a
quarrel, once tempers had cooled the old ties would be remembered.
A particularly close relationship existed between members of hamlets
that had a single origin.

By contrast with the hamlet, the village was not secure from feuds.
Children were warned never to accept food outside their hamlet
except from a clanmate, for fear of being "poisoned" by sorcery. The
main advantages of village structure were greater security from
enemy attack; the availability of specialists such as garden and
weather magicians; the ability to join forces for successful pig netting
and canoe races against other villages; and the possibility of putting
on impressive and enjoyable ceremonies and feasts.

Apart from shifts caused by quarrels, many adults moved at least
once during their lifetimes: a woman on marriage, though returning
home to bear the first child; and a man, first after having enough
children to be considered sufficiently adult to set up a separate household, and then after the death of his father, to whom he was indebted
for financing the marriage. While his father was alive, a married man
would remain in his hamlet, where his wife and small children had
previously been living under his father's roof, but after that he was
most likely to join men that he called by sibling terminology, either
members of his matrilineal clan or patrilineal parallel cousins. Alter-
natively, men married to each other's sisters often set up their own
hamlet. Almost always, however, such moves involved continuing
ties to the parent village.[6] These ties somewhat countered the tendency for hamlet affiliations to look much closer than intravillage
relations.

In sum, the family house protected women, children, and possessions from natural hazards and from intruders, both human and
supernatural. When occupied by an extended family, it also allowed
daily companionship among women and children even when bad
weather or darkness prevented them from sitting outside. Houses of
other kin and affines were very near, so that a woman working outside the house during the day would usually join one or two others
and the children they were looking after. It was not common for all

female hamlet members to gather together except on ceremonial occasions, but in mid-morning after the stone ovens had been prepared, both the women leaving for the gardens and those staying behind tended to assemble for a while in the shade to talk and play games. This practice helped link in-marrying women with their female coresidents. The men's house, as a center of male conviviality, similarly strengthened male bonding. But crosscutting these same-sex ties were those among members of each family. Men were not separated from women during the day for more than a few hours at a time, and many spent lengthy periods with their wives and children of both sexes.

Beyond the confines of the hamlet, the source of security and sharing was one's matrilineal descent group, but the usual residence pattern dispersed the living members (Chowning 1965–1966). Only after death did they live together in a ghostly village at their sacred place. Although the living members undertook some joint activities, mostly ceremonial, for everyday purposes ties among those who occupied the same hamlet were more significant.

Forces and Processes of Change, 1918–1954

In this period, three forces combined to affect Galilo housing and residence patterns: the Australian colonial government, the Christian missionaries, and increased involvement in a cash economy through work abroad as well as through local production of copra for sale. Some housing changes, such as new construction methods and regulations, were directly introduced by outsiders. More changes were indirectly generated, following cessation of regional warfare, new religious teachings about family life, and indirect exposure to novel ideas about what a "proper house" should look like. Yet changes were not unilateral; individuals quietly resisted some regulations, and households differentially adopted innovations or clung to previous habits.

The colonial government insisted that all houses be built on piles, with slat floors, because they considered ground-based houses unhealthy. They also forbade burial within houses and decreed the establishment of village cemeteries.[7] The missionaries, who initially came from Samoa and Fiji, taught a new method of "sewing" thatch from palm leaves, to form both the walls and roofs of the houses (figure 4.2). The cessation of warfare between villages made it safe to travel to the stands of palm trees to collect material. Initially the

4.2 Men with children on a typical sitting platform in front of a house type introduced by missionaries, with a cook house to the left. The house has an open verandah but no windows in the sleeping section. Ann Chowning, 1962.

Lakalai welcomed abandonment of the struggle with nettle tree bark, but over time they came to regard the task of sewing thatch as very burdensome. Some new houses had fireplaces and even stone ovens inside them, despite the constant danger of setting fire to the thin split-palm floors, but often there was a separate ground-based cook house. Some of these served more than one of the raised sleeping houses (see figure 4.3), and many had walls of poles or bark, like the more traditional family houses. Many old people, disliking the drafts through the floors of the raised houses, surreptitiously (and illegally) slept in the cook houses, usually accompanied by a grand-child or two.

Because it was difficult to build multifamily houses on piles, it became more common for each nuclear family to have its own house. In other Lakalai villages Roman Catholic missionaries, led by Ger-man priests, strongly discouraged shared dwellings, advocating in-stead their vision of European family life; they had some ability to enforce their decrees because everyone was married in church. Galilo, however, has always been Methodist (later called United Church), and those missionaries interfered little with traditional marriage pat-terns insofar as they affected residence. They may, however, have

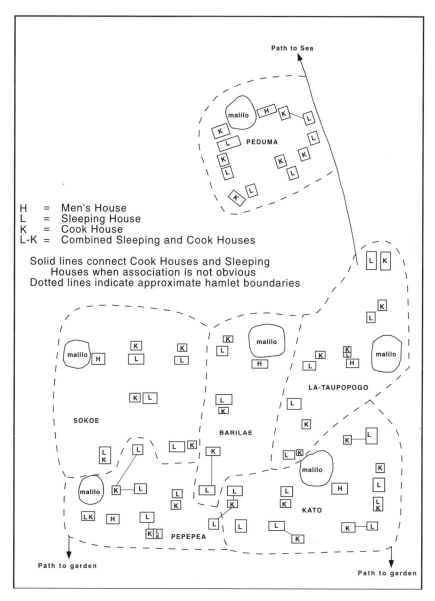

4.3 Galilo hamlets, 1954

been responsible for inculcating a new desire for privacy within houses[8] that led separate families to put up partitions between the rooms they occupied. Children still slept with their parents, however. Because sleeping mats were now usually laid directly on the floor and rolled up during the day, and because dogs could easily be kept away from food in elevated houses, some of them contained no internal furniture at all.

Wage labor outside Lakalai did bring in new goods, including pillows, the occasional foam-rubber mattress, and cloth. Traditionally Lakalai men went naked, but the missionaries insisted that they clothe themselves, and in Methodist villages women were also encouraged to wear clothing that covered their breasts. As new goods entered the village, places had to be found to store them that were secure and far from smoky fires. Most houses contained a lockable case, and some had doors that could be locked. Prevention of theft of manufactured goods, less individual and recognizable than traditional ones, became a continuing concern.

New Structures, and Alterations in Use of "Traditional" Ones

Both the colonial administration and the churches were organized to deal with large units like villages rather than with hamlets. Just outside Galilo, next to the missionary's residence, stood a combined church building and school; adjacent to it was the government rest house, used by government officers when they were on patrol (and occupied by members of the anthropological team in 1954). Village members had to construct all of these in addition to their new houses. A short distance down the road, but serving a much larger area, was an aid post staffed by a medical orderly. Galilo had also joined a cooperative society to market copra for Methodists,[9] and a smoke dryer for copra, owned by the society members, stood on the edge of the village, which was now also dotted with platforms for sun drying of copra.

Now that so many houses were elevated, pigs sheltered under them, and they no longer needed separate shelters. In a few cases houses were raised so high that seating benches were placed under them. These became gathering places, sometimes replacing the women's shady tree (figure 4.4). If it rained men might move from their grove to these spaces, still able to watch what was happening without retreating into the men's houses.

The administration also tried to introduce privies into Lakalai, ideally one for each family house. They reckoned without Lakalai male aversion to being seen defecating (Chowning 1989), and female lack of interest in changing their old ways. Most Galilo privies were in poor repair as of 1954 and seldom used (and never by men, except late at night).

4.4 Women and children of a hamlet gather in the shade provided by a new-style elevated men's house. In the background is one family house on the left, plus cook houses. Ann Chowning, 1954.

Administration Effects on Village and Hamlet

For census and other administrative purposes, government officers wanted units that were not only large but stable. Any outlying hamlet was simply assigned to a nearby village, and villagers were forbidden to break up or shift their sites. Crowded hamlets might, however, be ordered to divide. Each village was given two govern-ment-appointed officials, a *luluai* and his assistant, a *tultul,* to help enforce government policies. Galilo, as the largest Lakalai village, was uniquely assigned two *tultuls.* In the past, an occasional village, including Galilo, sometimes had an elected head who settled disputes (Chowning and Goodenough 1971), but the new system, which re-placed his office, ensured that for political purposes the village rather than the hamlet was always viewed as a single unit. Nevertheless, Big Men continued to put on hamlet-based ceremonies in an effort to outdo each other. The *luluai* of Galilo, a Big Man in his own right, was engaged in such bitter rivalry with the Big Man of another ham-let that almost surely they would have moved apart if the administra-tion had not forbidden it.

One precontact symbol of village unity, the racing canoe,[10] had been abandoned, reportedly because men now had too much "government work," including raising cash crops (an enterprise strongly promoted by the *luluai*). At the same time, joint work on official projects such as clearing roads and maintaining the government rest house kept up village-wide cooperation.

As the Galilo population recovered from a decline associated with Japanese occupation during World War II, hamlets expanded in size until, by 1954, only the last to be founded, Peduma, was physically separated from the others (see figure 4.3). Whether for hygienic purposes or in the interest of village unity, the administration had already advocated elimination of the uncleared strips separating them. Now it became possible for a man who had quarreled with his neighbor to change his hamlet affiliation without moving his house; the invisible boundary between hamlets was simply rethought.

The Methodist mission, in contrast to the Roman Catholics, generally supported all government policies. In addition, they tried to improve gender relations and promote a more Christian type of family life by preaching against all the taboos and patterns of avoidance that had often separated men from women. Their campaign was aided by the abolition of warfare, which they too helped bring about. No longer worried about the possibly fatal consequences of physical weakness, younger men tended to spend much more time in family houses than in men's houses, and the decline of the latter had begun. In public, too, men and women mingled much more freely in hamlet gathering places, including the spaces under both family and men's houses. Women still did not expect to sit in the grove attached to the men's house, but this restriction was the most visible remaining sign of the former differences in public areas for the two sexes. But the church was also worried about "immorality" among the unmarried, and boys and girls did not sit together in the village school.

Changes, 1954–1992

Changes continued during this period as the result of a number of factors. As more young people were educated outside Lakalai and took jobs away from the village, remittances made new purchases possible, and many imported materials, along with new ideas, were brought back by returnees. The rise and fall of local enterprises also impacted economic choices for individual families. The need to obtain cash for school fees, taxes, and contributions to the church, and the desire to buy an increasing number of foreign goods, increased concern about possessions and privacy. Christian teachings had greatly reduced fear of spirits, but fear of theft increased; while windows enlarged, locks proliferated. As the population continued to grow and as many of those who had lived outside married foreigners, hamlet unity declined still further. Both men's houses and the benches in associated groves gradually disappeared. The individual household became increasingly salient, but also likely to be physically separate from others. At the same time construction of a single meeting hall and a large church within the village reflect the salience of village identity in Galilo today. Although there have been far-reaching changes in family and social life, extended kin ties have not been abandoned, and many households accommodate more than the members of a nuclear family. A great variety in house styles and furnishings has emerged from increasing diversity in personal circumstances and preferences.

Education, Migration, and Remittances

The first government school in Lakalai was established in Galilo in 1962. From then on an increasing number of children, including girls, went on to secondary and even tertiary education. A number qualified for well-paid jobs outside Lakalai, from which they could, and were expected to, send money back to their parents and siblings, though not all did so. A number also married foreigners, whose influence was greatest if they returned to live in Galilo. At home a new cash crop, cacao, was added, and for a brief period most residents were fairly well off, gradually able to improve their standard of living, without great inequalities of wealth having yet become visible. But as time went on, housing and other personal property tended to reflect directly the success of individual children working elsewhere and the degree of responsibility they felt toward their kin at home.

Competition for Cash within Galilo

By 1968, when the *luluai* system was replaced by a local government council,[11] the combination of a steady increase in school fees and the demand for more foreign goods led to a drastic shift in values and behavior, toward the accumulation of wealth for one's closest kin only. Even within hamlets, food that had once been shared freely was now sold for cash. In particular, parents hoped that if they financed a good education for their children, in time they themselves would reap the financial benefits. Individuals varied in their willingness to abandon the old values of generosity, and it was still considered obligatory to contribute freely to major feasts sponsored by one's kin, as well as to their marriages, and also to the church. Otherwise, however, they sought opportunities to maximize their own wealth, adding to the cash crops of coconuts and cacao new enterprises such as trade stores and selling foodstuffs at the government station.

The biggest effect on residence derived from the introduction of oil palms as a cash crop, supplementing coconuts and cacao, which were no longer very profitable. The copra cooperative had collapsed, but some families had their own copra dryers and earned money from charging even kin to use them. Participants in a government-sponsored oil palm scheme were encouraged to abandon the village entirely and move onto separate blocks that contained very small houses of European style. In contrast to some other villages, Galilo showed little enthusiasm for the move; the few men who took up a block maintained a house in the village as well. Instead, Galilo cleared most of the old garden area, allocated a plot to each male resident, and planted it with oil palms. Vegetable foods were interspersed, but plots were not fenced, and village pigs constantly ravaged them, increasing the need for cash to buy food from the few trade stores that survived.

Oil palm is labor intensive, and planters who did well were those who could both muster the help of close kin and reward them enough to make their work worthwhile. Even without the differences caused by remittances, the amount of money available to individual households now varied to a degree that had not existed during the 1960s. Although much money was spent on purchases such as clothing and trade store food, some families could afford to improve their houses, even paying others to build for them. (Some younger men had been trained as carpenters.) Specific changes in houses are described below.

Changes in Hamlet and Village Organization

Official policy, though decided at the local level, did not always change with the lead-up to independence from 1968 to 1975 or even after Papua New Guinea achieved independence in 1975. The local government council demanded taxes, tried to get people to build and use privies, and insisted that the village maintain roads—an increasingly arduous task, as heavy vehicles replaced the bicycles used in 1954. But the council did not concern itself with the kinds of houses people chose to live in. Instead it concentrated on trying to maintain village harmony, holding weekly meetings to deal with a variety of problems. Council taxes were used to construct a large open shed with a concrete floor. Village meetings took place there, though because it would not hold everyone, the women had to sit on the ground outside. But the building was also used for meetings of the church-affiliated women's fellowship and occasional feasts (such as those in 1992 commemorating my departure and that of the head of the Methodist mission). Not far away on the edge of the old cemetery stood a large new church of permanent materials. The local missionary himself lived just outside the village, but the overall effect of these new structures, and the uses to which they were put, was to emphasize the unity of the village as opposed to that of the hamlets, already fragmented by economic competition.

Meanwhile, steady growth in population inevitably produced an increase in the actual number of hamlets. Typically new ones took the names of long-vanished ones that had occupied the same piece of land. As the population of Galilo increased from 265 in 1954 to 843 (of whom 683 were resident) in 1980, the number of hamlets grew from six to nine. One had split because of a quarrel, but two other new hamlets were established simply to escape overcrowding. Another hamlet had become so large that it operated like two when feast foods were dispensed, although men from all over the hamlet still fished together, maintaining ties established when they were younger. By 1991 a tenth hamlet was being constructed, and a few houses were now so remote from others that the old physical unity had vanished.

Hamlet membership is still of some importance, however. Galilo has divided itself into three groups, each comprised of hamlets of common origin, and labeled by the initials of these. The groups compete with each other to raise funds for village enterprises, from a bicycle for the minister to water pipes. At the individual hamlet level, it is felt that the office of village councillor should move from one hamlet to another. Women of a single hamlet, or a pair of related ones, take joint responsibility for looking after the aged and ill of their own hamlet(s), and have a bank account separate from that of the village-based church fellowship of which they are a part. It is also still expected that all hamlet residents will contribute to ceremonies sponsored by hamlet members, and food from a feast elsewhere in the village is still allocated to one man to dispense to other households of his hamlet.

Despite these centripetal forces, it is my impression that Galilo is dispersing as residents move farther apart. In several recent cases senior men have shifted to avoid close contact with juniors who have insulted them. Probably in the past the Big Men of the hamlet would have intervened, reproved the culprit, and kept the elders together. Now the decline in leadership in areas that lie outside the realms of government and church is such that it is hard to find anyone with the prestige and authority to intervene successfully.

Changes in Buildings and Uses of Space

As hamlets grew and spread, construction of men's houses was gradually abandoned, and the last remaining ones were identified as being the property of individual men rather than of all the male residents of the hamlet. As in the early period (though not in 1954), these were often under the same roof as a family house. The shady sitting places for men remained much longer but increasingly lacked benches, though these can quickly be constructed if they are needed. Where men's shady areas still exist, they are used ordinarily by women and children as well as, or instead of, men. For some ceremonies, however, only men sit and eat (and nowadays often drink beer) in one of these while the women stay outside. These are virtually the only occasions on which use of space separates men from women. Even in the church some pews hold both sexes.

The fact that some houses are now built completely out of sight of neighbors (which would not have happened prior to 1918) is a tribute to the diminished fear of enemy attack.[12] In some cases placement of new houses reflects their size; a few are simply too large to fit within hamlet bounds. Some moves have also been inspired by new concerns that particular parts of the village (low-lying areas that often receive debris washed downhill) are unhealthy. In fact, mosquitoes tend to be particularly bad around houses built in the bush, but there is still little understanding of the causes of malaria, which is the principal health problem.

The most striking aspect of present-day Galilo houses is, however, not their locations but their diversity in size, style, and material (figure 4.5). Some of this variety probably reflects house styles introduced by foreign spouses, and some reflects degree of exposure to so-called European types of house construction and a desire to emulate them. Above all, however, financial resources determine the kind of house one can live in. Because many people dislike making thatch and prefer the relative permanence of a metal roof, nowadays almost all family houses have one, though it may take a long time before

4.5 Mixture of house construction: on the left, a ground-based dwelling house of local materials except for metal strips along the roof; on the right, a house of imported materials. Posts for a new house lean against a felled tree in the foreground. Note weeds in the right foreground. Ann Chowning, 1990.

they can purchase the materials. Wall construction is much more variable. Houses with plank or fibro walls have usually been financed by people with good jobs outside Lakalai, often with a view to sharing the house when they themselves retire. A few of these differ from houses found in towns only in that they have privies and, often, cook houses of bush materials. Only one man, a government minister, has had constructed at vast expense a water storage system that will give him indoor plumbing.

But while some residents live in elevated houses of imported materials that look very much like those built by Australians in the tropics, others live in ground-based houses with thatch walls that, apart from the corrugated iron roof, outwardly resemble the ground-based cook houses that we observed in 1954. There are many other possible innovations, including the laying of a cement floor, the use of split bamboo for walls, and various combinations of bush and imported materials. Sometimes the flimsiest houses are intended to offer only temporary accommodation until something considered superior can be built, but in a few cases large extended families can live for many years in houses that show little in the way of change from much earlier patterns. The one consistent difference from 1954 is that most houses have large window openings, since fear of spirits has now been very much reduced (except in the vicinity of the cemetery, where it has increased). Almost all houses also have doors that can be locked as well (see below). It is common to see houses that are only partly finished because funds have run short; for example, part of the floor or most of the walls may be sawn planks, but the gaps are filled in with split palm or thatch while the owners try to accumulate money to pay not only for purchase but also transport of additional materials. In several cases, corrugated iron roofs have yet to be nailed down; flying sheets of iron during high winds are considered to be a major hazard of village life. Those trying to complete a house often write to various kin working outside Lakalai with requests or demands for further contributions, sometimes bolstering demands with threats that the noncontributor will have nowhere to stay on a return visit to the village.

Gradual changes in attitudes over the years have even led some men to enter privies openly (Chowning 1989), so that in contrast to the earlier situation, many, though by no means all, houses have well-built and well-maintained privies nearby.

Furnishings and Contents

Some men have relatively well-furnished houses because they retired early from working outside. When they returned to Galilo, they brought not only new ideas about what a house should contain, but also items of furniture. An extreme example is that of a man whose house has upholstered chairs on the verandah and a power mower for a tiny patch of lawn. My information about furnishings of elevated houses is mostly based on what I can see from outside and what people say, since there is no reason to invite a visitor into the house as long as there is sitting space under or in front of it. So I know that one house has a fairly typical mixture of thatch walls set with windows with glass louvers, wire screens, and curtains, but have no idea what furniture it contains. By contrast, some houses, especially those with fibro walls, have large openings cut for windows but nothing filling them in.

For a long time the most desired furnishings were those that provided a warmer and more comfortable bed than the traditional pandanus mat. Foam-rubber mattresses and blankets are used by almost everyone, along with pillows stuffed with kapok from village trees. A few people have mosquito nets. A new desire is for linoleum to cover the floors. In addition, everyone wants stout boxes in which to store their goods, away from rats as well as human thieves, and safe from careless damage by children. These boxes may also serve as seats. Although certain possessions are highly visible, notably personal clothing, many people do not want others to know how much they have; part of the shift away from sharing is evidenced by the practice of locking up, say, tobacco supplies so as to deny having them when visitors come.

Another contribution to security is the possession of a kerosene lamp. Apart from its other advantages, the light will repel intruders, including sorcerers and the ghosts that attack babies. Many people, however, cannot afford to buy the fuel to keep the lamps burning all night. In 1992 Galilo contained two or three generators, but one was used only to run the refrigerator in a trade store, and the others for the occasional showing of videos. The village did not contain electric lights.

In general, money is not spent on furniture. People are used to eating on mats laid on floors or on the ground; even if a house contains tables (normally built of timber scraps) inside or underneath it, they are not normally large enough to accommodate all the people who customarily share a meal. More often, they are used simply to keep new types of cooking and eating equipment, such as metal saucepans, enamel dishes, china cups and mugs, and foodstuffs, out of the reach of small children and, if under the house, pigs and dogs. The area under the house, for those houses that are tall enough, is usually furnished with built-in seats as well as a table, and all houses have outdoor seating available, often in the form of small movable stools together with one plastic chair. These are put in shady places; only the sick ever seek the sun. It is also common for elevated houses to have a shady verandah across the front, and many activities take place there, especially on rainy days, but their only furniture is mats.

Privacy and Property

Privacy is increasingly valued. This is not so evident in ground-based houses of perishable materials as it is in those with cement floors and several rooms. Space permitting, sleeping quarters occupy rooms not used for anything other than storage of personal possessions (and valuables people may wish to hide), and they are screened from public view by a cloth curtain or a wooden door. Depending on household composition and family circumstances, such as whether a man is temporarily avoiding intercourse with his wife for fear of getting her pregnant before a baby is ready to be weaned, each bedroom accommodates either a married couple and their young children, or a mixed group of same-sex kin. The growing concern for privacy can be seen even more dramatically in the practice of a few households constructing a fence around the house and treating intrusion within its bounds as an offense.

Only old-style ground-based houses have little provision for privacy, apart from shutting out the public at night. Not only the impoverished and the elderly but also the sick occupy such houses, which may be modified cook houses. The sick need warmth, ease of access for caretakers, and freedom from climbing stairs. They also receive many visitors, who show concern in a variety of ways. The desire to be cared for outweighs any concern for privacy in these circumstances.

Household Composition

New materials such as steel poles and new techniques learned by men trained as carpenters made it possible for large elevated houses to be built by those who could afford them. For those who could not, large household size made it necessary either to revert to a form similar to the pre-1918 dwelling, or to accommodate some family members in the cook house. Many households now need to look after husband-less women and their children, a new problem resulting from changes in sexual and marital behavior that have produced many cases of divorce and illegitimacy. With the disappearance of men's houses, single men ranging from older boys to widowers also have to be housed. So do married men whose wives have not yet reached menopause; avoidance is the easiest way of averting the shame of producing a child after one is already a grandparent. These new demands on family houses result in the great majority accommodating at least as many people as they did prior to the colonial period, though of a somewhat different mixture. It is a very rare house that contains only one nuclear family. But the population may also change from night to night. Particularly on weekends, Galilo people working in the provincial capital at Kimbe often make the two-hour trip to visit their kin, and the young and unmarried of both sexes often shift residence from night to night. Since a sleeper needs only a mat and a cloth cover, it is possible to turn up anywhere at nightfall and be accommodated with a minimum of fuss. The clearest indication of the decline in fear of sorcery as the result of mission efforts is that children as young as six may spend a night away from home without notifying their parents or causing concern.

Changing Values and Desires

Galilo in 1954 and 1992 looked completely different. A growing acceptance of European aesthetics was reflected in the placing of flowers and decorative plants around many houses, and the presence of patches of lawn around some houses and the church. Many people, however, though they no longer associated wild vegetation with dangerous spirits, disliked seeing patches of high grass on old house sites. The village councillors instructed people to cut the grass around the church, the government school complex, and the local minister's house, but they did not follow the colonial practice of insisting that weeds be removed from villages. To a foreigner's eye, the one blot on the present appearance of the village is the presence of several rusting cars and a scatter of other broken and unused artifacts, but these do not offend Lakalai sensibilities. Women still conscientiously sweep around their own houses and deposit their general trash beyond the edge of the hamlet.

With regard to desires for further change, everyone seems to want a metal roof. Corrugated iron has not been used long enough for people to realize that, like thatch, it will eventually need replacing. The other general desire is for a water tank to store rainwater, particularly because the single pump so often fails. (Only one man, the owner of the most successful trade store, has a water tap outside his house.)

Overall people seem to agree that the more "modern" and spacious a house is, the better, and indeed the more beautiful. One man, highly conservative in many other respects, stated that all objects of European manufacture simply look better than anything the Lakalai make. Funds permitting, it seems safe to say everyone would like a house built entirely of imported materials, but probably many remain content with other forms of housing so long as they satisfy basic desires for security and comfort. Certainly thatch houses are regarded as superior to the tiny houses on the oil palm allotments that, because of their size, are denigrated as "chicken coops."[13]

Where people do not agree is on the relative advantages of nucleated and dispersed settlement. One of the most sophisticated Galilo men, recently returned from three years in Brussels, argued that people need to live near each other if valuable traditions and a sense of Lakalai identity are to be maintained. He opposed the oil palm settlements, where one of his brothers had a house, and where his widowed mother frequently stayed. Many others, however, prefer to move away from kin with whom they have quarreled. I suspect that some of those with non-Lakalai spouses are particularly willing to separate themselves from others in the hamlet. There is, however, little further room for expansion in Galilo; what results may not accurately reflect people's desires so much as physical limits.

The Triumph of the Village

The erosion of hamlet divisions and the scattering of houses has not led to a weakening of the village as a sociopolitical unit. Possibly because Galilo is so large, it is very rare for a person who quarrels with fellow residents to move away entirely. Even those who do so frequently return to visit, since so many of their closest kin will remain behind. The fact that the neighboring villages are Roman Catholic also makes Galilo people tend to stay together; moving usually involves a large spatial shift to another United Church village.

Traditional ceremonies are still maintained, and participation in them binds the village together, as do church-centered activities and the fellowships of women and of young men (who maintain the roads). The village also has sports teams and a magistrate with authority to settle trouble cases. Finally, maintenance of extended kin ties tends to keep wealth imbalances from getting too large and to mute jealousy of those who, because they are able to seek and obtain help from their wealthy kin, are better housed and dressed than others. Despite the considerable variation that now exists in standards of housing between households, one well-traveled young man compared Galilo wholly favorably with what he had seen in another Papua New Guinea society, where he felt that differences in housing pointed to a shocking lack of community spirit.

Summary

The overall effect of culture change in Lakalai has been to weaken ties beyond the nuclear family, particularly to kin more remote than parents' siblings, first cousins, nieces and nephews, and grandchildren. Households, now incorporating men with women and children, often wish to keep what they earn for themselves, rather than share with hamlet mates. Differences in wealth, as well as in ideas about what constitutes an ideal house, have led to enormous variation in house styles throughout the village. The feature shared by most houses, in contrast to the past, is an area private to its residents in which they can demonstrate their separation from others, with the structure sometimes surrounded by a fence or a hedge. Spatially there is little left to signal hamlet identity except the old groves that marked the hamlets, and in a few cases even these have been cut down to make space for the expanding population. Nevertheless, people still identify themselves and others as residents of particular hamlets, and often use hamlet names rather than names of individuals in explaining where they are going or have been. As noted above, hamlet-based groups or coalitions of three hamlets act as units in some church affairs.

The village maintains its physical identity, and both church and political meetings unite village members in the two buildings that are not identified with a hamlet. The great size of the village means that only rarely does everyone attend even a major ceremony put on by any resident, but few people would stay away from a feast connected with church matters. These are held in the village hall or the nearest grove, which for this purpose loses its hamlet identity. Also, everyone attends church at least once on Sunday. The transfer of the church to the village proper has been an important factor in emphasizing village unity and in countering the increased individualism symbolized by the abandonment of men's houses and the new styles of family houses. Furthermore, as house styles have changed, for most people—those who do not maintain alternate residences outside the village—the emotional importance of being properly housed, and of providing housing for one's dependents, has actually increased. To a greater extent than in the past, the family house is becoming a semipermanent home, and at least a few men have a vision of constructing one that can actually be inherited by their children. If permanent houses are built, the frequent shifts that have characterized Galilo housing in recent years will become fewer, and new configurations will result.

Notes

1. The team consisted of four cultural anthropologists and a physical anthropologist. Ward Goodenough and I were based in Galilo, and Charles and Edith Valentine in the Roman Catholic village of Rapuri, to which they returned in 1956. Here I have not described some of the differences in housing between Galilo and Rapuri, which partly reflected mission policies. I am much indebted to Goodenough and the Valentines for relevant data.

2. *Malilo* is also the Lakalai word for hamlet.

3. Because it was formed from an amalgamation of two earlier villages, Galilo had two garden areas (see figure 4.3).

4. For an account of the male anal shame complex, see Chowning 1989.

5. For protection from soiling, men in particular either chose spots on which clean sand had been spread or sat on some sort of temporary seat, even a coconut husk. Women were protected by the leaf bustles they wore.

6. Village size permitting, many marriages also took place between co-residents, who were already called by kinship terms.

7. In other parts of New Britain one reason for official insistence on pile houses was to prevent burial of the dead inside them, but I do not know that this was the case in Lakalai.

8. The indigenous, though non-Lakalai, missionary resident in Galilo was particularly preoccupied with female modesty in dress, and may have influenced attitudes on related matters.

9. The Catholics belonged to a different society that marketed copra through a priest who urged them to spend the proceeds on corrugated iron for their houses.

10. Although each village contained several racing canoes, to avoid intra-village strife if one defeated another, only one canoe represented a village in actual races.

11. Each village had a single councillor elected by the whole adult population.

12. In recent years intervillage fights have again erupted, one of which destroyed the Galilo pump that had provided a new water supply. Some of those living near the outskirts of the village seemed to fear sorcerers rather than physical assault, however.

13. This is a term I have heard elsewhere in West New Britain for houses regarded as ridiculously small and cramped. Compare the use of terms for some homeless housing in Hawai'i (see Modell, chapter 9, this volume).

5

Transformations in the Domestic Landscape of New Zealand Homesteads

⌂

MICHÈLE D. DOMINY

AT THE SOCIAL and symbolic center of high country pastoralism in New Zealand's South Island lies the station homestead, the farm family's dwelling, and its encompassing domestic landscape—the driveway, cultivated garden grounds, farm buildings and yards, and tree plantings—that comprise the built environment of the Canterbury high country.[1] Beyond lie the station paddocks sheltered by land forms of high relief and planted shelter belts, and even farther removed lie larger higher altitude blocks extending out to the remote and rugged back country. While station buildings, gardens, and cultivated paddocks usually occupy freehold land, most of the holdings comprising these properties are Crown land, leased from the New Zealand government. "Station" refers to the entire property, although, according to Acland (1975, 385), in the nineteenth century "station" applied originally to "the hut, yards and buildings where a squatter stationed himself to work his run, but now [applies] to the whole property, including the stock and leasehold country." It also, he notes, can suggest a large property carrying several thousand head of sheep. For many high country people a high country property can only be called a station if it has Crown pastoral leasehold land and extensive areas of high altitude back country usually subject to severe snows and cold southerly rains; most simply defined, it is a property on which the production of wool is the main source of income and that might be liable to snow losses (see McLeod 1980, 9). The term "station" is not often used by high country people today, who prefer to refer to their properties as "farms"; they are equally as likely to refer to themselves as "farmers," "wool producers," "lessees," or even "stakeholders." The terminology, as well as changes in the use and

shape of the built environment, reflect the shift from the station of
the past with a large hired staff[2] to the contemporary station as a
family farm unit, with at most a couple of full-time shepherds or a
married couple as hired help. As properties have been legally subdivided between sons, they are also more likely to be called "farms"
rather than "stations."

Elsewhere in an analysis of high country toponymic and topo-
graphic systems, I argue for the centrality of an idiom of containment, and I suggest that the similarity of naming principles between
stations points to both predictable regularities of function and their
reflection in similarities in the design or mapping of different stations
(Dominy 1995a). Aerial photographs and maps point to consistent
symbolic regularities in spatial layout that reflect aspects of both the
social and conceptual systems organizing high country life. Such a
symbolic reading of spatial forms suggests that the dominant configuration is one of encompassment, of boundaries within boundaries,
characterized by what Kolodny calls a "geography of enclosures"
(1972, 55). My focus in this chapter is on transformations in the
innermost enclosure, that of the homestead and its immediate grounds
excluding the proximate farm buildings. More significantly, a closer
analysis of transformations in the use and design of domestic physical space reveals generational transformations in those social and
conceptual systems with implications for identity formation and the
configuration of the nuclear family and gender roles.

Cultural anthropologists, influenced by the work of Durkheim
and Mauss and Goffman, have explored the intimate association
of "divisions of space and social formations" and the mutual dependence of "behavior and space" as "space defines people" and
"people define space"; fittingly, Shirley Ardener (1993, 2–3) calls
the expression of these social relationships (such as kinship) and
structures (such as hierarchical systems) "social maps." Calling
for an integration of symbolic approaches and social production
theories, and stressing the approaches of Foucault and Giddens,
Denise Lawrence and Setha Low (1990, 460–465), in their review
of literature on the built environment, in particular encourage
explanations of the relationship between social organization and
dwelling form as it is embedded in larger sociocultural systems (also
see Chambers and Low 1989, 6). One avenue of approach for
understanding changing housing and social relationships is through
an archaeology of structures (see Behar 1986), maps, diaries, and
landscape.

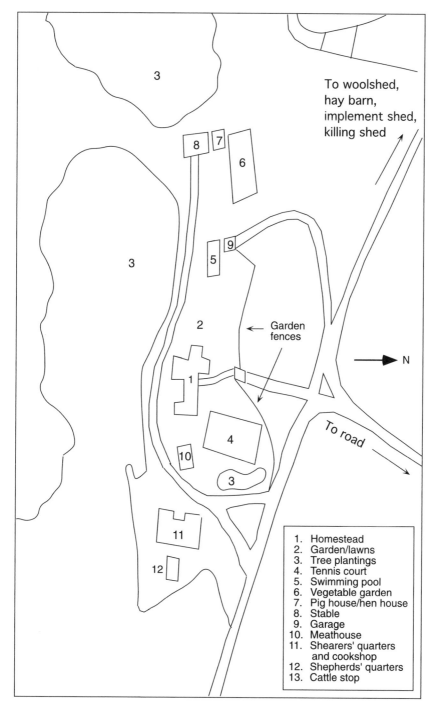

To woolshed,
hay barn,
implement shed,
killing shed

Garden
fences

N

To road

1. Homestead
2. Garden/lawns
3. Tree plantings
4. Tennis court
5. Swimming pool
6. Vegetable garden
7. Pig house/hen house
8. Stable
9. Garage
10. Meathouse
11. Shearers' quarters
    and cookshop
12. Shepherds' quarters
13. Cattle stop

5.1 Double Hill homestead (sketched from an aerial photograph)

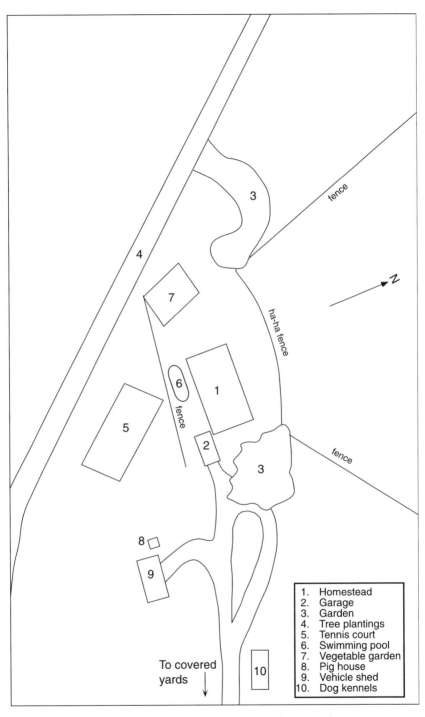

5.2 Glenaan homestead (sketched from an aerial photograph)

An Aerial View

Approaching two high country properties from the air and the ground —Double Hill, an old and well-established station first settled in 1869 and continuously evolving over the years, and Glenaan, a new station planned from scratch and built in 1974 after two brothers subdivided a property—reveals the layouts indicated in figures 5.1 and 5.2. Each homestead is surrounded by the garden, including tree plantings, shrubs, and flower beds, as well as the tennis court, swimming pool,[3] and vegetable garden this fenced landscape encompasses; these in turn at Double Hill are surrounded by farm buildings and enclosures such as the permanent shepherds' two-room bunkhouse, cookshop, shearers' quarters, hen house, pig house, and stables, and farther away are the woolshed, hay barn, killing house, and implement sheds. The older homestead, Double Hill, still has the facilities for a large staff, although today only two permanent shepherds are on the work staff; but the new homestead, Glenaan, is scaled back and shares a woolshed, cookshop, and shearers' quarters with a neighboring property called Glenariffe (the original station homestead now owned by a sibling and his wife), and only has a shepherd's hut and machinist's cottage to accommodate staff, and covered yards for stockwork. Beyond lie the airstrip, the gentler sheep paddocks on alluvial fans, and beyond that the access routes through saddles out to the back country, an expanse of high altitude tussock grassland leading out to alpine peaks that have been retired from farming or surrendered from the lease over the years.

From the air, station buildings are most identifiable by the extensive tree plantings of conifers, willows, eucalyptus, and poplar, all fast-growing trees that not only define the area around the homestead but also protect it from both the fierce nor'west winds that come over the Alps and the cold southerlies that bring rain and snow. The trees form distinctive lines running up and across the alluvial fans, although today many farm families are trying to break the straight lines and plant native species of trees in response to national environmental sensitivities about their visual impact. Environmental concern for landscape values points to the highly contrasting colors of conifers against the tawny tussock grasslands, the obscuring of landform details and lack of fit with the shape of the hills, the monotonous uniformity and nonindigenous nature of many windbreak schemes, and the dangers of "wilding" (uncontrolled spread) of introduced species (see Ashdown and Lucas 1987, 55–66).

The old houses tended to ignore the sun and sought protection from the wind. Many other factors determined placement of these early homesteads—proximity to water and firewood, aspect, and the limitations of building materials that were available (see Salmond 1986, 61). Early settlers typically located their homesteads in sheltered areas near streams, within hollows, and in the shadows of hills; frequently the homestead would surrender warmth, altitude, and a view for protection from certain natural elements. Sometimes its placement was determined by the land's having been bought from the provincial government as freehold rather than its being leasehold. One elderly woman who had moved to the high country with her husband to provide a larger property for their four sons described coming to the sad, old homestead: "It had straight rows of pines as shelter—they blocked the light—it had small windows, small rooms and was very run down. . . . Eventually the house was renovated. It had a concrete foundation and they said it was hard to extend but we did add to the living room and we extended all the windows."

There were exceptions, however, as some properties did favor the view (but not the sun); in his description of the Grasmere homestead, runholder and author David McLeod writes:

> The house stands, or rather crouches, beside a small glaciated hill in the very mouth of the Cass River where it emerges from its deep-cut valley between the Craigieburn and the Black Ranges. It is a poor place for a homestead, wind-swept and icy cold, and set on soil which is seventy-five percent stones. But oh, what a deeply rewarding view it has down the long slope of the fan to the beautiful pool of Lake Grasmere nearly two miles away! (McLeod 1974, 22)

But this location was not ideal in terms of placement for the view. When McLeod's son, Ian, sought a site to build a cottage homestead he noted that the freehold did not run up the side of the hill and was "by no means the best spot on which to have built a house" (McLeod 1980, 224). Like many of his generation, he sought the view and the warmth of the sun:

> Ian decided that he would like to get more sun and less frost, not to mention a better view. . . . [I]n due course the cottage was built, with a panorama of the whole Cass Valley spread out beneath it and sun beating straight on to it from early dawn until the great dark bulk of Misery cut it off in the late afternoon. Nothing could move in the whole wide basin; neither trains on the line nor traffic

on the road nor station work in the paddocks; not even ducks
upon the lake without being seen by a watcher from its windows.
There was one snag of course—the wind. The wind that whirls
over the Misery ridge from the west and, confined by the narrow
Cass Valley, emerges in a series of violent blasts like some great
trumpet player spewing out the whole contents of his lungs. . . . To
protect the cottage from these blasts we had to grow some trees as
quickly as possible. (McLeod 1980, 224–225)

Today when new homesteads are built, usually because stations have
been subdivided between siblings, they are carefully placed to mini-
mize the effects of nor'west winds and take advantage of the sun, but
because of cost, proximity to power lines or water supply is more
important in determining placement. The primary factor now, as in
the past, is cost (Salmond 1986, 61). The most distinctive contrast
between the old and the new is not only the placement of homesteads
—new homesteads virtually always stand higher and take account of
the view (see figure 5.3)—but also their compact design and construction from brick, concrete blocks, or stone. The omnipresent
verandah so characteristic of British colonial architecture is retained
for shade,[4] but windows are enlarged to frame and incorporate the
landscape into the interior; even additions to old homesteads feature
bigger windows, and many have replaced the original smaller windows with larger thermopane ones. Rather than avoiding the scale of
the landscape as the early settlers did, many contemporary families
want to be able to embrace it as part of their view and blend into it
with the architecture and garden design. The Glenaan family's environmental sensitivity is reflected in their contemporary homestead,
which has large windows to bring the outside inside, multiple verandahs to bring the inside outside, exterior paint the tawny color of
tussock grasslands, roof lines to reflect alpine peaks, and a raised
front lawn with a ha-ha, or dropped fence, between garden and paddocks that does not disrupt the continuity of the alluvial fan as it
stretches down toward the river (see figure 5.3; see also figure 5.2).
Whereas the runholder's mother told me that listening to the ava-
lanches in the mountains made her shudder and that she "never went
further than the garden gate" nor to see the rest of the property
because she hated the hills, her children and grandchildren in contrast are avid downhill skiers. Their recreational lives suggest this
most clearly as they embrace virgin ski fields and go jetboating, flying, wilderness tramping, camping, and fishing.
    One homestead especially illustrates this shift. Originally a five

5.3 The Glenaan homestead, now protected with mature shelter belts, was built on open alluvial fan paddocks above the Rakaia River. Large windows, multiple verandahs and doors, and ha-ha enhance the view of the river valley and mountains from the homestead. The homestead design, with its peaked roofline and tawny autumn tussock-colored paint, mimics the high country landscape. In 1994 the verandah was extended and the paint color changed to the flax tones of spring tussock. Michèle Dominy, 1988.

thousand-acre run when it was taken up in 1864, the homestead and station buildings were built in 1874 on twenty acres of freehold on a point at the confluence of two rivers. Over time the river shifted to flood the point; the homestead was rebuilt in 1917 in its present location on the south side of a two thousand-foot high hillside facing the river that provides its four-wheel drive access route. Sheltered from the nor'west winds but without the benefit of winter sunshine, the homestead was constructed by a well-known bush carpenter, Gideon Johnstone, who also constructed the woolshed—from the timber and iron of the original woolshed. Typically in winter the sun shines from 10:30 A.M. until 2:30 P.M., not even melting the frost before it is obscured by the hills behind. This is a hard property with fierce winds and bitter cold winters. To shelter the homestead a dense windbreak of conifers was planted in the 1920s directly between the kitchen and the glaciated alpine range of the main divide; by 1987 its height entirely obstructed the view. As Strongman (1984, 37) writes, the pioneer "seemed to forgo the wonderful view which he might have had of plains and mountains; he tended to surround his house and garden with trees." During my first visit a bulldozer man was working with the station owner to lay new four-wheel drive tracks on the property, and the owner's wife convinced her husband that it was time to take down the trees. They had replaced the original kitchen sash window with two identical windows side by side (while preserving the old wood-burning cooking stove), and she wanted to be able to see her view even at the risk of greater exposure to the winds. The next morning the garden and pear tree were severely windblown. The owners told me that today the homestead would never have been built in that spot; they have transformed it with the addition of a wing with full verandah angled to face the sun as much as possible, but their capital has been channeled back into improving the property for livestock, and they cannot afford to channel resources into moving or rebuilding a homestead. A high country family in an adjacent valley recently built a new homestead in a new location positioned at the head of a lake to absorb the view and was able to move the original homestead (now a staff cottage) from that site to another, windier site. In another instance, a couple purchased a high country property and have opted to live in the station cottage rather than the original homestead, in part because the homestead was rebuilt cheaply and unattractively after a fire, but more significantly because the cottage is well situated for the view, although they wish it were up the paddock just a little bit more in a hollow so that the sun would last slightly longer and the view would be slightly better. Regardless of when homesteads were built, varying practical constraints impeded the ideal.

The shifting location and design of homesteads suggests that a younger generation of high country people experience a greater control over their landscape, partly because of improvements in farming technology and changes in New Zealand housing design toward more organic homes, and easier transportation of heavier building materials such as brick and cinder blocks. These factors have contributed to a perceptual shift in which they have integrated vastness and the ruggedness of the high country into their lives in a way that their parents, and more particularly their grandparents, did not. The road, still subject to sudden rock slides and flooding fords, is much improved and better maintained with the aid of tractors and bulldozers. Also, all families use four-wheel drive vehicles, thus lessening the sense of isolation and vulnerability to mishap.

Early Station Evolution

Mary Nell, the wife of a station manager, came to the original Double Hill property (which was later subdivided) when she was first married in 1908 and kept daily diaries until she and her husband, who came first as a packman at the age of sixteen in 1900, left in 1912. In her diaries she describes the homestead when she first arrived: "At that time Gid Johnstone and Ted Wolfrey were adding on two rooms for us at the northern end of the homestead which by the way was only one room wide opening onto a verandah a chain long. The cookshop was out from the other end joining a large dining room used by the deer stalkers when there." As one of the original Canterbury runs first taken up in 1858, Double Hill station is classic in its design and its cohort of buildings. The first manager moved into a cob cottage as homestead in 1869—two other cottages were to follow with the current frame homestead being built around the third cottage.[5] Soon after, in 1882, the manager built the woolshed with pit-sawn beams, hand-cut rails, and no nails;[6] it had twenty-two stands for the shearers. Thornton (1986, 113) has referred to the woolshed as "the most striking symbol of the New Zealand pastoral landscape" and as a "vernacular building" that is "an essential part of our built environment." The stables and the first shearers' quarters of cob, which residents now jokingly call "the five star motel," were also built in the late 1800s. Mary Nell describes the shearers' cookshop:

> It was a long building with the kitchen and the cook's (at one end) bedroom opening onto a large dining room and behind that the same length of the dining room two bunks high was where all the old shearers slept as it was quieter. The rest of the shearers' accommodation consisted of three rooms with bunks two high but the partitions only went up to the eave.

In his unpublished history of Double Hill, Hugh Ensor's second eldest son, Peter, describes the high country homestead to which his mother, after the elegance of her North Canterbury property, with its billiard room and fine gardens, first came to live in 1930.[7] Mrs. Ensor is admired for rendering the high country environment more comfortable, muting the primitiveness through hard work, and adapting to harsh conditions (see Dominy 1993, 575).

> The old house was of sod walls[8] and snow-grass thatching,[9] later covered by corrugated iron and some weather board covering on the walls and matching lining on some of the inside walls. A long,

low verandah, one chain in length faced north with five rooms along it, with a big kitchen and cook's room on the east side, the sitting room on the north and west side going into a small kitchen and bathroom, but no connecting passage to the other rooms. It was all very dark with only some small windows and no glass doors. Again on the west side there was another verandah containing a laundry and big storeroom. These had been of later construction, not cob and thatch. (Ensor 1990, 13)

Kerosene lamps provided lighting, and every morning Mrs. Ensor would take away the six or so lamps, wash the globes, polish the stands, and trim the wicks. Not until 1948 was the first electric light turned on, when a water-driven wheel drove a six-volt generator, with a land line to the house, to produce power. The generator was later upgraded to twelve and then thirty-two volts with the addition of gearing mechanisms and a bank of sixteen two-volt batteries powering electric lights and fueling a vacuum cleaner, washing machine, and electric iron. In 1957 a hydroelectric plant was built two miles from the property with underground cables to the house to provide a good supply of light and power. A dam was constructed to raise the water level of a stream to operate a low-head turbine and generator that could produce thirty kilowatts of power. In 1971 power was reticulated across the river to Double Hill and its neighboring homesteads. Consequently, some of today's children, unlike their parents, grew up with television and fewer of the evening pleasures that previously had engaged the entire family, such as card and board games.

At the beginning of the depression in 1930, when many station owners were forced to take up residence on their properties, Ensor assumed active management of Double Hill, which he had purchased in 1916, and its two neighboring properties, Glenrock and Glenariffe, which had been purchased by his brothers-in-law in 1916 and 1917. At this time he and his wife had spent a week at Double Hill; Peter remembers making his first trip over the river in a spring cart with his parents several years later in 1921. Ensor appointed a manager and his wife to care for Double Hill in 1916,[10] and in the same year some improvements were made to the homestead. Although Mrs. Ensor was not the first woman to live at Double Hill, her husband was the first owner to do so.

Given lease restrictions, however, he could not hold on to more than one pastoral license, and so the lease of Glenariffe run was passed to his son; that of Glenrock was passed to another son, and

Double Hill and its freehold were retained in husband/wife partner-
ship. Effectively, changing land legislation reduced the size of pastoral lease properties, resulting in smaller station staffs. By 1934 twelve
permanent men were working on Double Hill and Glenrock,[11] including both Peter and one of his brothers, as well as shearers, cowman-
gardener, cook, and rouse-about.[12]

During 1938, 1939, and 1940 the Glenrock and Glenariffe diaries
were kept jointly, and the Double Hill diaries were kept separately.
Coincident with routine station activities noted in the combined
Glenrock/Glenariffe diaries for these years are those marking the
separation from Double Hill and the establishment of the Glenrock
homestead for a new family. These excerpted entries are typical of
the first months after separation when the homestead and station
buildings had to be made ready:

> "Transport arrived with rock salt, bricks and furniture" (6/VII/38).
> "Fireplace being built" (19/VII/38).
> "Reconstructing cow yard. Taylor made gate for same" (13/IX/38).
> "Teamster G. Fox arrived" (17/IX/38).
> "[Runholders] building yard for pups, killing" (30/III/39).

Tree plantings were an integral part of the process and, as at Double
Hill, they were concentrated primarily around the homestead
because rabbits, hares, and deer made it impossible to plant trees
away from the homestead.

> "Planted willow trees" (24/VIII/38).
> "Planting trees in Triangle paddock. Chambers fencing the trees"
> (30/VIII/38).
> "Finished fencing in the front paddock and planted 500 Douglas
> firs over the terrace in fenced section. . . . Chambers cleaning out
> under the shed" (8/IX/38).
> "Fencing young larches on the bank side of house" (29/VIII/39).
> "[P]ut in some poplars at Glenariffe" (29/VIII/39).
> "Smith making fence round the young trees behind the whare"
> (8/IX/39).

Some of these plantings were milled for timber in the 1980s. Over
the same period of time the Double Hill diaries note tree planting on
the west side of the old trees beyond the woolshed and stables to provide replacement windbreaks and timber over time. And perhaps
most dramatically,

> "Burrows, Wightman and Forrester bringing shed from across the
> river" (8–10/VII/39) with "Burrows constructing the shed" (12–
> 15/VIII/39).

Previously in 1937 new accommodations, required by law to a certain standard, were built at Glenrock. Six two-men bedrooms were located close to the Glenrock cook house.

Alterations and Additions

These homesteads have evolved considerably over the years, and changes in the homestead, gardens, and growth of trees mark the passage of time and serve as chronological landmarks for events. Mrs. Ensor's daughter-in-law, Louise, can describe the Double Hill homestead of the 1930s only in terms of today's rooms:

> What is the spare room down there was the family's dining room and there was a kitchen behind—this is before the house was altered—with a bakeoven, and the men were fed in the kitchen. The family were fed in the dining room, where we would sit on a cold winter's night. What is now the dining room was the sitting room, and the fireplace is where you now go into the sunroom. . . . [At dinnertime] there was a procession down the cold, cold verandah. . . . There was no back passage. [See figure 5.4.]

The station cook prepared meals for the family as well as the staff although they ate separately. This continued until 1942, when improvements to a small kitchen and the addition of a stove made it possible for Louise to cook for her own family, leaving them "independent of cooks and their dirty habits." Several years later in 1944 a new dining room for station hands was added onto the large old station kitchen (see figure 5.4). Today properties cannot afford large staffs or station cooks, and Lou's daughter's responsibilities are quite different. Like many high country women with a small staff, she cooks three hot meals a day plus morning and afternoon teas for her family and for the two permanent shepherds who eat with the family in the large farm kitchen; on Saturday evenings the shepherds cook their own meal. Casual laborers and workmen are also integrated into family meals. The cookshop is only used during shearing time for the shearing gang's cook to prepare meals, and although once the center of station life, today it is unused for most of the year.

Altered cooking spaces and eating arrangements result from a downturn in the farming economy, with consequent changes in social relationships such as the spatial diminution of class boundaries between owners and workers, the integration of workers into nuclear family life, and a configuration of roles for some women that circumscribes their activities to the homestead and its surrounds. Elvin

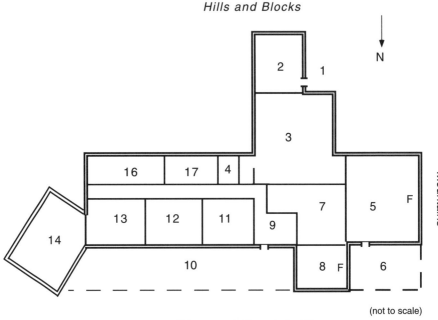

Hills and Blocks

N

2   1

3

16   17   4

7   5   F

Mountains

13   12   11
9

14

10

8   F   6

(not to scale)

River and Mountain View

1. Back door and patio [to store room]
2. Shearers' dining room [addition]
3. Family kitchen
4. Bathroom and WC
5. Sunroom [addition with fireplace]
6. Verandah to sunroom
7. Sitting room==>Family dining room
8. Sitting room, "front room" [1950 addition with fireplace]
9. Front door and entrance way
10. Verandah (one chain long) [route to original dining room #13]
11. Main bedroom [off verandah]
12. Bedroom [off verandah]
13. Bedroom [off verandah]
14. Bedroom [angled addition off verandah]
15. Interior hallway [added]
16. Bedroom/office
17. Bedroom
F. Fireplace

5.4 Floor plan for Double Hill homestead

Hatch (1992, 165) has written of this transformation from the two-table to the one-table pattern as reflecting post-World War II egalitarian pressures for social and economic leveling but also as suppressing "open expression of social distance on the one hand while implicitly confirming it on the other." The "one-table" is often large and special, sometimes original to the homestead, and carved of native wood, such as kauri.

At Double Hill the addition of a big sitting room with a stone fireplace on the northwest end of the house at a right angle to the rest of the house followed in 1950 (figure 5.4, room 8). Most homes have such a formal sitting room that is closed off from the rest of the house and used for large family gatherings at Christmas or Easter and for guests. Peter and Lou's daughter, who now lives at Double Hill with her husband, notes how smart the sitting room must have seemed at the time, with its "chapel-like" features; architectural ideas change, though, and she could imagine having extended the verandah around the house instead. Then in 1958 Peter and his wife rebuilt a section of the homestead. They began by removing many trees around the house and topping a lot of the old and tall poplar and pine trees that were too close to the woolshed. The station diaries follow the process closely, and Peter tells a dramatic story:

> We agreed to a plan which entailed demolishing all that part of the house containing the bedrooms and the old kitchen and replacing them with five bedrooms, an inside passage including a loo and an office for myself plus some other alterations. . . . We wanted to retain the character of the old house. . . . The first major job was to cut off and get rid of the part to be rebuilt leaving Lou and me to camp in the sitting room. The idea was to put a wire rope round and pull it down with a big tractor but at the first pull we saw the whole of the house move so that had to be stopped. We realised of course that the old sod walls were too solid and had to be dug out and what a mess it was getting the roof off with the old snow grass tussocks under the iron together with the possum nests and other vermin. [The builder] became concerned as to how he was going to match up the roofing of a bedroom to jut out at an angle at the far end of the verandah with the rest of the roofline. . . . In the end we had to get a dozer in to clean up the mess of the sod walls together with further excavation work for the extension of the house and, while it was on the job, preparing a site for the proposed tennis court among other things.

5.5 Built around the last of three cob-and-thatch cottages, the Double Hill
Station homestead was sited near water and sheltered by the then bush-
covered hills behind. The sunroom addition, with its vine-covered fireplace,
and the peaked-roof sitting room face west toward the Main Divide of the
South Island. Draped with wisteria, the verandah extends the living area of
the house out toward extensive lawns and garden plantings, beyond which is
the station woolshed. Michèle Dominy, 1990.

Also added on at the time was a big sunroom and fireplace on the
west side of the house (figure 5.4, room 5; see also figure 5.5). The
transformations of the Double Hill homestead were radical, but this
is not atypical. The expansion was prompted by increasing family
size[13] and by better economic conditions in the late 1940s and 1950s
resulting from war wool booms. As recently as March 1992, Peter
wrote to me of more changes to the current homestead, now occupied by his daughter and son-in-law, whose three children are grown:

> The whole place has been painted. My old office has been turned
> into another bathroom and a new office has been added on giving
> much more space for a computer plus more space to store all the
> paper work which is part of life these days.

Station families, however, are not always free agents to change the
homestead and often have to seek permission for the expenditure in
instances where the property is an incorporated family land company

with parents or siblings holding shares. Retired parents often call the shots, sometimes even selecting the setting and design of the homestead: One woman had no say in the design of her home, which was built upon her marriage; one bride gave up square footage for finished cabinets. Mostly, houses get the last of the resources because the farm gets them first, and many women wait years for a remodeled kitchen, additional bathroom, or revived front door. The homestead never really belongs to a couple but to the station; rather, they know they cannot stay in it past retirement or if a child wishes to return to farm. Accordingly, many changes are made with the needs of the next generation in mind—selecting a neutral color scheme or not overexpanding a garden.

Aerial photographs illustrate the formulaic pattern of growth of these homesteads through the years, seemingly "in a haphazard way as interiors changed with the times" with wings and attachments, creating structures likened by one high country woman to rabbit warrens. This woman's mother-in-law was known for "knocking out walls" and changing the shape of the homestead as her family grew to seven children; she said to me, "As the family grew so did the house." Another woman explained, "As children were born the house grew out, utterly transforming the original cottage inside; I was kept busy with children—I had six over the years." A passage from one of Ngaio Marsh's high country detective classics tells the same story in its construction of the fictional Mount Moon:

> Mount Moon homestead was eighty years old and that is a great age for a house in the Antipodes. It had been built by Arthur Rubrick's grandfather, from wood transported over the Pass in bullock wagons. It was originally a four-roomed cottage, but room after room had been added, at a rate about twice as slow as that achieved by the intrepid Mrs. Rubrick of those days in adding child after child to her husband's quiver. (Marsh 1973, 24)

Thornton (1986, 24) notes also that a century's evolution of country houses through use is apparent in the common practice of making alterations and additions to meet changing needs and circumstances, but houses were strongly vernacular and followed no common trend other than constant transformation (see, for example, figure 5.6). David McLeod echoes the Double Hill and Glenrock histories in his account of Grasmere and describes its construction:

> The homestead was, in part, one of the oldest-inhabited in the high country and like most of them, had been altered and

5.6 Clayton Station homestead, typical in its mix of construction materials (stone and wood siding), its architectural style, and eclectic angles, reveals the constancy of changing shapes through additions. Participants at a high country field day stand near the verandah that encircles the house on the edge of expansive and yet secluded lawns. Michèle Dominy, 1987.

enlarged. The original two-roomed cob and slab hut, built in 1858, is still (1974) contained within an enlarged house faced with limestone from the rocks at Castle Hill. This first hut had a roof thatched with snow grass laid on thin birch sticks crossing the round birch rafters. Bits of the snow grass remain after 115 years and the timber is still as sound as the day it was erected. Wings of timber have been added at different periods and the whole re-roofed with corrugated iron. (McLeod 1974, 21–22)

Today walls are removed to provide more light. Both the dining room and the sitting room at Double Hill have been provided with glass doors, and at a neighboring property the wall between kitchen and dining room was removed when the current generation began to make its mark, reconfiguring the interiors to create more centralized open family space.

The impression, as Ruth Behar (1986) notes in her analysis of the Leonese village house in Santa Maria, is one of "a house structure molded by the hand of time" (1986, 43) in which "the past and present, given shape in architectonic form, coexist in time and space"

(1986, 48) and whose diachronic aspects can be discovered through the exploratory process of doing "an archaeology" of the house (1986, 53).[14] Jane Adams, in her work on southern Illinois farm women, also examines the organization of space and time as a central structuring process through an analysis of homestead architecture:

> Farm structures are enduring; they tend to be remodeled more frequently than replaced, and many people relate to old buildings as repositories of memories. Buildings therefore can be usefully approached as maps to past social forms, suggesting through their spatial organization the ways in which the people who lived in them ordered their lives. (Adams 1993, 92)

Because such architecture is both a mix of permanence and modification, it provides a physical vehicle against which change and continuity in high country life can be measured. Earlier lives and times are evident in these old homes even as the spaces are transformed in each generation to meet new needs, and adapt to new domestic cycles, styles, economic situations, and technological possibilities.

The capacity of high country homesteads to incorporate people is not only structural but also symbolic. An elderly informant said of Glenrock, "It was like Paddington Station here often with twenty to a meal. It has always been like that, the walls were elastic. The walls stretch for [my daughter-in-law] also. That is high country hospitality." An improved road has lessened the need for such elasticity. Still there is space for visitors, especially siblings, who as adults always have the right to return to their childhood home even after their parents have left. Siblings (usually sons) on adjacent properties often take turns hosting Christmas as a tradition, as a symbolic gesture, incorporating those who have left back into station life and making them welcome through extensive and concerted preparations beginning months in advance. Homes absorb people easily; bedrooms are always available (often because children are away at boarding school), and because women have to cook large quantities of food for family and staff anyway, an extra person is easily accommodated. Workmen, children's school friends, journalists, and casual laborers are expected to stay. Walls that stretch defy a notion of closed nuclearity for high country families, and yet compared with their parents' generation, today's couples work much more closely and exclusively together as farm partners.

A key aspect of technology enhancing the nuclear family was the introduction of the telephone to replace the radio telephone that linked the valley's properties after the war. The old radio telephone linked all the valley twice a day as households signed on for messages, and calls out were heard by all. Even grocery lists, called into the village for weekly delivery on the transport truck, were public. Now families note how much more isolated from each other they are. Improved transportation makes trips to town possible, whether for a child's school game or play or a weekly game of golf. While this has lessened the mutual dependence of families on each other for a social life, wear and tear on vehicles on a rough and unpredictable road does limit such trips.

Social life in the high country is still actively constructed through dinner parties, riding expeditions, woolshed parties, dog trials, skating parties, rugby matches, and various school- and farming-related events down country. The size of buildings, from the homestead to the woolshed, can accommodate large groups, and ambitious outdoor events such as gymkhanas and overnight trips on horseback are organized. For instance, one station family with the longest continuous single ownership in the South Island celebrated its one hundred year anniversary by throwing a dinner party and dance in the woolshed for all their descendants and all of those who had ever worked on the property and their descendants; five hundred people attended. Isolation means that the children who have grown up in the valley have had to create their own amusements and seek each other out as friends; when they go to boarding school they often "stick together." Similarly, high country people, when criticized by others for visible signs of affluence—the pool and tennis courts, the elaborate gardens —will point out that they build these things themselves, that pools were originally put in to control the fires that so often devastated remote homesteads, and that they have to "create their own entertainment," although less so today with improved transportation in and out of the valley.

The Homestead Described

The back door and back porch where boots are left provide the usual entry to a high country homestead; one farmer told me that the act of removing his boots marks the spatial transition from farm to home. Typically near the back door is an outside toilet and a large sink, sometimes the washing machine and dryer, the pantry, the freezer, and storage areas. The central area of the homestead is the kitchen with an attached dining area and usually today an open familyroom or sunroom with a television, games, and comfortable sofas and chairs (see figures 5.4, 5.7, and 5.8). Newer homesteads often have a small office and sewing room off the kitchen; older homesteads convert unused bedrooms to office space; one old homestead moved the kitchen into a large, central sunny room that had been an office, turning the original kitchen into a sewing and laundry room. Formal living rooms are often additions to the homesteads and appear as well-lit side wings, often with fine views of the landscape. Bedrooms are usually set apart in wings to the homestead, making them private from the heavily trafficked central areas of kitchen and dining room. People were often able to tell me the progression of children who had moved through each bedroom, the eldest remaining child moving into the largest room as his or her predecessor left for boarding school.[15] It is not uncommon for old verandahs to have been covered over to provide additional rooms for sleeping or for teaching correspondence school, or to create an enclosed hallway to seclude sleeping areas. Older homesteads had verandahs off kitchens, living rooms, dining rooms, and bedrooms; many of the new homesteads follow this pattern. Today's interiors tend to use flecked natural and cream shades in rugs and wallpaper and paint. Similarly, exterior colors are tussock yellow or brown or cream, unlike the traditional white, and sometimes they are made of river stone or brick, better enabling them "to recede into the landscape."

Most high country properties have a cottage initially built for a returning son and his wife. As families grew, so would the cottage with the addition of rooms. But in many instances the son and his family (occasionally a daughter) would exchange houses and gardens with the parents and in time, as the parents moved down country, the cottage might then pass on to their returning grandson and his wife. The switch is never easy from either perspective, and there are many stories of parents running out from the cottage at the sound of a chain saw to protect a tree they had planted. Many high country women express their individuality and stake their claim to belonging through the imprint they make on both the homes and the gardens that they take over from their mothers-in-law. All families could tell me stories of how this was done, for instance by painting a kitchen purple (an aberration) or taking down wallpaper and ripping up carpets, assigning rooms for different purposes, relandscaping the grounds. Women told me how difficult it was to take over a mother-in-law's garden, and one told me that her mother-in-law would

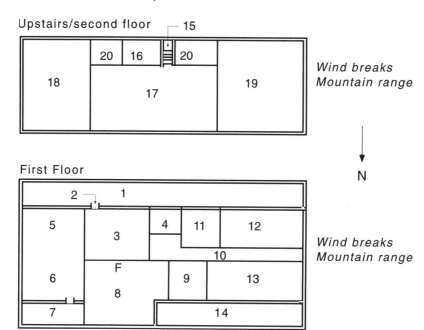

Hills and paddocks

Upstairs/second floor

18 | 20 | 16 | 15 | 20 | 17 | 19

Wind breaks
Mountain range

N

First Floor

2 | 1
5 | 3 | 4 | 11 | 12
10
6 | F | 9 | 13
8
7 | 14

(not to scale)

Wind breaks
Mountain range

River view and mountains
Ha-ha fence to paddocks

1. Back verandah
2. Back door
3. Entryway/storage/laundry
4. WC
5. Kitchen and eating area
6. Family dining room
7. Verandah/front entrance [off dining room]
8. Living room [with fireplace]
9. Main bedroom==>Office
    [and enlarged living room (off verandah)]
10. Passageway to bedrooms
11. Bathroom
12. Youngest child's bedroom==>bedroom
13. Eldest child's bedroom==>main bedroom [off verandah]
14. Front verandah
15. Interior stairs from back verandah
16. Bathroom
17. Central play and living area
18. Guestroom==>youngest child's bedroom
19. Guestroom==>eldest child's bedroom
20. Attic
F. Fireplace

5.7 Floor plan for Glenaan homestead

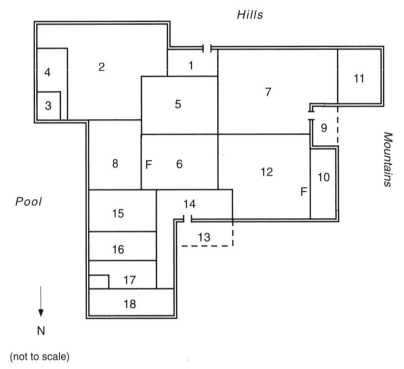

Hills

Mountains

Pool

N

(not to scale)

River and Mountain View

1. Back door and entryway/laundry area
2. Shearers' dining room [addition]
3. Bathroom
4. Child's bedroom==>Shearers' cook's bedroom
5. Kitchen
6. Family living area
7. Family dining area
8. Correspondence school room==>Sewing room
9. Verandah and side entrance
10. Verandah==>Bedroom==>Office
11. Guest bedroom [addition]
12. Formal sitting room [with fireplace]
13. Front verandah and entrance
14. Verandah==>Enclosed passageway
15. Child's bedroom
16. Child's bedroom
17. Bathroom
18. Main bedroom
F. Fireplace

5.8 Floor plan for Glenariffe homestead

notice with every visit if a plant was moved or went missing; the couple would just respond, "That's right, it's not there any more." One woman removed the furnishings of her sitting room from the homestead and re-created the identical room in her new home in a nearby village.

Gardens and Grounds

Well-planted New Zealand gardens, according to Thornton (1986, 24), assimilated the homestead into the landscape. They derived from an English stately home tradition in which gardens were indistinguishable from the landscape. Perhaps even more importantly for early settlers, as Thelma Strongman argues in *The Gardens of Canterbury*, they were reminders of home, integrating the familiar into the foreign environment: "The idea of the garden as fine art was part of the English culture which was imported into and impressed upon the new province" (Strongman 1984, 11). But the harsh tussock grasslands of the high country often seemed "sublime," inspiring settlers with fear and awe. Although common knowledge argues that early settlers eschewed indigenous trees and plants, it is not altogether true, as flax, toe-toe, and cabbage trees were used together with native plants brought from England (Strongman 1986, 42). Again Marsh's literary ethnographic idealization of Mount Moon reinforces the point:

> The house bore a dim family resemblance to the Somersetshire seat which Arthur's grandfather had thankfully relinquished to a less adventurous brother. Victorian gables and the inevitable conservatory, together with lesser family portraits and surplus pieces of furniture, traced unmistakably the family's English origin. The garden had been laid out in a nostalgic mood, at considerable expense and with a bland disregard for the climate of the plateau. Of the trees old Rubrick had planted, only Lombardy poplars, *Pinus insignis* and a few natives had flourished. The tennis lawn, carved out of the tussocky hill-side, turned yellow and dusty during summer. The pleached walks of Somerset had been in part realised with hardy ramblers and, where these failed, with clipped fences of poplar. The dining-room windows looked down upon a queer transformation of what had been originally an essentially English conception of a well-planned garden. But beyond this unconvincing piece of *pastiche*—what uncompromising vastness! The plateau swam away into an illimitable haze of purple, its boundaries mingled with clouds. Above the cloud, suspended it seemed in a tincture of rose, floated the great mountains. (Marsh 1973, 24–25)

Mary Nell notes in her diaries that the Double Hill homestead, situated on the south side of the river, was a "very healthy place to live—so open and you could see for miles especially the river away across the flats." The homestead was fenced, and Mary Nell describes her garden as lovely. Twenty years later, as Mrs. Ensor transformed the building from "shack" to homestead, she began to incorporate the landscape into a beautified domestic world with the addition of French doors and recultivation of the garden (see Dominy 1993, 576). Her daughter-in-law, Lou, sees both garden and homestead as beautiful symbols of cultivation, paralleling the beauty of the natural surroundings.

For many high country women their gardens are a visible sign of their creative lives' achievements. One woman who built a new homestead with her husband was able to transform a paddock into a garden that is expanding at present from two to three acres. She cooks willingly but would rather be outside where she has "something in which to focus her energies." She and her husband designed the shape of the lawn first, favoring curved edges and distinct garden sections; there is a rock garden, an azalea garden, vegetable garden, wilderness garden with pond and gully, and various flower gardens. Aesthetics and pragmatics, as in so much of the built environment of the high country, were combined. The lawn, for example, follows the contours of the land, and the trees throughout the property are treasured both for income and aesthetics, a mixture of domestics and exotics, unlike the pine plantations that provided timber for their parents' generation.

At Double Hill, while doing outdoor tasks as we went from place to place—taking garden rubbish to the dump, feeding the pigs and working dogs—Lou's daughter narrated, telling me that the garden is continually evolving. She and her husband took out the pines and poplars on the eastern side of the homestead in 1983, opening up the entire area to light and putting in the tennis courts. There were clusters of trees, poplars and firs, on the spur above the homestead—these hills and their vegetation dominate the old homestead—that have been cut down. She had plans to divert the stream and put in a pond but didn't know then if it would be done "during my time" at Double Hill; it was, in 1994. Given inheritance practices, her time is inevitably finite. Behind the kitchen there is a bricked area with daisies, and the old rose bushes are still growing well despite an age of over thirty years. Over the sunroom windows and verandahs roses and wisteria also grow well. She has changed the straight lines of the lawns. The flowerbeds would have very much the same flowers in them as in her mother's time, but her mother kept the beds very dense and the daughter, hating to work in them, opened them up. She has added shrubs that would not have been popular then but are more available now, and she has changed the lines, with the flower-bed curving out from the sitting room window into the driveway. The driveway curves round rather than forming its former straight line to the front door, and the old white gate has been replaced by a cattle stop (see figure 5.1). She wanted very much to have the garden different from her mother's; its transformation is an endless process, one that she says will never be done. She is mindful that if her son comes to farm Double Hill, his wife would not be able to maintain the expanded garden, especially with small children. The developmental cycle of the New Zealand high country homestead keeps the size of gardens in check.

Although women assert their individualities through the gardens they cultivate, this is not an entirely gendered domain as in the past but rather reflects the overall integration of women and men into the endeavor of farming as a nuclear family enterprise. Husbands and wives design the gardens together, and many women say how important "men, machines and money" are in the transformations of this landscape. On some properties men do the rotary tilling and take care of the pruning and vegetable gardens; on others their wives do; seldom are shepherds asked to do such tasks. One farmer told me that the vegetable garden is "the prime place where the domestic and business come together"; vegetable gardens as distinct from flower beds fall at the interface of the farm and domestic life. Toward the end of the life cycle many retired high country men turn their attention to gardening in lieu of farming, and those who move to cities, like their rural counterparts, continue to garden on a grand scale.

Conclusion

Geoffrey G. Thornton (1986, 10) has noted that New Zealand farm buildings are a "memorial to the early colonial economy," one founded on agrarianism, and "form an important element in the humanising and transforming of the landscape." They also reflect different social configurations emerging from the changing farm economy and changing value systems, as well as an evolving relationship with the New Zealand landscape.

New Zealand high country homesteads and their immediate built environment go through a developmental cycle in two ways as continuity of use and meaning is attached to buildings concurrently with shifts in use and meaning. In their consideration of the concept of household, Netting et al. (1984, xviii) point out that Goody's developmental cycle concept "takes no account of history" while opposing views treat the household as "fluid in structure and impermanent in boundaries." Both views can be synthesized in this consideration, not of household, but of homesteads.

First, their evolution reflects the stages of the developmental cycle of the family as aging parents move aside for their married children (who will eventually move aside for their children) to take over the farm. The walls stretch and contract as children are born and children leave; within the life cycle of a given family of procreation, rooms are transformed continually through use. As children are born, bedrooms and schoolrooms are created; as they leave the rooms become sewing rooms and gardens expand, reflecting the shifting focus of women's energies over the life cycle. Regularity of use over the years is fostered by persistent constraints of isolation, climate, and landscape and the continuity of the seasonal pastoral calendar.

Second, homestead evolution reflects the development of farming technologies, economic cycles, and environmental values, as each generation leaves a distinctive imprint on the design and use of physical space. For example, increasing pastoral productivity (and continuing landscape transformation) through the use of aerial topdressing, rotational grazing, and improved grasses means that more work can be done with fewer staff; the economic downturn in the world wool market makes farming more risky and less profitable, however, and today station staffs are pared down even more as many families run the farm with no hired help at all. Women without staff become more integrated as farm partners, but those with staff assume the primary role for cooking, and shift the focus of station life to the homestead kitchen. Changing attitudes to the environment are apparent in the placement and design of contemporary homesteads and the opening up of older settlement-dated homesteads. Expanded verandahs, bigger windows, natural colors, and gardens and windbreaks with curvaceous rather than straight lines have replaced the cold, dark, sheltered homesteads and formal gardens of the past. The new fondness for indigenous plants, the shift in environmental values, the use of more glass and light, the preference for curvilinear planting are all characteristic of New Zealand society in general, but these properties are particularly interesting places to see these changes because of the continuity of ownership and use.

The same buildings, though altered, endure, but no family can afford to get too attached to a building that they are only passing through, despite its link with the past and the future. In contrast, their attachment to the station as place is profound, and inheritance patterns protect the continuity of family ownership (see Dominy 1995b). Even daughters who leave will say that the station is still home, initially with an "H" and eventually fading to an "h" as they establish their own homes. One daughter told me that home is now elsewhere but her bones belong to her childhood home, a large station with its own burial ground. As a result of this kind of attachment, and the linking of family to place, the station homestead and its encompassing grounds continuously evolve over time through a process of accretion and reconfiguration as each generation asserts its sense of belonging by making it their own and leaves its marks for the next generation. The built environment is a cumulative identity marker denoting the continuity of family habitation over the generations as well as the particular historical and personal experiences of the individuals who move through it. The sense of belonging high country families share, however, is not based simply on material attachment to the built environment, but rather on an ideological attachment to the symbolic weight that family and the continuity of its attachment to property—the larger place, the station—carry.

Notes

Several field research trips to the New Zealand South Island high country between 1986 and 1995 were supported in part by the Wenner-Gren Foundation for Anthropological Research and Bard College. I acknowledge this support with appreciation. Helpful commentary was provided by Ann Chowning, Alan Howard, Cluny Macpherson, Judith Modell, Jan Rensel, and Margaret Rodman.

1. Lawrence and Low (1990, 454) define the built environment as an abstract concept referring to "any physical alteration of the natural environment" to include built forms, sites, and plans.

2. Hatch (1992) refers to this as a hierarchy of work force arrangements.

3. The Double Hill swimming pool, built in the fifties, replaced the old orchard that was ruined by a grass fire.

4. Salmond (1986, 77) considers the verandah a "classical colonial artifact" deriving in British settled countries from Jamaica and India. The verandah, sometimes extending around two or three sides of the house, shelters walls from the weather, provides cheap extra living space,

protects the front door, and serves as an outdoor room in the warmer months.

5. Many of the early homesteads were built of cob, consisting of a dampened mixture of earth, a proportion of clay, chopped straw or tussock grass, and cow dung (Thornton 1986, 15; Salmond 1986, 38).

6. Thornton (1986, 111) and Salmond (1986, 56) note that timber was the most common building material. In the bush the laboriously created and cheaper pit-sawn timber predated sawmill timber, which was produced quite early in New Zealand. Today corrugated galvanized iron has replaced timber, brick, and stone.

7. See the floor plans of Lilybank and the Orari Gorge homesteads, both classic stations well documented in Dick (1964, 15) and Harper (1967, 75), and typical of the type of homestead from which Mrs. Ensor had come.

8. Sod or turf was the most primitive of several available earth materials, dug out of the ground, and typically used in a double row with the space between filled with clay or "rammed" earth (Thornton 1986, 15; see Salmond 1986, 38 for more detail on sod construction).

9. This was the earliest and least common type of roofing in colonial New Zealand (Thornton 1986, 18). Snowgrass or rushes, whichever was available, were used in thatching.

10. The Double Hill diaries begin in 1916 and continue through the present.

11. Today the properties combined employ four men, including the two runholders.

12. In U.S. English it is "roustabout."

13. Peter and Louise had four daughters at the time, ranging in age from seventeen to eight. Other families in the valley had families of six or seven children. Today in the valley family sizes range from two to four children per property.

14. The Leonese house, unlike the high country homestead, is broken up into components or pieces as it is divided between siblings in this system of equal inheritance. In New Zealand the homestead remains whole, and when properties are divided a sibling is compensated with a new home of equal value.

15. A youngest son who had left the valley drew a diagram to illustrate which bedrooms each of the children used. As the youngest, he had been assigned all of them over the years. He had no memory of where his eldest sister had slept. His cousin, also a youngest child, told me that her room had often changed and said that she "had lived in all of them, just about."

6

Private Houses, Public Sharing
Pollapese Migrants Coping with Change

JULIANA FLINN

ALTHOUGH THE PEOPLE of Pollap in the outer islands of Chuuk in the Federated States of Micronesia pride themselves on practicing certain customs and keeping some valued traditions intact, one area that is rapidly changing nonetheless is housing. The changes are most dramatic in a migrant settlement on the main island of Weno, a place Pollapese perceive as an essential part of the Pollap community and where they consciously try to maintain customs from home. But housing is changing on the home atoll as well, even though access to building materials and consumer goods is more restricted there than in town. The changes in housing are related to and affect other aspects of their culture.

Changes to the "built environment," a term that encompasses housing, can be connected to social organization, symbolic systems, individual identity, and power and social practice (Lawrence and Low 1990). This chapter looks at changes in Pollapese housing as they relate to values, patterns of reciprocity, access to paid employment, educational opportunities, and structures of authority and rank. Thatched houses are symbolically associated with a communal kinship domain, tradition, and equal access to critical resources. The house of a chiefly kin group is essentially the same as any other house; higher prestige does not translate into a more elaborate structure. Thatched houses also represent self-sufficiency, being made of locally available materials and built by kin group efforts. Furthermore, all people have essentially equal access to land, building materials, labor, and household goods, and reciprocity, both within and between households, governs the distribution of most goods and services.

132

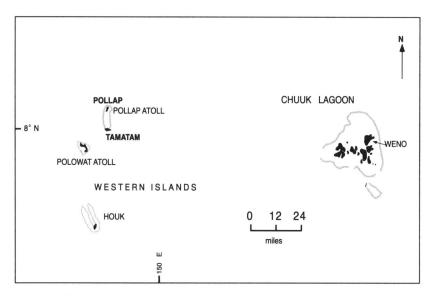

6.1 The Western Islands and Chuuk Lagoon

Even as Pollapese consciously strive to maintain values of generosity and communality, however, other forces, linked to external, foreign institutions, encourage social and economic differentiation that
disrupts patterns of reciprocity and traditional authority. These
forces are represented concretely on the atoll in the form of a church,
school, and municipal buildings and the construction of some houses
made of imported materials. Among the migrants, differential access
to building materials and labor has resulted in a wide range of styles
and has enabled some islanders to privately hoard some food and
goods while publicly displaying culturally valued generosity. Yet much
of this generosity cannot be reciprocated, challenging notions of
authority and rank that previously were tied to the kinship system
rather than to education and income.

Some of the differences between the home atoll and the migrant
community can be attributed to the setting and access to materials.
All the outer islands of Chuuk are low, coral atolls, and Pollap is the
northernmost of the Western Islands group lying in the western part
of Chuuk State (figure 6.1). Weno, the capital, is a high, volcanic
island in Chuuk Lagoon in the central part of the state. For lumber,
other building materials, and consumer goods, the outer islanders are
dependent on ships that travel in and out of Weno. Houses on the
home atoll include thatched houses made of indigenous materials,
others made of thatch and bits of purchased materials, and the rest

entirely in the new style. The older thatched style is gradually being replaced for residences, though not as yet for descent group canoe houses. In contrast, all Pollapese houses on Weno are constructed of imported, purchased materials.

Buildings on Pollap Atoll

Several types of structures have been built on the atoll. Canoe houses, dwelling houses, and cook houses are all versions of structures long common on the atoll, but a church, school, and municipal meeting house represent the impact of external forces, primarily since the beginning of the American administration of Micronesia. These larger structures are all centrally located in the settlement area adjacent to one another. Whereas the houses each are associated with a kin group, the larger community buildings represent and connect the islanders with outside institutions—the Catholic church, the educational system introduced and promoted by Americans, and the municipal government modeled after and established by the United States. All of these institutions and buildings rely on external expertise, money, and supplies.

The existence of these community buildings, along with changes in the nature of the building materials, are the major differences in built structures since the 1909 visit of an ethnographic expedition (Krämer 1935). Judging from the 1909 map and description (Krämer 1935, 253–255, 266–267), the settlement area looked then much as it did later in 1980, with residences, canoe houses, and cook houses at the southern end of the islet (figure 6.2). Many homesites had identical names in both 1909 and 1980. In 1909 there were four canoe houses; I found nine, four of which had the same names as on the 1909 map. Menstrual houses were absent in 1980, gone in the wake of conversion to Christianity. The other difference is that in 1909 there appear to have been no pan-community structures. A canoe house, perhaps one belonging to the chief's kin group, may have served this purpose, but this is not so indicated.

Thatched Buildings

The older housing style on Pollap, seen in figure 6.3, resembles the one found by Krämer (1935, 266–267) in 1909. Thatch is made with local materials, including sennit from coconut fibers, so that construction requires no money for purchase of imported supplies. If builders need materials or labor, they can turn to kin for assistance.

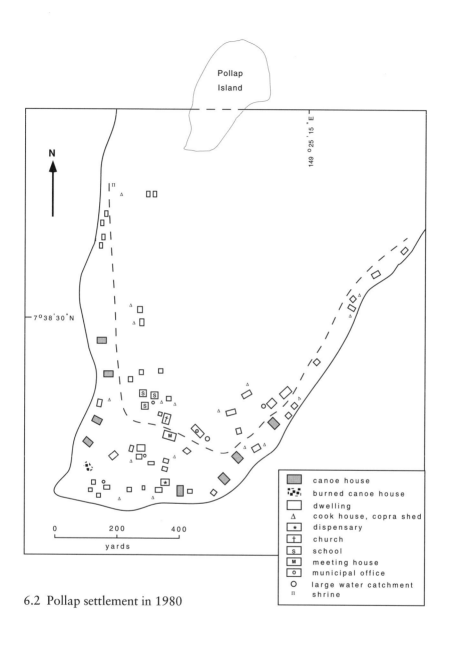

6.2 Pollap settlement in 1980

Legend:

- **canoe house**
- **burned canoe house**
- **dwelling**
- Δ cook house, copra shed
- ∗ dispensary
- † church
- S school
- M meeting house
- o municipal office
- O large water catchment
- Π shrine

Pollap Island

149 °25 ′15 ″E

7°38′30″N

0   200   400
yards

N

6.3 Thatched houses such as this one on Pollap represent self-sufficiency and communal kin relations. All materials for constructing thatched houses are available locally, including coconut fiber for sennit. Although the interior space is small, many activities take place outside the structure, extending living space. Juliana Flinn, 1980.

Thatched houses represent self-sufficiency and a very close connection with land and kin, highlighting cooperative, communal relations. The Pollapese perceive a disadvantage in the lack of durability of these houses; they require frequent repairs, and do not stand up well in typhoons. Building and repairing these houses are collaborative, not individual, endeavors, however, and a variety of kin are likely to assist. In addition, everyone has equal access to this type of assistance without needing any cash income.

Thatched houses on Pollap are one-story, one-room structures, occupied by matrilineal, matrilocal extended families. With little space and many people, they provide essentially no privacy; instead, they enable considerable social interaction. The style of construction keeps them relatively cool during the day, providing shelter from the sun while allowing some breeze to come through, but the houses also harbor bugs and need frequent upkeep. Some of the thatched houses incorporate bits of imported materials, especially a strip of metal across the top of the roof, which more effectively prevents leaking.

From an American perspective the houses may seem crowded, but they are used quite differently from our dwellings and serve fewer purposes. Cooking, eating, and visiting, for example, are not regular indoor activities; houses serve primarily as places to sleep and to store clothes and other personal items. (This practice seems to be common across the Pacific; see for instance Chowning, chapter 4, this volume.) Much of daily life occurs outside the houses themselves. Women use outdoor cook houses for food preparation and cooking, and other work such as preparing pandanus for weaving or making sennit takes place outside as well. Even a good deal of visiting and socializing takes place in the open, in cook houses, or under the shade of trees. The cook houses are little more than shacks or lean-tos made of scrap materials to provide relief from the sun. Except for special feast foods, most cooking today is done in metal pots in the cook houses rather than in earth ovens. Food preparation thus takes less time, but the cook houses nonetheless serve as places for women to work and visit when they are not in the gardens. The open structures ensure that these activities are quite public and visible, keeping the isolation of women to a minimum.

Pollap homesites embody a number of cultural notions connected with kinship and reciprocity. First of all, the members of a household at a named homesite theoretically are the female members of a matrilineal descent line, their husbands, and their unmarried children. The men of the descent line are called *mwáánefót,* and when this term is combined with the name of the homesite, it refers to the men's descent line membership, regardless of his current residence. A single homesite may consist of one or more separate dwellings, although this may mean little more than separate places for parts of the descent line to sleep and store clothing. As long as they continue joint food production, they constitute a single homesite. A new homesite is established when a couple moves to a piece of land the husband brought to the marriage; two separate descent lines emerge, however, only when the members consistently prepare food separately and cease sharing resources. Although a couple may establish a separate residence, the two of them may continue, at least for a time, to share food with the original homesite members.

In fact, those who live together share resources and are said to "eat from" each other's land. The residents of a homesite routinely prepare food together, although members of a nuclear family sometimes cook a small amount of food, such as a pot of rice, for themselves, especially if they live in a separate dwelling. It is this daily sharing of food that delineates a homesite and the establishment of a separate descent line. The term for a dwelling or homesite, *yiimw,* also refers to a unit of food contribution and distribution for feasts and other public occasions. One homesite may consist of more than one *yiimw* for these purposes; among the twenty-one named homesites in 1980, there were forty-two food contribution units. New units form when members of a homesite or one section of it, such as a nuclear family, feel they have the resources to make a separate contribution. No separate dwelling is necessarily implied, and the food is likely to be prepared and consumed together within each homesite.

Members of homesites with dwellings built of imported materials follow essentially the same patterns of behavior. They, too, are oriented around descent groups and shared land and resources. Yet the homesites with thatched dwellings have stronger symbolic connections with kinship and land, because the materials and labor necessary for construction and maintenance come from shared kin land and labor. Structures of authority and respect within kin groups and customary relations with patrilateral and affinal kin govern access to and use of resources with the thatched houses. Access to money and imported materials remains largely irrelevant.

The same is the case with canoe houses, which are larger structures and serve as residences as well as canoe shelters, although Pollapese say this use is a fairly recent development in response to a need for more housing. The population certainly has increased dramatically over the past three decades. In 1909, the population was recorded as only 60 (Krämer 1935, 248); from 1925 to 1949 the population remained quite stable, varying only between 153 and 159 (Japan 1931, 1937; United States Navy Department 1948; Fischer 1949). From then on the population began rising and has increased steadily, reaching 432 in 1980 (United States Department of State 1980). The loss of previous functions of the canoe house is probably another factor promoting their use as dwellings. For example, men used to be trained in navigational lore in canoe houses, away from the presence of women. This is no longer the case.

Canoe houses are even more open than the regular houses, affording less privacy while they accommodate more people. Although these buildings serve some of the functions of a men's house, women are no longer excluded, and all but one is also a residence for a family. This one, at least in 1980, was inhabited by a number of single or separated men, whose sisters provided them with food.

In both the canoe houses and dwellings, plaited pandanus mats—several layers in some cases—over the dirt floors, provide a soft

6.4 Some houses on Pollap incorporate materials, especially plywood and corrugated metal. Although newer houses may have interior walls and several rooms, they generally have no more furnishings than thatched houses. Juliana Flinn, 1980.

cushion for sitting. Sleeping mats kept packed away during the day are rolled out in the evening. These provide for relatively comfortable sleeping because of the cushioning layers underneath. Like the houses themselves, the mats, too, embody kin and land connections. They also represent cooperative female labor and provide visible reminders of the value of women's work. Mosquito nets, a trunk or two, a kerosene stove and lantern, and perhaps a back-strap loom for weaving lavalavas and loincloths are a few of the other goods in these houses. Otherwise they have no furniture.

Houses of Imported Materials

More often now, people on Pollap are building houses from purchased, imported materials (see, for example, figure 6.4). Typhoon relief funds have made it possible for some; others rely on money from wage labor, although most Pollapese on the atoll are subsistence gardeners and fishermen. A few people earn money from teaching in the elementary school. When the price is reasonable, Pollapese sell copra, bringing in some funds, and in more recent years they have been selling fish. Otherwise, they rely on seeking money from relatives employed on Weno. Even though almost all Pollapese can turn to relatives for funds, only a few islanders have full-time paid employment, so access to the new style of housing is uneven. Materials and labor for the thatched style are essentially equally available to all, with one house similar to another. But the new style of housing provides a stark contrast, because those without jobs and those only distantly related to employed people find it harder to purchase the materials. Labor is yet another consideration. When building a thatched house, people rely on the reciprocal assistance of kin. When building the new style, with purchased materials, they often pay for help instead, with some more able to pay than others. Thus the new houses are visible symbols of incipient differentiation and declining importance of reciprocal kin relations.

Another consideration is that women's contribution to the construction of the new houses is not as clearly valued. Although some women have a cash income, more men than women are employed, and at better wages. Furthermore, much of the construction activity of the new style is male work, without activities comparable to the female work for thatched houses of gathering and preparing materials, weaving thatch panels, and preparing mat floors.

There is much more differentiation among the newer houses than with the thatched style. Some are little more than plywood and corrugated metal shacks; others have cement floors, and some are painted, with louvered windows. One is even a two-story building.[1] Unlike the thatched houses, the newer ones usually have several rooms, with interior walls so that nuclear families have separate areas within the structure. These are modeled on houses built elsewhere in Chuuk, especially the port town, associated with prestigious and powerful people, and consistent with missionary emphasis on the conjugal couple and nuclear family. The thatch houses have one open space providing for several nuclear families, although if a family grows large, an additional small thatch house may be built close by, on the same land. Building a larger house with imported materials, subdivided into rooms, has some continuity with this practice. Household composition remains essentially the same, however, for either type of house, and daily gathering, gardening, cooking, and other activities are communal and involve all members of a homesite, regardless of house structure. Tendencies to hoard private stores of goods remain minimal.

Despite the structural differences, the new houses are not likely to have many more goods than are found in the thatched houses. Since inhabitants of the new houses are more likely to have funds, they are consequently more likely to be able to purchase a few more items— perhaps another lantern or stove, more clothes or a suitcase—but not furniture. Nor are new houses necessarily more comfortable than thatched houses. They may or may not have a layer of mats, but even when they do, the cement or wooden floor is much harder than the dirt floors of the thatched houses, and the metal roofs heat up the interiors by about twenty degrees.

Economic activity on the atoll is still oriented primarily toward subsistence horticulture and fishing; even those working for wages continue those activities. Kinship relations dominate in this arena, while market exchange involves outsiders and imported goods (see Philibert 1984, 1989). By tapping the money income of relatives, most people have access to some imported goods while the general subsistence economy still thrives. A modest amount of differentiation is growing, however, with increasing interest in acquiring imported building materials. Ideologically, people are nonetheless still constrained to avoid flaunting their houses and possessions as symbols of higher social status. This parallels an emphasis on having the educated and employed young people, the incipient elites, continue to observe and respect their higher ranking kin and acknowledge the authority of the chief.

Pollapese Houses on Weno

Where differentiation is most marked is in the migrant settlement on Weno, where no thatched houses have been built.[2] (For example, see figure 6.5.) The new house styles range from very tiny and rough shacks to painted, louvered, and air-conditioned houses. Some have no more goods than might be found in a thatched house on Pollap, whereas others have major appliances. The contrast can be striking: A house with a plywood floor, metal walls and roof set over beams, windows simply cut in the metal, and three small rooms, sits next to a much larger one with a painted wooden exterior, cement foundation, finished roof and ceiling, screened and louvered windows, tiled floor, curtains, two refrigerators, washer, dryer, and air conditioner. All houses are wired for electricity, which is inconsistently available on Weno, but none has running water. One house has been prepared, however, to have a private bathroom attached to one of the bedrooms.

Further evidence of change, especially a heightened concern for privacy, is provided by the sight of locks on so many rooms and

6.5 All of the houses of Pollap migrants on Weno are built of imported materials, though sizes, styles, and contents vary greatly. Juliana Flinn, 1980.

buildings. On the atoll, people might lock a trunk, but they can't lock a thatched house. On Weno, people regularly lock their houses and sometimes rooms inside houses as well. These are visible signs of increasing privatization and limited access to resources.

Pollapese even lock outhouses. With an outbreak of cholera in Chuuk in the early 1980s, Pollapese on Weno abandoned use of the shore area they had traditionally used (without outhouses). Since they were not supposed to build outhouses over water on the shore, they built them close to the houses instead. Outhouses vary considerably, exhibiting as much differentiation as the houses themselves. One outhouse, belonging to someone with a relatively substantial income, is large and equipped with a purchased toilet, table, and a vase of flowers and plants, with barrels of rainwater for flushing. This contrasts with an outhouse that is little more than a few pieces of plywood and hole in the ground.

Access to house sites is also unequal on Weno compared with Pollap, because land is a commodity that can be purchased, and only a few Pollapese have been in the position to do so. Several contiguous plots in the village of Iras, near the airport, have become the focus of the Pollapese settlement on Weno (figure 6.6). Those plots

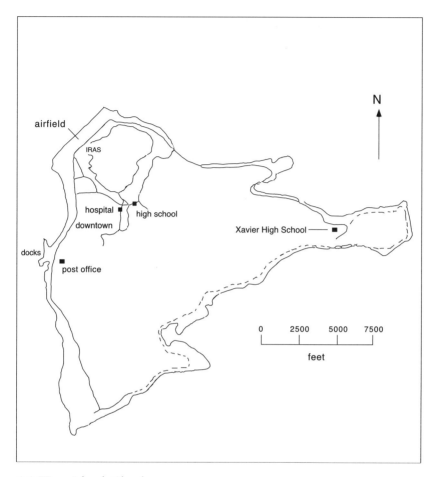

6.6 Weno Island, Chuuk

that have been bought provide for a wide range of kin, but most
Pollapese nonetheless cannot choose to build on their own land but
have to find a connection through one of the owners. A few have
chosen to look elsewhere on Weno, using ties through non-Pollap kin
for housing or access to a site to build a house. Some prefer to be less
directly dependent on the owners of the land and the authority of the
community's leader, but another motivation is the increasing crowding. Although space is certainly becoming more limited as more
houses are built, supporting those numbers is even more burdensome. Living elsewhere relieves some of that pressure, although Weno
as a whole is growing quite rapidly with islanders from throughout
the state migrating to the capital.

Some government employees have access to government housing or can have other housing subsidized; their employment also makes it feasible to rent housing. One of the Pollapese migrant families lived for several years in a subsidized house. It had a stove, refrigerator, furniture, and fixtures for an indoor bathroom. That house was quite close to the rest of the community, but later the family moved back to the Pollap land plot. At times, some of the members of that family talk of moving to the government housing area of Weno while continuing to spend considerable time in the Pollap community, especially on weekends. To maintain a leadership position, the family cannot move far away physically, despite the availability of other housing. Instead, they spend money to improve the house on the Pollap land, establishing a strong claim to leadership, especially since the superiority of the house matches the high position the man has managed to achieve.

Although in the past house size was not an indicator, now it has become a major cost and thus a sign of status. Those who can afford to do so build better houses and furnish them with more goods. They continue to share resources with others, but the access is no longer equal, so that older reciprocal patterns have shifted or faded entirely. For example, only those with monetary income can contribute money for food distribution, purchase clothing for relatives, store food in refrigerators to serve relatives and visitors, or offer the use of a washing machine. These forms of reciprocity cannot be matched by those without an income. Nor are there activities comparable to communal efforts to build or repair a thatch house or work in the gardens. Instead, employed migrants work in their offices or shops, students attend school, and others pursue their goals in coming to Weno (such as purchasing imported goods for use on Pollap). Instead of gardening or making mats, women are more likely to be preparing imported food for their immediate family, washing clothes, or playing bingo. Men often visit other Western Islanders living on Weno.

Houses vary more on Weno than on Pollap, a pattern connected with increasing inequalities. But one structure, explicitly designed to parallel the purpose of an atoll building and to represent common concerns, is a meeting house. (Pollapese do not feel a need for other parallel structures because although Pollap has an elementary school and church of its own, the islanders use Weno schools and churches when in town.) Both the atoll and Weno buildings are new and connected with external institutions, but the Weno meeting house nonetheless is construed as one that represents commonality, not differentiation. Pollapese built the meeting house on Weno with municipal funds, not communal contributions, and placed it in the center of the community, parallel to the atoll situation. Part of its function is to provide a place to house some of the men coming to Weno only temporarily, until the next ship back. In some respects, then, it serves traditional functions of the atoll's canoe houses. On the other hand, whereas some families on Pollap now use canoe houses as residences, women and children do not sleep in the new meeting house on Weno. People believe women and children should have a more sheltered and less public place to sleep.

Pollapese are concerned about the issue of adequate housing on Weno as migration—still largely circular—increases. The two plots of land that form the center of the Pollap migrant community each held a single house in 1980, deemed almost adequate at the time. Six years later, six more had been built, yet they still felt a need to house people in the meeting house. Three other houses are situated on an adjacent plot, one man built on land close to the community, another built on land in another village, and a few Pollapese live with other kin scattered elsewhere on the island. Some Pollapese aspire to obtaining their own land on Weno, but it is increasingly difficult to do so. Islanders are either reluctant to sell, or the price is too high. Pollap as a municipality has purchased a plot, but it is primarily for food, not housing. Furthermore, those able to purchase land and those leading the efforts to obtain communal land are the newly emerging elite, not those with traditional rank in the clan system.

Even with the new buildings, housing is perceived as insufficient. The houses are clustered very close together now, and the crowded situation contributes to sanitation hazards. Without a good refuse collection system, garbage (increasingly cans from imported foods) usually ends up simply being dumped near the houses. Outhouses are now close to the residences, since Pollapese no longer use the beach, and most are not maintained for proper sanitation. Water is yet another problem. Some people collect water in barrels from roofs, but there is no adequate sanitary system. The new houses at least allow for water collection, which is not feasible with the thatched houses. On Pollap, however, people often drink coconuts instead of water, whereas on Weno they have very few trees they can use. Pollapese in the migrant settlement bathe and wash clothes under a small waterfall coming from a pipe draining water from up the hill, but the area is awash in mud. Frequent rainfall contributes to the problem, so with little space between the houses, and soil that does not drain quickly, the entire vicinity is constantly muddy, making keeping the houses clean a difficult undertaking.

Even crowding appears to be spread unevenly. The better-built houses often have fewer residents compared with the other houses. In fact, those with the most money can build both an expensive house for their own family and another, more basic, structure for other kin. Thus they technically continue to support their kin, though not in the same fashion as on the atoll.

The social differentiation suggested by the variation in housing is related to new differences based on employment, rather than traditional kinship, gender, and age principles. Those who traditionally had higher prestige were clan elders and others who had acquired expertise in areas such as canoe building, navigation, and curing. But today it is the younger, formally educated islanders who are finding employment and thus acquiring direct access to money.

For years, some young men have been spending a few years as sailors, employment that usually does not require much education. But other than this option, formal schooling is seen as necessary for employment, especially for the better-paying jobs. And the money people can earn through these jobs is far more than what others can earn through selling copra, fish, or handicrafts. The first of the educated young people were able to obtain teaching positions at the elementary school on Pollap, but now high school graduates and returned college students look for work on Weno if they intend to remain in Chuuk. Others are leaving for Guam, though it is rare for anyone to plan permanent emigration. It is not clear yet whether or not workers outside Chuuk will become a source of remittances. Most of those leaving have been young people attending college, and they seek funds from parents and kin rather than send remittances.

Not only can those with jobs more readily build houses, but some have even gone into debt to build them, borrowing money from a bank. At least one worker also borrowed money for household goods, such as beds and an air conditioner. Those without a secure source of income do not have this sort of access to mortgages or loans. Different types of jobs also affect access to household goods, because some of the positions enable Pollapese to travel outside Micronesia to places such as Guam and Japan, where they can acquire household goods that are scarce, expensive, or unavailable in Chuuk. These are further examples of factors contributing to the increasing differentiation in housing.

The houses in Weno are divided internally inside, with rooms occupied by a nuclear family or other small kin unit, such as a group of closely related female students. In one case, a nuclear family has an entire house, with separate rooms for the parents, sons, and daughters. This contrasts strongly with the open construction of traditional houses on Pollap, and their clear connections with extended kin groups.

The Meeting House and Communality

Whereas the new houses represent more emphasis on privacy and individuals or nuclear families rather than on a group orientation, the meeting house and municipal land purchase represent to Pollapese continuing commitment to communality. Pollapese built the meeting house not from communal funds, however, but from municipal funds. This purchase and the building of the meeting house are both examples of how community projects are coming to be perceived more as government rather than Pollap community responsibilities. Pollapese speak of these actions as symbolizing their unity and communality, but they nonetheless represent a shift in responsibility from themselves to the government, with more dependence on money and external options. The government is looked to for assistance that previously would have been communally donated.

The meeting house flanks the two central plots of land, symbolizing unity, and Pollapese view it now as a community resource. It serves some of the purposes canoe houses serve on Pollap as well as those of the home atoll meeting house. On Pollap the cement meeting house is located in the center of the settlement area, together with the church and school. It is used for weekly meetings and other community events such as feasts, whereas canoe houses serve as descent group meeting sites and provide shelter for families and canoes. The meeting house in the migrant community operates in similar fashion and is used for community events as well as additional housing.

On Weno, however, a boy past puberty may be given his own room, allowing a separation from his sisters that is traditionally valued. Thus a teenage boy on Pollap can live in the canoe house, but on Weno he is likely to live with his own mother and sisters. Furthermore, an event that might have occurred in a canoe house on Pollap —a clan meeting, for example, that did not involve the whole community, or dance practice—is more likely on Weno to be held in the meeting house. On Weno houses are too small for large groups, and there are no canoe houses. The meeting house may have been constructed of materials purchased with money from the government, instead of indigenous materials contributed by community members, but Pollapese emphasize the communality of its use as evidence of their continuing commitment to cultural values.

Inequality, Prestige, and Privacy

With increasing differentiation and unequal access to goods come new problems and potential conflicts with traditional values. For those with more goods, especially more expensive ones such as refrigerators, the issue of continuing to share property with kin and to allow access to their use is becoming a thorny one. The issue is problematic in a manner not paralleled on the atoll, where islanders continue to have essentially equal access to land, food, and most household goods. Pollapese values stress continuing patterns of generosity in Iras, especially in the wake of efforts to create a strong sense of identity and unity in the port town.

On the one hand, allowing access enhances prestige. One man, for example, bought a VCR, rented movies, and showed them for the entire Pollap community in the meeting house on Weno. Displaying such generosity is valued. On the other hand, the new construction allows for more privacy, which in turn allows for hoarding food and hiding goods from public view. In some houses, for example, one room—the first one that people enter—is more public than the others. Here are likely to be the publicly shared goods. Other rooms, with walls and doors to separate them from each other and from the public room, are private, with goods and food reserved for closer family members.

The more public and front room is not necessarily where the expensive imported goods are displayed (cf. Robben 1989); a bed and air-conditioner, perhaps even a refrigerator, may be put in a bedroom. These are for private use, not to be shared with others. The public room is not so much for the display of valued items as it is for display of valued behavior—generosity. Pollapese on Weno can no longer afford to be generous with all of their possessions, so only selected food and other items appear in this arena.

Cooking still sometimes takes place outdoors on Weno, but families more commonly cook rice and other purchased foods on kerosene stoves inside the houses. Separate nuclear families often cook food for themselves, although they may still operate as an extended family cooking larger quantities of indigenous food in outdoor, more public, cook houses, as they do on Pollap. Thus opportunities for cooperative cooking are reduced in Weno. But public sharing still continues, especially on Saturday, when the women cook food together outdoors in a cook house. Usually they cook indigenous food from Pollap land or that of relatives on Weno or nearby islands. In other words, in the public view—outdoors and in easily entered, visible rooms—sharing continues; the smaller, more hidden rooms allow for keeping scarcer food and goods from the public view.

Generosity and sharing food are so valued that to publicly refrain from doing so is socially dangerous. The changing economy is making it possible for people to acquire new goods, with the result being unequal access to them. But then sharing these goods becomes more problematic. The newer buildings make the combination of public sharing and private hiding feasible.

Change and Continuity

Older patterns of Pollapese reciprocity are shifting in a variety of ways on Weno. The newer houses require less regular maintenance and repair, requiring less frequent requests to kin for assistance. Building houses is often based on wages rather than kinship. And reciprocity with other property and food continues in one arena—a public, visible one—whereas reciprocity is becoming more restricted to closer kin in the more hidden one. Furthermore, those with the money incomes are more able to be generous and provide for others, bringing them prestige that previously was accorded to more senior members of descent groups. Now junior members can successfully exercise a measure of authority that otherwise would not be feasible.

Similarly, with the growing tendency to keep scarcer food and goods reserved for close family—behavior that conflicts with stated values emphasizing reciprocity and generosity—Pollapese nonetheless assert continuing commitment to those values by the more public sharing. They especially point to the joint efforts on Saturdays to prepare large amounts of food to be widely distributed. Continued generosity is also said to be evidenced by the way collections are made to purchase food for the community, even though it is only those who are employed who can contribute. Traditionally on Pollap, food contributions are based on households, and each has essentially the same sort of access to food as any other. Those without a money income on Weno obviously benefit, but their standing is more of a dependent one than would be the case on Pollap.

Despite all these changes, Pollapese continue to assert that this way of life is consistent with their customs. They contend that as

others in Chuuk eschew old ways in favor of individualism and mate-
rialism, Pollapese continue behavior that represents valued, traditional ways based on generosity, reciprocity, and respect for kin.
Having a land base on which to physically build a community makes
it possible for them to share a sense of community, a sense of being
Pollapese on Weno. Those who are employed use their income in
traditionally valued ways—by being generous—even as they purchase
goods for private use as well. A sense of community is maintained
through the weekly public preparation and distribution of food,
punctuated by other feasts and parties. Public rooms in houses where
food is still shared allow for some continued reciprocity, even as private rooms shelter other goods.

The Pollapese are experiencing what is happening elsewhere in
Chuuk, including growing dependence on money, more social and
economic differentiation, heightened interests in education and
employment, migration to Weno, and health problems, all reflected
in shifting housing patterns. At the same time, they distrust the values represented by these changes and struggle both to take advantage
of jobs and goods newly available and to maintain an older way of
life. At the moment they do so by separating the newly created private space from the public space. It is the use of the public space that
allows Pollapese to demonstrate to others and to themselves a public
commitment to old values, as they quietly pursue avenues to exploit
new possibilities.

Notes

I wish to thank Jan Rensel, Margaret Rodman, Michèle Dominy, Cluny
Macpherson, and other participants in the ASAO sessions on "Changes in
Housing and Social Relationships in the Pacific" for their helpful comments
on earlier drafts of this paper. I also wish to thank Scott Curtis for drafting
the maps of the Western Islands and Chuuk Lagoon, Pollap in 1980, and
Weno.

1. Pollapese women couldn't use this second floor, however, because they
would then be higher than their brothers, violating patterns of respect. I
stayed with my family on this second story.

2. For a discussion of another migrant community on Weno, see Reafsnyder 1984.

7

A Samoan Solution to the Limitations of Urban Housing in New Zealand

CLUNY MACPHERSON

SAMOAN MIGRANTS in Auckland, New Zealand, face difficulties in finding suitable venues for various activities central to Samoan social and religious life. The problem arises from the fact that housing in Auckland was designed to meet needs of domestic groupings of the dominant ethnic group that differ in important respects from those of Pacific Islands migrants. *Pākehā,* or European, domestic groupings are typically smaller, nuclear family units with a generally stable composition that are only loosely affiliated with various kinship and community groupings (New Zealand Department of Statistics 1986, 1991). *Pākehā* households lead what has been described as a "privatized" lifestyle, and private dwellings are typically used more or less exclusively for nuclear family activities (Koopman-Boyden 1978). By comparison, Samoan migrant domestic groupings are typically larger, extended units with constantly changing composition (New Zealand Department of Statistics 1986, 1991). These domestic groups are also more tightly affiliated with and involved in the activities of a range of corporate activity connected with village of origin, extended kin group, and church congregations. The lifestyle of migrant Samoan domestic groups might be described as "communitarian," and they use dwellings more frequently for activities involving much larger groups of people. Thus while Samoan migrants have access to quality homes, there is a mismatch between their requirements and the design of available homes. Finding appropriate venues for activities necessary for social cohesion poses difficulties for migrant communities.

This chapter explores an increasingly popular solution to the problems of space for a number of activities at the center of Samoan social organization: the use of garages as social spaces. The creation

of an inexpensive, multipurpose building close to the house has provided a versatile space that Samoans routinely employ for a whole
range of activities. The difficulty with such multiple use is that some
of the activities are, at least in cultural terms, incompatible. A space
that is slept in may also be a venue for worship. Thus the space must
be periodically redesignated in ways that make its purpose at any
given time seem both unambiguous and appropriate. The chapter
also discusses a set of procedures and markers for designating a
generic space suitable for a specific activity and ensuring the authenticity and force of activities performed in it. But first, the chapter outlines the origins of the difficulties faced by Samoan migrants in
finding adequate housing in New Zealand.

A Brief History of Samoan Migration

Samoans began migrating to New Zealand in the mid-1800s to train
at theological training institutions as pastors and teachers for the
Pacific mission field. The Samoan migrant community in that period
was a small, transient one whose members were generally committed
to changing rather than reproducing Samoan customs and usages
(Pitt and Macpherson 1974).

A second, more significant wave of Samoan migration that commenced shortly after World War II and continued until Western
Samoan independence in 1962 comprised two distinct components.
One group, composed largely of Samoans associated with the New
Zealand administration and Samoans who had served with New
Zealand forces in World War II, moved to New Zealand in relatively
small numbers. The other was made up of a number of *afakasi,*
people of mixed Samoan-European parentage who, uncertain about
their status in a newly independent Western Samoan state, moved to
New Zealand to observe social and political developments in Samoa
(Pitt and Macpherson 1974).

While the motives of people in this second wave differed, their
orientation to Samoan worldview and lifestyle was similar and might
best be described as ambivalent. In many cases their primary cultural
orientation was to elements of their European cultural heritage.
Their ethnic identity was usually shaped by two factors: the ethno-
centrism of European colonialists with whom they had associated in
Samoa, and the fact that most had resided in the capital Apia, where
opportunities to observe and participate in Samoan custom were
limited.

The third and most significant wave of migration commenced in the 1960s and continued until the mid-1980s when it slowed dramatically with the contraction and restructuring of the New Zealand economy. It consisted principally of migrants from rural villages who were drawn into the unskilled and semi-skilled positions created by successive New Zealand governments' drive to expand secondary industry and to establish an import substitution program. The majority of Samoans in this wave were thoroughly committed to a Samoan worldview and lifestyle. They were assertively Samoan and in a relatively short time replicated many elements of Samoan village social organization (Pitt and Macpherson 1974).

Housing Policy and Home Ownership

The Samoan migrant population grew rapidly in the 1960s and 1970s; intercensal increases of 75 percent were not uncommon during the period (table 7.1). Although basic wages in the sectors in which most Samoan migrants found work were relatively low, they were significantly higher than wages in Western Samoa. There were also ample opportunities for work, a well-established labor movement, protective labor legislation, and a comprehensive social welfare system.[1] A central element of the social welfare philosophy was a commitment to the importance of private home ownership. Government policy of the day sought to achieve high rates of private home ownership for all New Zealanders,[2] and government agencies were established to assist low-income groups to obtain homes.

Assistance took one of two forms. Families with low incomes and little or no savings were assigned housing in various state-owned housing complexes. Rents in these complexes were related to income and were typically much lower than in the open housing market. A series of government policies encouraged families placed in these homes to save money in order to buy them or to buy private housing.[3] Families with some savings were offered several incentives to purchase new homes. First, low-cost, long-term (typically longer than twenty years) mortgages were provided by a government home financing agency, the State Housing Corporation. Second, families were permitted to obtain cash advances on social entitlements such as the child allowance to enable them to meet deposit requirements. The policies were successful and many New Zealanders were assisted into their own homes during the 1960s and 1970s.

Many Samoan migrant families who arrived in the third wave had

Table 7.1
Migrant Samoan Population Features, 1936–1986[a]

Year	Total Population	Intercensal inc. (%)	Born in Samoa	Intercensal inc. (%)	Born outside Samoa	Intercensal inc. (%)	Proportion (%)[b]
1936	362	—	279	—	83	—	22.9%
1945	716	97.8	592	112.2	124	49.4	17.3%
1951	N/A	211.2[c]	1,336	125.7	—	250.4[c]	—
1956	3,740	211.2[c]	2,995	124.2	745	250.4[c]	19.9%
1961	6,481	73.3	4,450	48.6	2,031	172.1	31.3%
1966	8,663	33.7	7,447	67.3	1,216	–40.1	14.0%
1971	22,198	156.2	12,354	65.9	9,844	709.5	44.4%
1976	27,876	25.6	19,711	59.6	8,165	–17.0	29.3%
1981	42,453	52.3	24,141	22.5	18,312	124.3	43.1%
1986	66,254	56.0	33,864	40.3	32,390	76.9	48.9%

Source: New Zealand Censuses of Population.

[a] The figures are derived by deducting the Samoan-born from the total Samoan population.
[b] Those born outside Samoa expressed as a proportion of the total Samoan population. Those born outside Samoa are almost all born in New Zealand.
[c] Estimate arrived at by calculating ([1956–1945]/1945 * 100)/2.

relatively low basic incomes and limited savings,[4] and thus qualified for government housing assistance. Financial concessions from government and incentives offered by construction companies[5] persuaded many Samoan migrants to buy new homes in the low-cost subdivisions that were developed on the fringes of many New Zealand cities during the 1960s and 1970s. The decision to take advantage of government housing finance packages, however, effectively determined the size and style of Samoan family housing in the short and medium term.

Housing Design

Government, or more correctly the government's housing advisors, had made assumptions about the lifestyle and requirements of the "typical family" that had been incorporated in design briefs ever since the state became involved in financing home ownership. The State Housing Corporation was charged with financing sound basic homes built to acceptable standards for "typical" low- and middle-income families, supposed by the government to consist of two parents (and later, one parent) and 2.11 children. Construction companies wishing to win this business had to produce designs that would meet the corporation's standards and that could be built for the sum routinely lent by the corporation as a first mortgage plus the buyer's down payment, ordinarily between 5 and 10 percent of the total price. Companies typically produced a range of designs, intended primarily to meet the needs of different types of site, but all variations on the same theme.

Homes financed and built under these housing assistance programs were typically free-standing, single-storied, wooden, three- and four-bedroom homes with floor areas of around 100 square meters, set on freehold lots of between 750 and 1,000 square meters. The emphasis was on provision of housing, and few, if any, additional facilities were provided initially. On sloping sites, storage, or occasionally garaging, was provided under the house, but paths, fences, storage sheds, and garaging were not financed under government loans, and few low-income families had the resources for such improvements in the beginning.

The homes were sold from the plans and built later by private construction firms. As part of the process, construction companies sold the sites, arranged the loans from the State Housing Corporation, completed legal formalities, and obtained necessary building permits on their clients' behalf. To migrants with limited cultural capital and English, the one-time payment was a simple solution, obviating the need to deal directly with bureaucracy. Building firms, aware of the rapid growth in the Samoan population (table 7.1), realized the market potential and started to employ Samoan salespeople and to sell quite deliberately to Samoans.[6]

Emergent Problems

Homes designed to accommodate nuclear families were not well suited to the needs of Samoan migrant *'āiga,* or family. The composition of the Samoan domestic group was fundamentally different, and typically very much more fluid, than that of the European nuclear family for which the houses were primarily designed. The makeup of the Samoan household was constantly changing as new migrants joined and others rejoined households in which they had relatives (Macpherson 1974; Pitt and Macpherson 1974). But in the end, the amount of space and the cultural proscriptions influencing spatial requirements both limited the size of households and shaped their composition.

The day-to-day problems with design quickly became obvious. There were often too many people in spaces designed for four. Households of eight to ten adults with additional children using facilities designed for two adults and two children produced a range of problems. The size of households put unforeseen pressures on the physical facilities. Overworked cooking and hot water systems failed and left families with neither hot water nor the resources to repair the systems. Infectious illnesses and, in winter especially, influenza and respiratory complaints spread rapidly, and such cramped spaces were not ideal conditions for either nursing or recuperation. Tensions arose over the allocation and use of space within the house. Those who were at least nominally owners of the house were regularly required to offer their bedrooms to others determined by culture to have prior claim. Thus younger working people were routinely expected to surrender their beds to older, vacationing family members. Other members of the household whose incomes also contributed to the mortgage payment similarly found their space periodically reassigned to visitors. Despite general acceptance of the imperfect fit between ownership and control, strains did build in households. As one young woman who had to vacate her bed to make space for her uncle and aunty noted:

> My back is so sore from sleeping on the floor. I don't know why I go out to work in the cold to pay for this house. I can't even find a comfortable place to sleep when I come home! If it was not for the fact that it is my father's brother and his wife [who need my bed], I would throw them out of the house, so I can have a sleep again.

There was also tension over the use of particular spaces. The largest single room in these homes, the lounge *(potu mālōlō)* was usually around 4.5 meters by 4.5 meters. This space was normally reserved to welcome and entertain guests, and to display symbols of wealth such as stereos and televisions, and markers of status such as certificates commemorating educational or sporting achievements. New furniture, art prints, and encyclopedia sets, signs of conspicuous material success, were also displayed in these rooms for all to see. In this space at least the impressions that guests formed of the family could be and were managed. But as spatial pressure increased these markers periodically had to be shifted to permit people to sleep in the room. Thus a space normally reserved for one use was being used for others.

Families who were required to host visitors at short notice were constantly shifting sleeping mats and bedding elsewhere in the house to accommodate their *mālō*, or visitors. The standard furniture in the *potu mālōlō* consisted of a lounge suite seating five to eight persons. To create space for larger parties, furniture had to be removed so that guests could be seated on the floor. People who wished to host even small numbers of visitors had to remove some of the very symbols of success that were essential "props" for performances and that gave the room the appropriate formality. Tension over the use of space generated pressure for the creation of new households.

While Samoan etiquette made it difficult to ask relatives to leave one's home, several factors provided incentives for people to leave at certain times. First, immigration regulations required that "suitable accommodation" be available to those who wished to migrate. Suitability was calculated, among other things, on the basis of a complex formula that required a minimum volume of breathing space per occupant in bedrooms. Those who wished to sponsor immigrants had to establish new households complying with these regulations and have them inspected before applications for immigration could be processed. Second, Samoans preferred living with close kin and eventually left households to whom they were not closely related to establish new households comprised of closer kin. For instance, as the number of siblings and first cousins in the community increased, they would leave households that they joined initially for expedience and constitute new ones with closer relatives with whom they had more in common. Third, as members married they too often set up new households to which a couple's siblings often then attached themselves. There was thus a period in the late 1960s and 1970s during which the number of Samoan households in New Zealand grew rapidly.

Interim Solutions

Increasing the number of households reduced pressure on existing households and partly resolved some of the day-to-day problems outlined above. Despite some racism in the rental housing market (McDonald n.d.), the availability of private rental housing, government rental housing, and private home ownership schemes allowed families to constitute new households. With large numbers of single people working and earning, it was relatively simple for groups to collect the bond necessary for housing rental and the deposits for home purchases.

New Problems

There were, however, other intermittent problems with the arrangement of space in these houses that were not as easily solved. In the early phases of settlement in the 1950s and 1960s many preferred to commemorate life crises *(fa'alavelave)* in more familiar social and physical surroundings. Many migrant *fa'alavelave* were "taken to the island," often at considerable expense to those involved. As the Samoan immigrant population became larger and more established in New Zealand, many of the *fa'alavelave* that punctuated Samoan village life were replicated in New Zealand (Macpherson 1974). Events such as *fa'aipoipoga* 'weddings', *saofa'i matai* 'chiefly title conferments', and *oti* 'funerals' brought together relatively large groups from various sides of the *'āiga* involved.

The major, public parts of these events could be held in the growing numbers of Samoan church complexes that mushroomed between 1965 and 1990, and in public halls. The public parts of these events, however, represented only the culmination of a considerable amount of forward planning and organization for which suitable space was not readily available.

Many of the family-to-family meetings that necessarily preceded *fa'alavelave* lasted for forty-eight to seventy-two hours and called for uninterrupted access to a space large enough to receive and entertain a number of visiting parties of ten to thirty people. Most events also required a space for use after the formal public ceremony for the private completion of formalities and final redistributions *(le tālatalaga)* of ceremonial goods (*tōga* 'fine mats' and *'oloa* 'money and food') within families.

In Samoa these activities would have been conducted in the residence of the *matai* 'chief' or in large guest houses *(faletele* or *fale talimālō)* where these were still maintained, but such buildings were not readily available in New Zealand. Church and community halls were too large and often heavily booked, and the lounge, the only large room in the house, was neither large enough nor appropriately designed for the purpose. Even when furniture was removed and guests sat on the floor there was insufficient space for groups to face each other; for *'ie tōga* 'fine mats' to be displayed and stored; for visitors to be served refreshments and to be given food gifts such as barrels of salt meat *(paelo povi māsima)* and biscuits *('apa masi)*. To make even that space available, furniture had to be stored in other rooms, meaning that for the duration of the event, the routines of other members of the household were upset.

The removal of furniture to accommodate the *mālō* created some anxiety for hosts about the way this might be construed by guests. People were generally reluctant to be seen to be *fia pālagi* (a derogatory term that means 'emulating the European')[7] by keeping the chairs and preventing people from sitting easily on the floor. On the other hand, people did not want to be seen to be slighting their guests by removing the chairs and implying that their guests were not comfortable in European furniture. As one young woman said during a furniture rearrangement:

> Don't take all the seats out there. Leave two for the old man and lady in case they don't want to sit on the floor. Leave the dining chairs close to the door. We can bring some back in here for the others if they don't sit on the floor. If we take everything they'll think we think they aren't used to sitting on chairs. There's no point in offending them.

Furthermore, formal events invariably draw a number of *mālō*, visiting parties who must wait their turn to make their speeches and to present and receive gifts. In Samoa waiting *mālō* are accommodated in houses belonging to other members of the family near the *matai*'s until their turn comes around. In New Zealand there was no suitable ancillary space for the increasing numbers of *mālō* that arrived on such occasions. The situation was made worse by the fact that New Zealand winters are inhospitable and not times when older people wished to wait around outside houses. As the size of the migrant Samoan population increased, the number of such occasions multiplied very rapidly and the problems of suitable space for these activities became more and more apparent.

Solutions were not immediately apparent. Larger homes in other districts were available but generally much more expensive, and few Samoan families had either the income or the equity to "trade up" to these homes. Even families with large combined incomes were reluctant to invest in larger dwellings, especially in areas dominated by *pālagi*, or Europeans.

It was, of course, technically simple to add to existing houses, but this option presented certain practical problems. The first of these was financial. Insistence on high construction standards and cost inflation over the period combined to push building costs up rapidly. While many families had relatively high incomes, commitment to a steadily increasing range of village, family, and church activities in both Samoa and New Zealand consumed considerable amounts of migrants' disposable income (Pitt and Macpherson 1974; Macpherson 1974). Furthermore, financial institutions, unaware of the nature of Samoan kinship obligations, were reluctant to include the incomes of nonowners in their calculations of a family's ability to repay loans and mortgages.

There were other problems as well. The need to deal with *pālagi* professionals to complete necessary design, legal, financial, and construction formalities was a daunting prospect for many migrants.[8] The building companies that initially had handled all the formalities were not interested in the less-profitable additions. Some families added areas of decking to their homes that provided a relatively cheap additional outdoor space, but this was of limited value because it was public and was exposed to the rain in winter and the sun in summer.

The Garage: A New Solution for an Old Problem

One solution to space problems emerged as car ownership became more widespread among Samoan migrants. In sprawling New Zealand cities where work is often some distance from dormitory suburbs where people live, private transport rapidly became a necessity. Large Samoan households with diverse work and leisure requirements made car ownership a necessity, and with rising incomes it became more feasible. As people sought ways to protect their cars, they looked to companies building detached garages for the growing numbers of home owners who had bought the basic housing package from the government earlier. A number of firms were established to produce and sell sheds and garages to this group, and competition grew rapidly.

These builders were usually small companies offering plans for a range of small buildings, from 3-meter square garden sheds to 12.5-meter square garages. The basic building was an unlined shell, clad in galvanized steel weatherboard with a galvanized iron roof on a concrete floor pad. The buildings were versatile and could be modified to the customers' specifications with virtually any number and type of doors and windows. Some of the various configurations can be seen in a sampling of advertisements (figure 7.1). Because the regulations governing ancillary buildings were less strict and construction was simpler, the cost of building these structures was approximately 15 percent of the cost of adding a comparable area to the house.

To sell these buildings, companies arranged either second mortgages over the property or loans from finance companies, handled legal formalities, and obtained necessary construction permits. Such package deals, usually provided by the garage-building companies and associated finance companies, again obviated the need for the owner to deal with bureaucracy and were very popular with Samoan and indeed many other families with limited incomes and resources.

As with housing companies ten years earlier, many of these firms recognized a growing market and employed Samoan salespeople to sell directly to it. Before long many Samoan families were signing up for *fale ta'avale* 'garages'. In fact, garage ownership followed home ownership and car ownership as the third wave material status symbol. But status was not the sole motive for garage construction.

The possibilities presented by these buildings were obvious to people who were by now well aware of the limits of their available space. While there were of course formal, legal limitations on what could be added to garages without consent, local government officials paid little attention to what happened to them after the final construction inspection. Families could then line the walls and ceilings, build internal partitions, and add water, electricity, and other amenities as funds permitted. At this point the garage became a far

7.1 Sample of advertisements for garages from the Auckland 1996 yellow pages. Reproduced with permission of Telcom Directories Limited.

more versatile space in which some of the shortcomings in the house design could be addressed.

Furthermore, the large garage-type doors could be opened to provide easy access to the outdoors. With the doors open there was in effect continuity between the space occupied by those at the center of activity and the periphery occupied by those who served, and observed, the people and activity taking place in the center. The doors served other practical purposes that made the garage a dramatic improvement on spaces in the houses (with their narrow openings) and an ideal venue for many formal activities. The arrival of visitors could be observed, coffins could be carried in and out by multiple pall bearers, kava strainers used in kava ceremonies could readily be thrown outside for cleaning, food could be brought in and out with ease by several people working together, fine mats and barrels of salt beef could be taken in and out during ceremonial exchanges, and, in good weather, children and others could watch through the large doors without disrupting the activity.

Competition developed to build larger and better appointed garages. Before long, garages that were once envied were overtaken by larger and more luxuriously fitted ones. As one woman said:

> I used to like playing housie [bingo] in that garage at S. . . . 's place. It seemed big and very nice. But we are now playing the village housie in K. . . . 's garage which is much nicer. It has carpet on the floor. The walls are lined so it's warm inside, and there are heaters on the roof like the ones at church.

The competition was fueled partly by rivalry within families and partly by some Samoan salespeople who were able to exploit their understanding of Samoan concern with prestige to increase their sales and commissions. Some salespeople would tell prospective buyers about of the sorts of options that well-known people were requesting in their buildings and then suggest, albeit obliquely, that they probably would not want that sort of thing. Thus a family might be told:

> We do offer a range of optional extras. We are presently building a 10 meter by 10 meter garage for the senior deacon in the church at. . . . In that one, we're lining the walls and ceiling, installing translucent roof lights, awning windows, strip lighting, wall heaters and that sort of thing. It's a little more expensive but I suppose it's important because he and his wife have to entertain groups from the congregation regularly and need to provide a suitable venue for office holders in the church. Still it's probably more than you want in your garage.

The garage would not have become as popular as it has if it had been only a status symbol. In fact it represented a very simple solution to a number of the practical problems posed by the layout of the standard house.

The Garage in Family Life

First, these buildings provided a space in which young unmarried men could sleep while married adults, young children, and unmarried women slept in the house. Such an arrangement was more like that which prevailed in Samoa, where young unmarried men slept in a space known as the *faletama,* or unmarried men's house, while young and unmarried women slept under the watchful eye of parents and elders.[9] In fact, the garage was increasingly referred to as the *faletama.*

The spatial separation of these groups relieved the tension that developed as people, especially young men, continually had to watch their language in the presence of female kin. They constantly had to avoid saying certain things in front of their true and classificatory sisters in order not to provoke family crises. Within relatively small, crowded houses chances were high that such lapses would occur and be overheard, provoking increased tension. Furthermore, the risk grew as more and more complex groupings were thrown together by chain migration and as the "rules" that governed the style and content of conversations became ever more complicated. Within the new "men's house" conversations that could not be held elsewhere could go on without fear of giving offense.

Second, lounges in houses could be reserved for the display of symbols of status and the formal entertainment of smaller groups. In Samoa an area is reserved to entertain formal guests, traditionally the *faletele,* or guest house, but increasingly the front room in European-style houses. In New Zealand, increasing use of the garage for sleeping, informal entertainment, and larger meetings meant that a space that was often both symbolically and physically in the front of the house could now be reserved exclusively for formal reception and entertaining.

This arrangement was both practically and symbolically more appropriate for Samoans and their guests. Guests could be invited into a space where family photographs and certificates, audio and video equipment, encyclopedia sets, the ubiquitous china cabinet, and musical instruments were on permanent and carefully staged display. The family was always prepared for the unexpected guest and was no longer caught bundling mats and bedding out of the way.

Third, for the larger groups of visitors taking part in the preliminaries for many social events, the larger garage was ideal. There was room to store and display the *'ie tōga, siapo* 'bark cloth', and food that was often collected and later redistributed on these occasions. Large numbers of people could sit in comfort on the floor, and those who had to bring food to feed them periodically during these occasions could enter in appropriate ways and circulate easily.

Fourth, *mālō* who were required to wait their turn could be moved into the back of the space to watch proceedings and to size up the hosts' orators before moving forward to make their speeches and presentations to the hosts and their representatives.

Thus a number of events that brought representatives of families together could be accommodated easily in these new and relatively inexpensive spaces. But family-to-family events were not the only ones to make use of these spaces.

The Garage and the Village

As time went on, villages' migrant chiefs and orators constituted overseas branches of village *fono,* or councils, to plan and manage activities of migrants from their villages. In the early period when few *matai* lived in New Zealand, council meetings could be held in the sitting rooms of private homes. As *matai* migrated and as younger people were given *matai* titles in recognition of their *tautua,* or service, to their families, the number of *matai* grew rapidly. Meetings of the *fono* could no longer fit into sitting rooms.

Furthermore, as villages in Samoa increasingly called on their migrant members to mobilize resources for various projects, meetings of the migrant "branches" of village *fono* became more frequent and the need for appropriate spaces for these meetings became more pressing.

Further difficulties emerged as *'ava,* or kava, ceremonies became a central part of the more formal of these meetings.[10] The formal preparation of the *'ava* usually involves a woman *(tāupou),* often unmarried, stirring and straining the ingredients in a bowl *(tānoa)* with a strainer made of shredded bark of the *fau,* or hibiscus. The strainer is periodically thrown over her shoulder to a man outside the house who shakes out the residue and returns it. Throwing strainers over one's shoulder and out a small window to a person three meters below and out of the line of sight is not an easy task. The return throw is even more difficult, and a poorly aimed return could obviously cause serious offense.

Garages are now frequently used as meeting places for these village *fono*. Beds, clothes, and evidence of human habitation are moved out of the way and even, in some cases, screened off to provide a large open space around which *matai* can assemble. The best mats available are placed around the perimeter. But the spaces are transformed in other ways to increase their authenticity and to give force to decisions made in them.

The *matai* titles associated with a village are ranked and the relative importance of each is embodied in a statement known as a *fa'alupega*. Each of the titles in a *fa'alupega* is assigned a seating position within the house, and when the *fono* is convened these positions are to be observed. When formal *fono* meetings are convened in garages the order of precedence is invoked and the relative seating positions of the various titles is observed. In places where meetings are held frequently the seating positions of various *matai* are known and assumed without comment. But in places where meetings are held less frequently, people jokingly direct each new arrival to an imaginary post. Thus one hears conversations like the one below:

> Host: Seiuli sir, Welcome to our *fono*. Thank you for coming. Your post is over there under the window.
> Seiuli: Thank you for your welcome. Where is Seiuli's position?
> Host: It is under the window.
> Seiuli: Thank you. But under which window? The inland one or the coastal one?
> Host: Under the inland one [gesturing]. The village V. . . . is over here!
> Seiuli: I can't see it!
> Host: It might be because it's too dark!
> Another: Or possibly because Seiuli is getting too old and can't see it.
> Seiuli: That's enough. I've found my position.

Of course, once several people are seated, new arrivals who know the seating arrangement of the *fono* can locate their positions in relation to them. Occasionally newly installed *matai,* and especially those who have been born in New Zealand or who have lived in New Zealand or away from the village much of their lives, have to be directed to their seating positions. But after a short time their positions are known.

Thus the building that at other times may be referred as the *fale ta'avale* 'garage' or as the *faletama* 'unmarried men's house' is redesignated the *maota o le nu'u* 'village meeting house'. For the duration of the meeting the protocol of the *fono* and of the *maota* are observed. It is easy to shut one's eyes and listen to the speeches and conversations and imagine being in the village on the island, forgetting that the *maota o le nu'u* is in fact a garage ten meters square in suburban Auckland. When the *'ava* ceremony becomes incorporated in these meetings the illusion is complete. The *tāupou* mixes the *'ava* and throws the strainer to an untitled man sitting outside the door; the caller announces the people to be served *'ava* and an untitled man moves back and forth between the *'ava* maker and *matai* and other guests who are served *'ava*.

The Garage as Chapel

Samoan migrants have remained committed to the Christian faith. Intracongregational political tensions have also remained a feature of Samoan migrant churches. There is, however, a significant difference in the potential for resolution of tensions within migrant congregations and comparable disputes in Samoa. Village political tensions that spill over into religious organization and life in Samoa can be resolved by the church elders' council *(fono a ti'ākono)* and the village council *(fono o le nu'u)*. These two organizations often have overlapping memberships and are anxious to preserve the appearance of unity within the village in the face of other villages. Where there is a will on the part of these bodies, decisive and occasionally dramatic solutions can be reached and imposed on parties to disputes.

In New Zealand, in contrast, congregations and villages are not coterminous units with a common concern on the preservation of the appearance of unity. Thus when political issues surface within migrant congregations they may be more difficult to manage.[11] As a consequence a series of splits have resulted where grievances were not satisfactorily resolved, leading to the formation of new congregations. Some of the dissident groups grow eventually into new congregations and build their own churches, while others will exist only until a compromise is negotiated between the factions. In the short term the splinter groups need places both to worship and to organize their affairs.

In a number of cases garages have been pressed into service as chapels (*fale sā*), highlighting yet again the versatility and importance of this structure. With the correct "dressing,"[12] a small modern keyboard, and appropriate leadership and discourse, the humble garage becomes an adequate chapel until such time as a new church is built or a reconciliation with the parent congregation is effected.

The Garage as Language Nest

In the past ten years Pacific Islands communities have become concerned about the speed with which their languages are being lost among the first generation of New Zealand-born Pacific Islanders. The readily apparent example of the relatively rapid loss of the Maori language has made many parents determined to ensure that Pacific Islands languages are taught to the New Zealand-born children. The impressive, recent success of Maori preschool language immersion programs known as *kōhanga reo* 'language nests' have provided the Pacific Islanders with a model for their own language retention programs.

Samoans have established a number of *ā'oga 'āmata* 'preschools' that are conducted entirely in Samoan by trained parents and untrained assistants.[13] These are often part of church congregations' activities and are held in church building complexes where these are available. But where these complexes are either not available or are overused, or where there is some opposition to these activities, *ā'oga 'āmata* have been established in garages. With carpet, toys, musical instruments, and keen parents, garages have proved an inexpensive and congenial venue for the new Samoan language nests. In these cases the *fale ta'avale* has become a *fale ā'oga* 'school' and has proven yet again the versatility of these structures in meeting Samoan-defined social objectives.

The Garage as Casino

As the demands for funds for family, church, and village activities has increased and the style of fund-raising has changed with circumstances (Macpherson 1994), housie, or bingo, has become an increasingly popular form of fund-raising.[14] Growing numbers of families, villages, and churches are now organizing regular bingo schools.

People play the game for either cash prizes or grocery prizes provided by the organizers, who then take as profit the difference between the cost of the prizes and the value of tickets sold. The key to profitable bingo is to increase the numbers of people buying game cards and playing. While the numbers of players buying game cards in each game increases, the cost of prizes remains more or less constant since there is only one prize per game. An additional key to profitable bingo among Samoans is to provide regular refreshments between groups of games.

The sitting rooms of houses were too small to accommodate many players, and church halls were in some denominations not available for gambling, and in other cases not congenial and liable to be taken over by groups whose needs had greater significance. Thus a group catering for a wedding would normally have precedence over a housie game despite the formal booking systems that operated. Housie games are supposed to be licensed and inspected periodically by inspectors to ensure that the management of the game meets certain standards of fairness. Unlicensed games in public venues invited the possibility of prosecution and forfeiture of equipment and proceeds of the games.

The garage provides an ideal alternative venue for housie for fundraising. It is private and yet large enough to accommodate enough players to yield a reasonable profit; it is large enough to be able to serve refreshments conveniently; and it makes it easy for parents to bring their children, who play with hosts' and other guests' children. To even out the costs of providing the refreshments, games float between the garages of the various members of the organizing group.

The Garage as Music Studio

As the Samoan migrant population grew, so too did the number of events for which Samoan music was required. Most weddings, socials, and fund-raising activities require Samoan music at certain parts in the festivities. Part of the music played on these occasions are Samoan standards. But the number of opportunities for popular music and the number of bands writing and playing Samoan popular music also expanded.[15] A new genre of migrant music was born in New Zealand garages. Many of the songs were ballads about lovers separated by migration, life in an unfriendly environment, separation from family, and a longing for return to Samoa. But an increasing number of fun songs are being written and practiced by young Samoan migrants.

Some bands that composed and played music in Samoa regrouped after migration, but many new bands were formed in New Zealand. The bands' objectives varied. Some intended following in the foot-

steps of the successful Pacific Islands dance bands and playing pro-
fessionally; others aimed at becoming semi-professional and taking
advantage of the growing number of opportunities to make a little
extra money out of a recreational activity. Still other bands were
purely recreational and exhibited more enthusiasm than talent. The
growing number of opportunities for casual and untaxed income, the
increasing number of live and television talent quests, the activities of
professional Samoan impresarios, and the success of well-known
Samoan bands contributed to the increase in the numbers of Samoan
bands in the 1960s, '70s and '80s.

But Samoan musical development is not static, nor is it confined
to works written and performed in the Samoan language. There are
at least two other genre that reflect somewhat different universes in
which various sections of New Zealand-born youth exist. At one end
of this musical spectrum is the increasing number of groups performing both traditional and modern gospel music in close-harmony style.
At the other is Samoan rap and a new wave of Samoan rap and local
reggae music, rooted in urban New Zealand, now being written and
performed by both Samoan and mixed groups.

Without connections in the music world through whom to hire
practice space, and in many cases without the money for hiring such
venues, Samoan bands were forced to practice at members' homes
until they were good enough to take their practice sessions without
embarrassment into more public venues such as church halls. The
halls were so often heavily booked that they were not readily available at convenient times to groups not directly connected with the
congregation. Private homes were the only other available venues
and were less than ideal. Additionally, with many families comprised
of shift workers, it was often difficult to find times when band practices were convenient and would not disturb sleeping household
members.

The garage solved these problems. Garages provided inexpensive
venues in which bands could develop both song repertoires and the
dance steps that went with them. Bands that were determined to
carve out more professional careers had to make "demo tapes" to
circulate among potential promoters. Commercial recording studios
were expensive to hire, and before long garages were being converted
into "recording studios." The walls and ceilings of the "studios"
were filled with insulation and lined inside with gypsum board. Then
egg cartons were fastened to the walls to improve the spaces' acoustic
properties for recording. It was interesting to be sitting in a church

service in a garage filled with the hastily hidden trappings of a recording studio.

There is a vein of songs in Samoan popular music that was conceived, written, practiced, and finally recorded in the double garage. These have become an important element in the Samoan migrant lifestyle and provide interesting insights into the Samoan perception of the migrant life and identity. The garage may be said to have contributed to the continuity and evolution of the Samoan ballad.

Conclusion

Samoan migrants in New Zealand were provided with homes designed around the lifestyle of the European, or *pākehā*, nuclear family. While these provided adequate physical shelter they were not well suited to the larger and more fluid Samoan domestic unit. The solution was a simple one: the construction of inexpensive ancillary buildings that could be adapted to meet a variety of Samoan migrants' needs. These buildings, intended originally as garages *(fale ta'avale)*, have been adapted to a number of other uses and have doubled as unmarried men's quarters *(faletama)*; meeting places for migrant village councils of chiefs *(maota o le nu'u)*; a home for newly formed church congregations *(fale sā)*; venues for housie-based fundraising; sites for the new language retention movements *(ā'oga 'āmata)*; and practice venues and recording studios for the production of a new genre of Samoan migrant music.

These simple, inexpensive, and versatile buildings have played a significant role in supporting the continuity of elements of Samoan social organization and the reproduction of Samoan culture and tradition for four main reasons. First, their size and lack of partitioning made them an ideal venue for certain activities that were too large for a house but too small to warrant using a hall. Second, they were inexpensive to build, and large numbers were erected at a time when the demand for such venues was growing. Third, they were spaces that could be used in a variety of ways simply by rearranging props and redesignating their purpose. Finally, unlike public and church buildings controlled by other agencies, the garage remained readily available to, and under control of, the family. This certainty allowed for confidence in planning. The humble garage has long since ceased to be a garage; it has become anything and anywhere that Samoan life demands and the imagination can reach.

Epilogue

The contraction and restructuring of the New Zealand economy (Macpherson 1992) has led to a dramatic decline in the demand for un- and semi-skilled labor. This has in turn produced high levels of unemployment among migrant Pacific Islanders and declining real and disposable incomes among Samoan families.[16] A number have experienced difficulties finding and keeping both private and rental housing and increasingly, garages are being pressed into service to house relatives who have nowhere else to go. The same economic forces that led to housing problems also have contributed to a curtailment of certain kin-based and community activities that expanded and elaborated as long as people had relatively high disposable incomes. Thus the growing demand for garages for temporary accommodation has coincided with a reduction in demand for these spaces for communitarian activities. Although there is inevitable competition between the two sets of demands, it is not as marked as it might have been had it not been for these coincidental trends. Optimists point to the recent renewed growth in the New Zealand economy and argue that the present situation is a temporary aberration. They argue that within five years Samoans will once again be fully involved in the economy, and if this is the case, garages will once again become the venues for an ever evolving range of activities limited only by Samoan ingenuity.

Notes

I am grateful to Margaret Rodman, Jan Rensel, and Tim O'Meara for comments on an earlier draft of this paper. *Fa'afetai fo'i Sisi mo le fesoasoani ma le onosa'i.*

1. New Zealand Official Yearbooks (NZOYB), published annually, contain details of social welfare provisions existing at various times.

2. Government policy was not wholly motivated by altruistic concerns. Building and construction industries have always made significant economic contributions to the total national output. In 1975, for instance, these industries generated 40–45 percent of gross domestic capital formation (NZOYB 1975, 505).

3. New Zealand Official Yearbooks contain summaries of the policies prevailing at various points during this period.

4. In fact, while individual incomes were typically low, Samoan household incomes, which often included the incomes of numerous adults, were relatively higher than European nuclear families' household incomes.

5. The incentives included, for example, discounts on home and land packages purchased during slack periods, deferred land repayments, waiving of certain legal costs, and occasional "specials" such as "free" clotheslines, mail boxes, and paths.

6. Some companies seeking to capture this market produced radio advertising campaigns in Pacific Islands languages that sounded very much like Pacific Islands radio advertising. Some also mounted newspaper advertising campaigns in the Samoan language press.

7. It is derogatory because it implies that *faʻa-Sāmoa*, that is, one's own Samoan custom, is not considered good enough for the occasion. It is a rebuke that is not used lightly.

8. A series of building scams prompted a campaign by government-sponsored consumer organizations warning people to be careful of dealing with certain people in building. In a well-intentioned move, consumer organizations publicized these warnings in Pacific Islands languages and made the perceived risk appear even greater.

9. Shore's (1982, 49, 144) description of the layout and symbolism of various elements of both the house and the village is instructive.

10. *ʻAva* is a drink made from root of the *Piper methysticum* and widely used in the Pacific both ceremonially and socially.

11. There is a history of migrant congregations splitting over a range of theological, organizational, personal, and family issues. There is even at present a serious, long-standing dispute in the Samoan section of one of the largest Pacific Islands churches in New Zealand.

12. The "dressing" consists often of a series of wall hangings depicting Jesus, the Last Supper, and the Crucifixion; brass crosses, candles, flowers, and ornate chiming clocks; and pulpits and tables with white lace and/or linen coverings.

13. It is not possible to estimate the numbers of these *āʻoga ʻāmata* with accuracy since not all apply for registration and funding and because these are continuously splitting and amalgamating.

14. Fund-raising projects have changed over time. Early on people were brought from the island in groups to work. As the labor market contracted, smaller groups of entertainers were brought to tour New Zealand to raise funds. As Samoans' disposable incomes shrank in the late 1980s (Macpherson 1992, 1994), one or two *matai* were brought to explain projects and solicit funds for them in censuses *(tusigāigoa)*.

15. The establishment in 1993 of a powerful and popular Pacific Islands radio station, 531PI, has both provided an outlet for airing and generated a market for this new Pacific Islands music.

16. It is difficult to obtain reliable figures for Samoan unemployment beyond the 1991 census, at which point it was running at 21 percent against a figure for the entire New Zealand population of 10.8 percent (New Zealand Department of Statistics 1992, 21). Since then the levels have risen, but

it is not possible to disaggregate the figures for individual groups. The figure for all Pacific Islanders is high, however, with women experiencing levels of around 29 percent and men levels of 31.5 percent unemployment. It is likely that Samoan levels are fairly close to this figure; they are by far the largest group among Pacific Islanders in New Zealand, so have a disproportionate impact on the unemployment figure.

8

From Houses without Walls to Vertical Villages
Samoan Housing Transformations

⌂

ROBERT FRANCO

SIMEAMATIVA MAGEO AGA

SINCE THE EARLY 1950s, large numbers of Western and American Samoans have been leaving their home villages and moving to and through Hawai'i in search of improved socioeconomic opportunities. In this search they discover distinctly different housing structures and spaces, requiring substantial adaptation in patterns of social organization developed in village Samoa. As Samoans leave the public, open housing configuration of their home villages and move to the private, closed housing of urban Honolulu, they face growing challenges, particularly in areas of youth social control, appropriate parental discipline, and community policing. They also find it difficult to host visiting kinsmen coming through Hawai'i on their way to California, or returning from California to Samoa. The housing forms available to Samoan migrants have direct implications for each of these challenges, by interfering with village-based strategies for social control and hospitality.

In this chapter we assess transformations in Samoan housing and social organization along a continuum from rural Savai'i to urban Honolulu. This assessment is based on the ethnographic research of Keene (1979), Sutter (1977), Gerber (1975), Shore (1982), and Franco (1991), and the community participatory research of Franco and Aga over the last fifteen years. Shore examines the spatial orientation of houses within the Western Samoan village of Sala'ilua. Keene and Sutter both focus on housing and social relations in rural Western Samoa. Further, Sutter's research provides a comparative analysis of housing in a periurban village outside of Apia. Gerber discusses the relationship between open housing, child discipline, and socialization in American Samoa. The ethnographic research of these authors provides a comparative framework for the more in-depth analysis of social and housing transformations in Honolulu.

Integrated into this comparative framework is data from Franco's own ethnographic research in Western Samoa in 1975, and in American Samoa in 1984 and 1989. Franco has also worked in Samoan "public" housing areas in both California and Hawai'i. Working closely with Ms. Simeamativa Aga, a Samoan social worker, parenting educator, and community leader, he conducted a survey of fifty Samoan households in Kalihi Valley Homes. Aga and Franco, as members of the board of the Fetu Ao Organization, have also conducted parenting and youth workshops in Kalihi Valley Homes and Kūhiō Park Terrace. The primary work of the Fetu Ao Organization, established in 1980, has been to provide youth cultural programs in the Kalihi area, advocate culturally appropriate parenting education, and deliver HIV/AIDS prevention education to the Samoan community in Hawai'i.

In contrast to the public nature of housing in Samoa, public housing for Samoans in Honolulu is extremely private. Our primary concern is the social transformations that occur as Samoans move from open-public housing in Samoa to closed-public housing in Honolulu. These transformations involve new patterns of youth supervision and discipline, problems of youth gang violence, and more general security and safety concerns. In addition, since these transformations are occurring within the broader context of Samoan global migration and circulation, we examine the social hosting of Samoan families in Honolulu public housing.

Samoans: Their Global Family

Contemporary Samoan mobility occurs within a single movement system linking Samoa to New Zealand, Australia, and the United States. Within this movement system Samoans make decisions involving educational, family, labor market, and retirement considerations at multiple destinations. The Samoan 'āiga is a localized segment of a widely dispersed descent group. Numerous extended families may overlap in one localized segment, and an individual always belongs to more than one 'āiga through relations with both mother's and father's family.

The 'au 'āiga is a wider extension of kinship ties covering great genealogical and geographic distance, and there is considerable movement between localized kin groups. Ceremonial and church observances, labor requirements, and *malaga* 'group visiting' all work to reinforce family ties, keeping family relations warm (see Tiffany 1974).

Children are loved and valued by the *'āiga*. As they grow they come to represent additional wealth for the chiefs *(matai)*, and they are expected to support and care for their parents and grandparents in later years (Keene 1979). Adoption is a common practice in Samoan families, with children frequently moving into households of different kin where they help with the supervision of younger children and take care of the elderly (Shore 1977). This movement outside the nuclear family household reinforces in the child the concept that an individual's family responsibilities and opportunities extend far beyond nuclear and immediate kin (Franco 1991). These opportunities and responsibilities now extend across a global network of family connections.

The Housing Continuum: Western Samoa

In most Western Samoan coastal villages, housing appears to be linearly organized along the main coast road, with plantation lands extending inland. Shore (1982, 49–50) details the linear configuration of housing within his fieldwork site, Sala'ilua village, and then discusses the ideally concentric orientation of the Western Samoan village. In Sala'ilua, the seaward side of the village is generally associated with light work, cleanliness, and "decorous and controlled behavior" exposed to the gaze of the entire village. Important guests are housed and important meetings are held in the *faletele* 'guest house' seaward of the family compound. The *faletele* is also where the young girls of the family sleep under the watchful eye of the chief and his wife. By contrast, the interior bush lands of Sala'ilua are thought to be populated by ghosts *(aitu)*, not people. To go into the bush is to leave the center of chiefly control, and to expose oneself to the dirtiest and heaviest work, and the greatest threat of danger.

The same principles of controlled/uncontrolled behavior can be seen in Shore's depiction of the ideal concentric village orientation, which revolves around a *malae* 'sacred political ground', where all dignified activity can be easily viewed. A secondary ring of houses *(fale)*, with a large guest house at the center, then radiates out to include smaller huts and cook houses. At the periphery are village boundary areas, the bush, and the sea, all areas outside under less direct chiefly control.

Shore goes on to identify those prestigious villages where the circular village model continues to provide a powerful conceptual pattern. Within the villages of high-ranking *ali'i* 'noblemen with formal powers to command' there is a special house *(maota)* attached to the title, and all senior chiefs have their main title homes. Chiefly houses command a view of the *malae* and the wider village. Subject to chiefly supervision, the *malae* is a place where careful, controlled behavior is expected. Similarly, Shore notes that in recent years such behavior has come to be expected along the village road, with some village regulations as well as government laws applying exclusively to comportment on the road (1982, 50).

Keene (1979) and Sutter (1977) studied social organizational features in two rural villages in Western Samoa. Both researchers emphasized that within the village numerous adult members of a child's family oversee his or her behavior. The child is aware of an overarching social control structure, ascending from older siblings and cousins to parents, uncles, aunts, ministers, and *matai*. In rural villages, this supervision is facilitated by the wall-less construction of Samoan houses and the open public nature of the central *malae*. Many individuals play a parenting role, and discipline for misbehavior is swift and sure. Overdisciplining is curbed because other family members, who have observed the misbehavior and the disciplinary response, can intervene.

As Samoan children grow up they move progressively into more formal social and work groups. Adolescent males become members of the *'aumāga*, or village men's group, where they are directed in communal work endeavors by the village chiefly council. A young Samoan may belong to his *'aumāga* for twenty years or more, and only upon assuming a *matai* title does he formally leave the *'aumāga.* Young girls move into a parallel organization called the *aualuma*, or village women's group. This group includes unmarried women, and the wives of untitled men, and is headed by a *tāupou*, the daughter or sister's daughter of a high-ranking chief. Their responsibilities are primarily related to maintaining the clean and ordered appearance of the village and hosting visiting *malaga*. These activities are supervised by the *faletua ma tausi* 'organization of chiefs' wives' in conjunction with the chiefly council. Young Samoan men and women socialize and work in their respective youth groups in the open arena of village life, largely under the public supervision of their families and their chiefs.

Keene (1979) found that Samoans maintained social order by subjecting much of their lives to public scrutiny. People living in the rural villages were much concerned about their reputations with their kin and neighbors. The wall-less houses in which they dwelt rendered much of their lives public. For Keene the houses instantiated a systematic feature of the society—a kind of collective strategy for controlling behavior by providing an audience for it, an audience whose approval mattered a great deal to the performers.

Shore also links the public character of Samoan social life and the wall-less features of Samoan housing: "Probably the most striking aspect of Samoan personal identity . . . is its strongly social and public nature. . . . Samoans live most of their lives in a very public arena. The more private aspects of experience are strongly discouraged by the absence of walls in a Samoan house, and by powerful norms of social life, which keep people in almost constant social interaction" (Shore 1982, 148). Later, Shore adds: "[T]he Samoan *fale* . . . is open to public view. Life in such a *fale* is, even by communal standards of most Polynesian societies, strikingly public" (Shore 1982, 179).

Shore argues that for Samoans the association between open housing and social control is largely an implicit understanding, "which informants readily recognize when presented with relevant hypothetical situations" (Shore 1982, 179). Some of Shore's informants remarked on the important relationship between open housing and specific social behaviors and values associated with sharing, and in particular, sharing food. Another informant compared Samoan- and European-style *(pālagi)* housing: "In a *pālagi* house, which is walled up, you cannot see the kind of behaviors that go on inside. If people do bad things you cannot see them. But you can always see from one Samoan house the sort of behavior that is going on inside another" (Shore 1982, 180).

Sutter (1977) vividly describes the open quality of life in the village of "Vao": "In viewing the village arrangement, the primary impression is of openness. . . . Movement between houses is unhindered. This same feeling of shared space is reflected in the open architectural style of the fales or houses, 91 percent of which, at the time of the study, were traditional, without rooms or walls. . . . For this reason it is possible to stand at one end of the village and look through virtually all of the houses almost to the other end" (Sutter 1977, 14).

Sutter's description of the periurban village of "Nu'u" provides a stark contrast: "The primary impression of Nu'u . . . is one of closed private sections. Households are separated and made more private by individual lanes leading from the roads . . . borders are emphasized.

... The theme of exclusion, separateness, and privacy is further reflected in the closed, European style of construction. Over half the houses have outer walls, and within these homes the space is further divided into separate rooms which are again divided by tables, chairs and beds" (Sutter 1977, 58).

Sutter reports that Nu'u residents prefer a more exciting life near the urban center, better opportunities for advanced schooling and employment, and "independence from the control of relatives" (1977, 59). He clearly argues that the spatial change from rural to periurban Western Samoa is accompanied by greater household separation, higher proportion of European walled houses, and declining kin-based social control.

Since Sutter's 1977 study, greater emphasis has been placed on the bidirectional character of Samoan internal and international movements (see Franco 1992, 1991, 1987). Samoans move back and forth across numerous rural and urban environments. Generally, as they move closer to cities, they experience more closed and private housing and a greater degree of freedom from kin-based social control. Conversely, as they move into rural villages, they experience open and public housing and a greater degree of kin-based social control. A thick web of social relations now extends across numerous rural and urban places, and although many Samoans are removed from kinship entanglements such as *fa'alavelave*, most are still strongly influenced by Samoan kin-based social controls and cultural values.

The majority of Samoans living overseas send substantial amounts of money home to Samoa. This money is often conceptualized as a form of *tautua* 'service' to the family and chiefs residing in the home village. These remittances are frequently invested in improving the existing home, perhaps adding on a new room, or adding modern plumbing and electrical features. Additionally, these remittances are used to build entire new homes for parents or other family members, or for the migrant when he returns to Samoa to retire. The newly constructed homes tend to be *pālagi* style with Samoan housing features merged into the design. Uniformly, the homes are large, enabling household heads to support and host large numbers of family members.

Housing Transformations: American Samoa

In Tutuila, American Samoa, all villages might be considered periurban, that is, within easy reach of the Pago Pago–Fagotogo urban area. The villages of Tutuila share the same linear and concentric configurations that Shore observed in Western Samoa. The coastal road usually defines the seaward boundary of the village, while the interior bush lands are often steep and mountainous. Most of the villages have a central *malae* where social interaction is generally open to public observation.

Samoans in Tutuila enjoy substantially higher income levels relative to their kinsmen in Western Samoa, and this contributes to a much higher proportion of *pālagi* housing. The higher prevalence of *pālagi*-style construction means that Tutuilans depend more upon auditory than visual cues in trying to assess the nature and quality of social interaction behind closed walls.

Yet higher income levels also contribute to higher noise levels. Television, as a visual and audio medium and a focal point of social-spatial relations, plays a large role in most American Samoan homes. The television targets individual attention away from the broader social interaction of the *malae* and disrupts normal patterns of family communication and socialization. Within *pālagi*-style living rooms, the television is the focal point of an implicitly identified viewing area, wherein hierarchical social interactions are often clearly observable.

In recent years, in the Tafuna area near the airport on Tutuila, a new type of community housing model has developed. In this area Samoans have been purchasing freehold lots and constructing large homes. Here, and in some areas of Upolu and Savai'i in Western Samoa, Samoans are opting to move off communal land, and thus away from the strict land use oversight of the *matai*. On these freehold lots Samoans build large homes (a few with swimming pools), enabling them to support and host many kinsmen. These new homeowners support and practice the *fa'a-Sāmoa* 'Samoan custom' but in a much more selective manner.

Gerber (1975) focuses on the relationship between housing and child discipline within her larger elucidation of the cultural patterning of emotion in Samoa. She posits that Samoans believe it is their biblical duty to administer corporal punishment; physical punishment is an expression of love and concern for the child. However, punishment can increase in intensity until the child is injured if relatives or neighbors with recognized authority are not present to intervene. She emphasizes that the open character of American Samoan villages, and the close proximity of openly constructed houses, makes it possible for observers to "monitor the progress of the conflict with considerable accuracy," with both visual and auditory evidence (Gerber 1975, 58).

From her larger perspective on emotional patterning, Gerber discusses the temporary and permanent forms of adoption so common within and beyond Samoa. These adoptions connect households and contribute to the thick web of social connectedness across the Samoan movement system. She first outlines the adoptive history of a girl who lived with various kinsmen over the course of her childhood and early adolescence. Gerber then examines the "disciplinary use" of adoption. She provides an example of parents "exiling their daughter to the United States" and comments: "Children are also sent in the other direction—Samoan families in the States send unruly youngsters to their more conservative Samoan relatives 'to teach them how to behave'. . . . The disciplinary use of these separations from one's family is reflected in the constant parental threat to send away disobedient children" (Gerber 1975, 81).

In sum, Gerber concludes that one of the most feared forms of punishment for Samoan children and youth is to be kicked out of the house: "The worry about being separated from one's family seems often to be cast in physical terms. A person without a family is pictured as having no food to eat and nowhere to sleep" (Gerber 1975, 82).

The move from Samoa to Honolulu involves a dramatic change in the housing context. As Samoans move to and through Honolulu, various types of housing continue to provide a central, physical space for Samoan familial and cultural identity.

The Housing Continuum: Honolulu

Approximately 98 percent of all Samoans residing in the state of Hawai'i live on the island of O'ahu. Geographically, the Samoan community extends westward from Kalihi in urban Honolulu through the Wai'anae Coast area to Lā'ie-Hau'ula on the north shore. The Wai'anae and Lā'ie communities are largely rural in orientation. Residents face challenging commutes to urban Honolulu for education, employment, and excitement, as well as to keep family relations warm. Most Samoans in Wai'anae have spent some time in central Honolulu or Kalihi before relocating westward to Wai'anae. On the Wai'anae Coast, Samoans, native Hawaiians, Filipinos, and others interact in a largely agricultural, fishing, and service economy. Lā'ie-Hau'ula community life centers around the Mormon Temple, Brigham Young University, and the Polynesian Cultural Center. Generally, Samoans in this north shore community enjoy a rural coexistence with Hawaiians, Tongans, Cook Islanders, and Tahitians, and have a relatively strong employment and housing base.

Approximately 28 percent of the Samoan community on Oʻahu lives in the Kalihi area. Many of these Samoans live in three public housing areas:

1) Kalihi Valley Homes (KVH): Located just off the Likelike Highway and Kamehameha IV Road, KVH (also called Kam 4) provides 400 single-story units (figure 8.1). In some of the small adjoining front- and backyards, banana and other tree crops are planted. The units are arranged in two parallel rows along the highway, on a gently sloping hillside that affects parking, traffic congestion, and safety for children playing in the streets. Security concerns about break-ins are greater in the *uta* 'landward' row (row 2 in figure 8.1), because the *tai* 'seaward' row (row 1) is more open to casual observation by passersby. In 1990, the Hawaiʻi Housing Authority invested in the installation of two patrol guard stations at each entrance to KVH. This has substantially reduced the flow of random, undesirable traffic. Because of this additional security measure, Samoans have a far more favorable impression of KVH today than they did in the 1980s. A community hall, built over a basketball/volleyball court, serves as a center for educational, counseling, and referral services, as well as tenant association meetings.

In 1994, because of the increased security, Samoan residents at KVH were able to build and maintain a traditional *fale* near the eastern gates. On any given morning, elderly Samoan men and women could be seen playing, working, and conversing within the open *fale*. In 1995, Samoans under the direction of a *tufaga fai vaʻa* 'master canoe builder' used the ground around the *fale* to carve and construct a traditional Samoan *paopao* 'fishing canoe', which they carried over two miles for its initial launching at Keʻehi Lagoon. Although the *fale* was dismantled in 1996, such activities were important in building solidarity within the Samoan community at KVH.

2) Mayor Wright Housing: This 364-unit housing complex is located on the corner of Liliha and King Streets, where King Street merges with Dillingham Highway, near downtown Honolulu (figure 8.2). Samoans express preference for housing in Mayor Wright because of the greater availability of larger units, the flatter lay of the land, and better policing and security. Samoans also relate that there is a greater sense of community at Mayor Wright, that it is friendlier, more

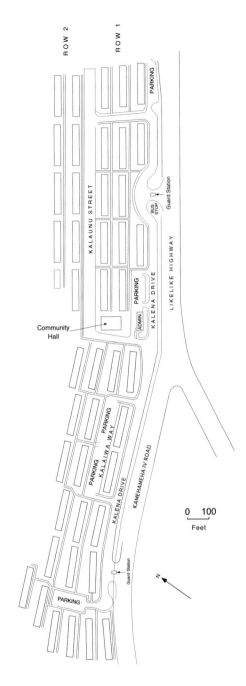

8.1 Kalihi Valley Homes

neighborly. Within this housing complex, the entire community comes out for Samoan song and dance performances. An effective Neighborhood Watch program contributes to a greater sense of security for Samoans at Mayor Wright.

3) The third Kalihi housing area, Kūhiō Park Terrace (KPT), presents the greatest adaptive challenge to Samoans in Honolulu. KPT, a 614-unit housing complex, is located off North School Street, about a half mile west of the Likelike Highway (figure 8.3). KPT housing is dominated by two sixteen-floor high-rise towers, Buildings A and B, with small apartments accessible by elevator. Across Linapuni Street from the twin towers is a series of low-rise housing units called Kūhiō Homes. Samoan residents at KPT clearly prefer the latter units because they have upstairs-downstairs configurations with three to four bedrooms and small yard areas. The surrounding group area includes space for making the *umu* 'earth oven', an exercise park, playground, baseball field, and family center, with a small stream near the eastern boundary.

Throughout the 1970s and 1980s KPT had a very bad reputation in the Samoan and wider communities in Honolulu. There was a great deal of concern about the unsanitary conditions of the buildings. The stairwells smelled; the handrailings were unsafe; the garbage chutes were too small, improperly used, and inadequately cleaned and maintained. Samoans have always been accustomed to cleaner, nicer, larger homes, and many felt they had to swallow their pride to live at KPT.

Samoans also linked the housing situation at KPT to social problems such as child abuse and neglect, drug use, and gang violence. A large number of the KPT households are headed by single Samoan women with children, who qualify more easily for public housing. Many of these women work in part-time, low-income jobs that frequently require them to arrange for child care within the housing area. Occasionally, the children may be hurriedly dropped off with a neighbor who is supposed to be looking after them, or in the worst case, the children are left in the apartment alone and unsupervised.

If discipline problems arise while a female or male parent is away from the household, the parents, upon their return, may react with a high degree of corporal punishment. Because of the closed, confined nature of the housing and the absence of close kin in the near vicinity, the physical punishment can become excessive and no one may intervene to stop it. Hearing a noisy ruckus through closed walls, a nonkin neighbor is compelled to telephone housing security officers

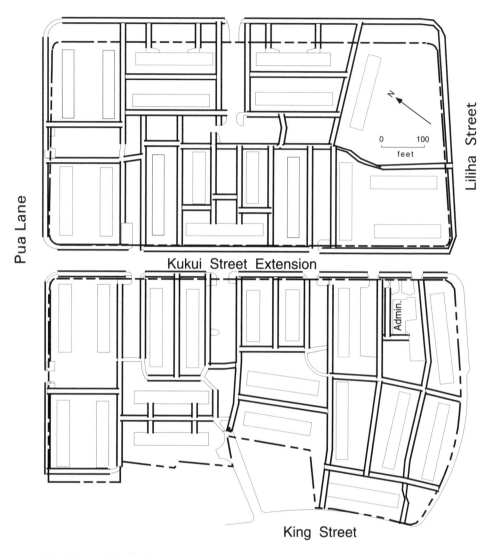

Pua Lane

Liliha Street

Kukui Street Extension

Admin.

King Street

8.2 Mayor Wright Housing

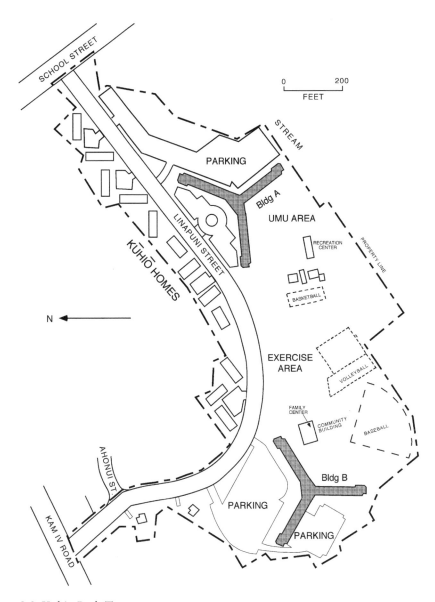

SCHOOL STREET

0   200
FEET

STREAM

PARKING

Bldg A

UMU AREA

RECREATION
CENTER

PROPERTY LINE

LINAPUNI STREET

KŪHIŌ HOMES

BASKETBALL

N

EXERCISE
AREA

VOLLEYBALL

FAMILY
CENTER

COMMUNITY
BUILDING

BASEBALL

AHONUI ST

Bldg B

PARKING

KAM IV ROAD

PARKING

8.3 Kūhiō Park Terrace

or the Honolulu Police. Samoan parents may then be arrested for child abuse, separated from their children, and evicted from their housing.

Samoan parents are concerned that the wider community does not understand traditional Samoan methods of disciplining children, and that there is an unfair bias on the part of professionals in the child welfare field. Samoans are at a distinct disadvantage in that they emphasize a group orientation where parental responsibilities are distributed throughout the extended family and the village. Many parents are therefore poorly prepared to assume total responsibility for their children in a crowded public housing context.

These parents are bewildered and highly stressed by the problems they are experiencing with their children. An added complication is that a large percentage of the Samoan parents in public housing are not bilingual; thus language barriers limit their opportunities for professional counseling. Further, many Samoan parents complain that they cannot get counseling assistance until they have committed an alleged offense, at which point they are referred to an English-speaking "crisis worker."

Fetu Ao professionals indicate that ten to twenty Samoan parents a month are ordered by the courts to attend parenting education courses because of alleged child abuse. The parents attend these classes held in English, quit because they do not learn anything, and later return for new sentencing from the courts. This judicial revolving door may ultimately affect the parents' access to the public housing unit.

In the recent past there was great concern that transitory Samoan men visiting women in KPT were bringing and consuming illegal drugs and alcohol in the housing units. Again, the closed, confined nature of the apartments allowed this behavior to go unnoticed for long periods of time. Many parents were concerned that drug sellers and drug users were able to establish a base of operations in KPT and that this was particularly detrimental to young children.

Samoan youth gang participation is a major problem in public housing areas in both Hawai'i and California. Samoan parents are concerned about youth gang activities, and they want to learn new strategies for effectively dealing with this problem. In more open villages in Samoa the collaborative work and service of other 'aumāga reflect directly on the status and prestige of the matai, the 'āiga, and the village. The malae and the government road are areas where careful and controlled behavior is expected. At KPT, the surrounding grounds provide an area where there has been little oversight by adults, and the street has clearly been a stage for gang solidarity and antisocial behavior.

In 1991, the Fetu Ao Organization submitted a proposal to a state program entitled "Strengthening Families: The Youth Gang Response Committee," requesting approximately $6,000 for a Samoan Parenting Program in KPT and the other housing areas. The problem of Samoan youth gang participation and drug-related activities has been a long-standing concern for the wider community as well as for Samoans themselves. From the wider community's perspective the Samoan population accounts for a disproportionate share of the total number of reported and confirmed cases of youth gang crime, child abuse, and neglect. A 1990 report by the Samoan Service Providers Association (SSPA, a largely Samoan-managed community organization) states: "While Samoans represent two to three percent of the state population, they comprise seven percent of the state incarcerated population, twelve percent of the gang population." This latter figure is tentative at best, but it does reflect growing Samoan concern about the gang behavior of their youth. In response to this concern SSPA staff worked with younger Samoan housing residents to paint a beautiful mural representing life at KPT on the wall of the Community Education Center, a wall that was previously covered with graffiti. Although the mural now needs to be refurbished, it has not been defaced by graffiti since its creation.

Marlene Shiroma, a part-Samoan student, conducted fieldwork among the "Sons of Samoa" at KPT in spring 1992. The Honolulu-based Sons of Samoa (SOS) originated in Los Angeles fifteen years ago (Del Rosario 1989). Many of the current SOS members were sent by their families from Los Angeles to relatives in Hawai'i because it was felt that a stronger or better disciplinarian in Honolulu would "straighten them out." The majority of the SOS members are Samoan or part-Samoan, although some non-Samoans are allowed into the organization. There are four "generational sub-groups" within the SOS: the Original Gangsters (OGs), the Pee-Wees, the Junior SOS, and the Baby Gangsters (BGs). The OGs are headed by a "Godfather." The Junior SOS members range in age from fourteen to twenty.

Junior SOS members were most concerned about their living situation at KPT, and they felt that a few of the KPT security guards were unfair in reporting certain families to the housing management. These reports could lead to eventual eviction of their families. Within

KPT, a new nonkin-based authority structure, lacking legitimacy in the eyes of SOS members, can enforce sanctions behind closed doors without the public confirmation of youth misbehavior prevalent in an open Samoan village.

A recent public television special on Hawai'i's youth gangs showed an initiation into the Pee-Wee SOS at KPT. The youths were drinking a good supply of beer. SOS members danced and handsigned "SOS," "Blood Killer," and "Crip," to a reggae beat. They swore and repeatedly said, "Fuck you, bitch. Fuck you, Pālolo, Mayor Wright and Kalihi Valley Homes." This severe derogation of other housing areas with substantial Samoan populations suggests that the SOS members are creating a group identity based on their unique KPT experience rather than on their shared Samoan cultural backgrounds.

Fetu Ao requested funding to provide parenting education classes in Samoan, and in the Samoan way. Fetu Ao received $1,500, which is being used to purchase radio air time. Radio is an effective educational medium for several reasons. Over the years Samoans have listened to radio for significant news (title changes, small craft advisories, hurricane warnings, international mail arrivals, college entrance exam results). Radio as an audio medium requires verbal skills highly valued in Samoan culture. Though a highly personal medium, radio also allows a certain degree of distance and anonymity. Further, nearly all Samoan households can afford radio, whereas many cannot afford cable television to watch the *Sāmoa i Hawai'i* program. Although the radio broadcasts do not officially support the court-ordered parenting education, the Fetu Ao program is a modest start.

Samoans in public housing often host smaller visiting groups of family members. Larger *malaga* are supported by substantial church congregations closer to Honolulu airport, or in the Lā'ie-Hau'ula area. Samoans residing in public housing often provide financial support and hospitality for the visitors at larger church facilities. One of the main complaints of Samoans in public housing is that the units are too small and confining, making it difficult for them to properly host kinsmen visiting from Samoa or the U.S. mainland. *Malaga* visit KPT but cannot stay long because they impose spatial constraints on other KPT residents. Further, each household has an a approved list of residents, so Hawai'i Housing Authority officials can intervene to have visitors removed.

Since the fall of 1993 a community policing effort has contributed to an improved sense of security and safety at KPT. Residents trained by Honolulu police officers conduct nightly patrols and enforce a

10:00 P.M. curfew. Vaopele Samoa, a volunteer for the night patrols, commented, "There's a lot of changes, there's a big difference. The teen-agers started to stay inside where they're supposed to and there's a lot less trouble. Before, the kids would be out painting the walls, scratching cars, fighting, getting in trouble. Now they've started to behave." According to Lui Faleafine, KPT Project Manager, "Today, for instance, you won't find drugs on the streets at Kūhiō Park Terrace. Sure, it's in the house, but you won't find any dealing on the streets, and we have a 10:00 P.M. curfew that's working" (*Honolulu Advertiser*, November 14, 1993, A8). The success of community policing at KPT has led to similar programs at eleven other public housing projects on Oʻahu.

On October 14, 1995, the Kūhiō Homes and KPT residents joined together to celebrate the completed construction of their own *paopao*, which they carried over a mile to launch at Keʻehi Lagoon. The carrying was made easier by the pounding rhythms of Samoan teamwork songs, American military march cadences, *'aiuli* 'clowning that focuses attention', and laughter. On this same day the Kūhiō Homes and KPT residents also dedicated the "Kūhiō Homes Security Gate" and the "KPT Security Gate." More than two hundred residents, many donning "Neighborhood Security Watch" hats, joined the canoe launching and gate dedication ceremonies.

These ceremonies were intended to give Samoan residents a greater sense of solidarity and control over their housing areas. Additionally, the ceremonies were designed to build stronger relationships between Samoans and native Hawaiians. A Hawaiian *kupuna* 'elder', knowledgeable in canoe-launching traditions, led the Samoans down to Keʻehi Lagoon, and another *kupuna* blessed the canoe before it entered the water. Back at the housing a third *kupuna* joined in the dedication of the security gates that will protect Samoans living in public housing on Hawaiian land.

Finally, in 1995, the Aloha United Way (AUW) campaign chose Jesse Sapolu, a Kalihi-born Samoan and four-time Super Bowl champion, as one of its spokespersons. The SSPA-KPT mural, graffiti-free, provided the backdrop to Sapolu's AUW campaign address.

Conclusion

As Samoan families move from rural to periurban villages, and from port towns to major urban centers, they must adapt to changing housing forms. The primary changes are from open and public to closed and private housing, with a concomitant decrease in overall house space. These housing transformations have resulted in a profound change in the nature and quality of youth socialization and discipline. Further, smaller housing units, both private and public, make hosting large groups of visiting *'āiga* more difficult. Samoans in Honolulu rely heavily on their churches and congregations to coordinate the hosting of these *malaga*.

As Samoan populations continue to grow in urban centers such as Honolulu and San Francisco, they will continue to seek low-income and public housing opportunities. In these housing areas community policing is a promising new practice, in part because it mirrors the community-based social control practices still prevalent in most open Samoan villages.

Community policing at KPT works outside the confines of individual public housing units. Developing new youth socialization and disciplinary practices within small, walled structures is a much more challenging problem. Nothing in Samoan housing structures, or in the structure of open village life, prepares Samoan parents for the youth socialization challenges they are experiencing in American public housing. In the short term, a Samoan-conceived parenting education program, utilizing skilled Samoan social workers and educators, is urgently needed.

At KVH, the frequent use of the *fale* for work, play, and conversation suggests the need for open community centers modeled on Samoan architectural and cultural principles within each public housing area having substantial numbers of Samoan residents. These centers should overlook a central meeting area, a *marae,* where youth and adult activities could be planned and implemented; dances and the arts could be practiced and performed; and community development directions could be debated and decided. Since native Hawaiians as well as Samoans reside in public housing, both groups could share the *marae* and the activities it would support.

The governments of Honolulu City and County and the state of Hawai'i serve a multicultural population continually absorbing new Asian and Pacific immigrants. It is not surprising that they have not built public housing specifically to meet the social and cultural needs of Samoans. But attention to the characteristics of healthy communities, whatever their ethnic origin, is essential to the success of any housing project. Concepts of public housing and village life that emphasize community-based responsibility for child rearing and social control; earning status through service to the community; and performing political, economic, and cultural activities in a central, public arena could productively be incorporated into the vision and planning for future public housing in Honolulu and Hawai'i. If this were done, it would serve not only Samoans but those of other ethnicities as well.

Similarly, as the urban centers of Apia and Pago Pago continue to grow and pressure on limited urban and periurban land increases, the governments of Western and American Samoa will consider traditional concepts of public housing and village life in their visions and plans for future urban housing. Fortunately for both Western and American Samoa, marvelous examples of Samoan architectural design and communal village life can still be drawn on to help bring these visions and plans to reality.

Note

This research was supported by a fellowship at the East-West Center Program for Cultural Studies, the Population Program, and the Pacific Islands Development Program. We are very grateful to Tom Keene for his advice and insight on earlier drafts of this paper. The phrase "Houses without Walls" is borrowed from his doctoral dissertation.

9
(Not) In My Back Yard
Housing the Homeless in Hawai'i

JUDITH MODELL

WE RECOGNIZE that homelessness is a deep-seated social ill which has resulted from the actions and inactions of many people and institutions. But precisely because homelessness is a result of human failings, we are confident that it is within the power of a compassionate, concerned society to take the steps necessary to eliminate it. (Waimānalo Task Force on the Homeless 1991, henceforth WTFH 1991)

In the summer of 1991 I was doing fieldwork in Hawai'i.[1] One night in July, I arranged to meet friends of mine in Waimānalo, a town about fifteen miles from downtown Honolulu (see map of O'ahu, figure 9.1). There seemed to have been a misunderstanding, and when I arrived they were on their way to a town meeting called to discuss the problem of homelessness in the area. I went along, stayed through the three-hour meeting, and learned a good deal about community responses to housing people who have no homes.[2] The issues raised that night suggested links between my work on family and kinship and the changing social construction of "home" in a Hawaiian cultural context.

Waimānalo was one of six sites on O'ahu designated for a cluster village, the state's response to the increasing number of homeless people.[3] Presentation of the governor's plan prompted the formation of a task force on the homeless in Waimānalo, and the group had been holding meetings to assess the implications of constructing such a village in the community.

The general consensus was that a cluster village was a bad idea. The evening's discussion made it clear that this did not represent the NIMBY-ism[4] some commentators said it did. Rather, the people at

194

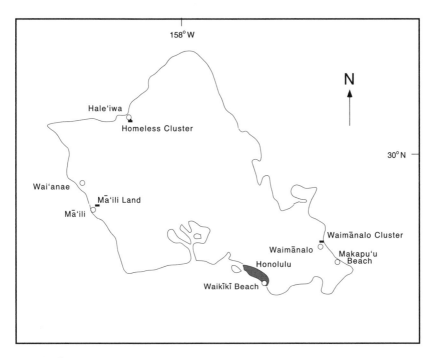

9.1 Oʻahu, Hawaiʻi

the town meeting included in their rejection of the cluster idea an exploration of the meaning of "homeless" and a concern for the recognition of the humanity and dignity of those who were without homes.

I would put it this way: The residents of Waimānalo (at least those who came that night) embraced a kind of "IMBY-ism." They did not want the homeless to go away and be someone else's problem. They proposed instead that the homeless be given housing *in their own backyards*—within the community and incorporated, not separated and stigmatized. The acronym IMBY is not part of the literature on housing and homelessness, indicating the novelty (in an American context) of the suggestion that homeless people be moved "into my backyard." Even more notably, the suggestion was not just figurative but literal: The residents of Waimānalo intended to "house" people in the backyards and frontyards of existing structures.

With its connotation of protected property, NIMBY evokes the whole of an American state policy toward housing; with its connotation of acceptance, IMBY reflects a contrasting perspective on the "openness" of household boundaries and the fluidity of property interests. And while the Waimānalo Task Force plan emphasized inclusiveness, it also responded to modern notions of housing that grant people privacy and the option of closing the door when the time comes. Like other Pacific Islanders, Hawaiians in an American state (and in an urbanized area of that state) modified the idea of "openness" in household boundaries to suit new conditions. Inside their own (physical) structures, Waimānalo's homeless would also be enveloped within the surrounding community.

> After careful deliberation (and consultation with the homeless themselves), the Task Force has rejected the State concept of cluster villages on the grounds that such clusters are not responsive to the real needs of Waimanalo's people, and will tend to isolate and stigmatize their formerly homeless tenants. (Executive Summary, WTFH 1991)

The homeless are folks just like you and me, said the coordinator of the task force at the meeting I attended, "except they just can't afford a house." Behind the discussion lay culturally distinct definitions of the homeless, of a home, and—concepts that were clearly connected —of family, kinship, and "belonging." These concepts determined the content and form of a multifaceted plan to be presented to the state as an alternative to the cluster-village idea. The Waimānalo plan reflects Hawaiian cultural values and sheds light on the links between housing and social relationships more generally. In this chapter, I use the Waimānalo town meeting as a focus for exploring what happens to interpretations of "home" when housing policy is called into question—as it has been in Hawai'i in recent years.

The chapter, then, is about how homelessness defines "home." And it is about the responsiveness of that definition to cultural values and social positions: Hawaiian people developed a definition of home in the context of competing interests as well as contrasting viewpoints. Finally, it is about the way Hawaiian cultural values concerning social relationships—the importance of affiliativeness and *aloha*, or generosity—imbued a concrete plan for housing people who have no place to live.

There are, in addition, two further strands that connect the Hawaiian instance I describe to broader issues of housing policy, ideas about what makes a "good" home, and notions of a proper household. One strand has to do with the significance of community responses to policy, however community is constituted. (Community may be a town or a neighborhood or a segment of a population—a coalition of people who have interests in common. I consider the Waimānalo Task Force to be representative of particular community interests.) In considering the establishment of a new, and planned, built environment, how much attention is paid to such groups? How do such groups get attention from those officially in charge of housing? How do they translate values into the practical considerations of constructing a home?

Another strand has to do with the relation between "home" and "homeland." In the contemporary political context, native Hawaiians interpret history and their present condition in terms of the loss of a homeland. This formulation influences the arguments made by Hawaiian people who confront the problem of homelessness. The definition of a home, then, is explicitly tied to issues of cultural identity. But what still bears inquiry is the way in which cultural self-consciousness, coupled with the loss of a homeland, determines actual proposals for "handling" the homeless. These strands weave through my discussion and can, I hope, suggest a basis for comparative approaches to interpretations of home in the context of homelessness.

Housing and Social Values

In a recent review essay, Denise Lawrence and Setha Low (1990) summarize the main themes in literature on the built environment: the built form as object of social organization, as symbol of social and cultural belief systems, as a means by which the individual defines the self, and as a means of social production and reproduction. When a community is faced with the necessity of building homes for those who lack them, these issues come to the fore, influencing the planning process. Under such conditions, constructing and marketing homes become a matter of public debate and controversy. The political and economic forces that always at some level affect housing (see Rabinow 1989) are likely to be blatantly visible in a housing "crisis." Moreover, as literature on housing describes, factions emerge; notions of a good home and a humane housing policy are no longer matters of consensus but of competition (Lang 1989; Pynoos, Schafer, and Hartman 1980). This literature, too, points to the role of grass-roots movements in establishing the desirable qualities of a built environment (Ward 1982; Hopper 1990). Such a perspective implies (if it does not focus on) the significance of cultural diversity and social hierarchies to the evolution of a built environment. Housing policy does not just happen, but is the result of strategic maneuvering on various levels.

Recently, literature on the homeless has taken a turn in the direction of recognizing that people are not passive in the face of changes in housing and housing policy (Hopper 1990; Lang 1989). This represents a modification of conventional approaches that concentrated on categorizing and counting the homeless. Identifying and enumerating was, in turn, usually accompanied by an account of the causes of homelessness (e.g., Momeni 1990; Rossi 1989; Erikson and Wilhelm 1986). Causes tended to be personalized; homelessness was attributed to particular characteristics of individuals rather than to the social, cultural, and political conditions that might make it impossible for some people to have homes (e.g., Redburn and Buss 1986).[5] From this point of view, the homeless are *not* "folks just like us." Another body of literature deals with the provisions that are made for the homeless—whether these are shelters or homes, cluster villages or separate dwellings (e.g., Caton 1990; Hoch and Slayton 1989).

Literature on the *built environment* in the context of homelessness has mainly described emergency or temporary housing since that accords with the portrayal of the phenomenon as both aberrant and caused by unusual events or characteristics. This way of responding to the problem cuts off consideration of what a "home" might mean, and what a certain kind of housing can mean over time for its occupants and for its neighbors. That was one of the themes in the Waimānalo Task Force report. The task force did not regard housing the homeless as a temporary response to an emergency, but as a way of providing homes to people without them. In this, too, they asserted a definition of homelessness that did not assume character traits, sickness, or disability, but an external condition in which housing was not available to everyone. At the same time, the task force recognized there might be special qualities in a homeless population that merited special attention. This did not, however, make the homeless "abnormal." As urban planner Peter Marcuse puts it: "Housing for the homeless must be provided with their particular needs in mind, just as all housing should be provided with the particular needs of its occupants in mind, so that such housing will provide homes, not just shelters" (Marcuse 1990, 152).

Who are the people who need homes in Hawai'i? The population is not, in one sense, the consequence of an abrupt and violent displacement or a natural disaster. The homeless who provoked intense discussion were not created by industrial expansion, a technological accident, or a typhoon or hurricane; responses to disasters like the 1992 Hurricane ʻIniki, in fact, suggest that those rendered homeless by natural disasters are viewed as different from the ordinary homeless, subject to forces beyond their control and thus worthy of help. Ordinary homelessness in Hawaiʻi—the rule, not the exception—is a consequence of the steady rise in housing costs, the replacement of low-income by luxury housing, and the erosion of residential space by resort space (see Chun and Takeuchi 1983). "When will the supply ever meet the demand?" headlined *The Honolulu Advertiser* one Sunday in 1994, despairing of the possibility of housing Hawaiʻi's permanent residents and suggesting that "change" had only been for the worse in this respect (*The Honolulu Advertiser,* April 17, 1994).

But if not a natural or industrial disaster, the relentless loss of homes *is* a social and cultural disaster. "Those who will venture an educated guess at the number of people who are homeless in Hawaii vary their estimates between 5,000 and 15,000, with about 60% of these being on Oahu" (Institute for Human Services, *IHS Newsletter,* Spring 1994). A rising number of unhoused people disrupts conventional social order and disturbs the provision of social services. It also challenges cultural values about place and "belonging."

Hawaiʻi is not alone in suffering this crisis. Homelessness is increasing throughout the United States, as any newspaper reveals (Lang 1989, 3; Caton [ed.] 1990). Low-income housing is scarce in all major American cities (Lang 1989, 16), and there are virtually no federal funds for redressing the scarcity; according to advocates, as long as housing is in private hands, profit, not altruism, is likely to spur building efforts. And, as elsewhere, the plight of being without a home falls unevenly: In Hawaiʻi, Hawaiians form a disproportionate number of the homeless.[6] That was true, too, in Waimānalo: "A majority of those surveyed (approximately 60%) are native Hawaiians" (Executive Summary, WTFH 1991).

State Power/Native Resistance

There are also some elements that are distinct to the homeless situation in Hawaiʻi. In general, these have to do with the way a state bureaucracy means to recognize the significance of a *Hawaiian* population—whether defined by ancestry, blood quantum, or culture.[7] Specifically, the problem of homelessness cannot be separated from the controversies over rights to land in the state of Hawaiʻi. A homeless person who identifies him- or herself as "Hawaiian" may claim a parcel of the land allotted to the Hawaiian people by a Congressional Act of 1921. This Act was an attempt to redress the injustices that followed upon land distribution in the late nineteenth century (the *Mahele*), when the land was divided into royal lands, government lands, and public lands. "Under the act, about 188,000 acres of public lands were designated as 'available lands' and put under the jurisdiction of the Hawaiian Homes Commission to be leased out to Native Hawaiians, those with 50 percent or more native blood, at a nominal fee for 99 years" (MacKenzie 1991, 17). The Act, however, brought in its wake a huge amount of administrative confusion that results, some commentators say, in keeping land out of the hands of Hawaiian people.[8]

In 1978, the Office of Hawaiian Affairs (OHA) was created to protect Hawaiian rights. OHA is a multipurpose agency that adds red tape and rules to an already complicated and politically tense debate over land allotments (MacKenzie 1991, 19). In claiming land, an individual has to prove his or her "Hawaiianness" and then wait for an available parcel to be granted. The waiting can last for decades, only to be followed by difficulties in actually constructing a livable residence on the property. With a new tract of Hawaiian Home Lands acreage lying empty and bare before their eyes, in that summer of 1991 the people of Waimānalo were well aware of the impact of tangled bureaucratic regulations. The task force's written report commented pointedly on the phenomenon of Hawaiians being homeless in their homeland.

Though homelessness can almost always be linked to the rising cost of housing, in Hawai'i this too has a distinctive character—partly because the situation reflects the dominance of other than native people in the construction and marketing of living spaces. Building seems to go on expansively, without cease, in Honolulu and increasingly in surrounding areas. When a new house typically costs more than $350,000 and rents average around $1,000 a month, few families can easily afford adequate living arrangements. Housing and rental costs in Honolulu average more than two and a half times the U.S. median. So, for example, a four-bedroom home in Honolulu costs $451,600, compared to the national median of $173,500; annual rental costs average $12,480, in contrast to the national average of $5,100. "Those who can buy typically pay more than they should out of their monthly paycheck for less than they want" (*The Honolulu Advertiser*, April 17, 1994). With annual median income that tends to be one-third that of Caucasians or Japanese, Hawaiians and part-Hawaiians are not major home buyers.[9] A Hawaiian person might well feel doubly dispossessed: The land is no longer his and the wherewithal to live on the land is denied to him by a discriminatory economic and political system.[10]

Recognition of the tightness of the housing market and, specifically, of the difficulties Hawaiian people had getting adequate housing, issued in a modification of laws about occupancy. In 1981, the Honolulu City Council passed a zoning regulation that borrowed from traditional Hawaiian living arrangements to allow for what is termed ʻohana housing: incorporating relatives into an existing structure or building an " ʻaccessory to the principal permitted single-family dwelling' for extra residents" (Kea 1991, 505). Less than ten years later, in 1990, a moratorium was put on such ʻohana housing, with the argument that it was being exploited by people who shared for "gain" or lived with "strangers." This moratorium has contributed to the current crisis—though people can continue to make informal ʻohana arrangements and hope not to be discovered.[11] Further demonstrating how rapidly the social construction of home can change, during the fall of 1993 sympathy for ʻohana housing once again appeared in city council deliberations, and ʻohana zoning was approved for specific areas of Oʻahu (*The Honolulu Advertiser,* December 12, 1993).

The concept of ʻohana, with roots in Hawaiian tradition, thus continues to have ideological and practical implications for housing policy in the state of Hawaiʻi. In *Nānā I Ke Kumu (Look to the Source),* a book of Hawaiian customs and beliefs, the ʻohana is described as composed of people connected by ties of love and loyalty, duty and obligation. Members of an ʻohana may or may not be blood kin; they are related by virtue of sharing sustenance and support. The definition suggests a permeability of household boundaries and an expansion of the meaning of "co-resident." The ʻohana also recalls that "home" is more than a roof over one's head and "residing" more than a matter of having a place in which to eat and sleep (Pukui, Haertig, and Lee 1972, 171). The concept of ʻohana, I show, profoundly affected the plan put forth by the Waimānalo Task Force.

Data for my paper come from several years of fieldwork in Hawaiʻi. Waimānalo is one of three areas in which I work. Its important characteristics, for this chapter, include a substantial Hawaiian Home Lands neighborhood, recently expanded—though in the summer of 1991 no one had yet begun to build on the new lots.[12] The significance of the Home Lands and of "being Hawaiian" was discussed with intensity at the task force meeting I attended. Another distinct feature is Waimānalo's beautiful beach, long attractive to tourists, residents, and, as well, the homeless whose tents dot the ocean front. In the past five years, rules about living on the beach have become stricter; regulations, however, did not so much diminish the number of people as reduce the stability of housing on the beach. There is still a good deal of camping on the beach, but now tents must be folded up once a week to prove the temporariness of settlement.

Tent clusters did not become squatter settlements or receive recognition as "self-help housing" (Ward 1982). The ambiguous status of tent housing was apparent in other parts of Oʻahu, prompting diverse responses in occupants and observers. On the Waiʻanae Coast, where I also work, and in downtown Honolulu, tent "cities" were constantly threatened with destruction, presumably to be replaced by "real" housing. Some of my data come from residents of the replacement housing on the Waiʻanae Coast, a cluster village called Māʻili Land. Other data come from reports on the dismantling of tent-housing in ʻAʻala Park, near Chinatown in Honolulu.[13]

Throughout Oʻahu, developers continue to develop, tourists to arrive, and elegant condominiums to displace affordable housing. These developments, and the attitudes they imply, make a large impact on communities like Waimānalo, attractive both to tourists and to migrants from urban centers. As in other parts of the United States, too, high-rent housing is built without any policy of replacement for those who are thereby deprived of a place to live (see, e.g., Gans 1991, 214). For Hawaiians, the disaster may be gradual—a continuation of practices that are decades old—but it is also utterly devastating. Early in 1991, Governor Waiheʻe, the first Hawaiian governor of the state, had proposed measures for providing housing for those who were displaced by what he deemed progress. These measures were received, not surprisingly, with less than enthusiasm in many places. And that brings me back to Waimānalo.

Hawaiian Culture and the Homeless

Any plan for dealing with the homeless has to establish the client population. That can be done more or less humanely and more or less absolutely. The Waimānalo Task Force was not an exception; its first task was to define the homeless.

> A person or family shall be considered "homeless" if, at the time
> of evaluation, such person or family shall either (a) lack a fixed,
> regular and adequate residence, or (b) have a primary residence
> that is a supervised publicly [sic] or privately operated shelter . . . ;
> (c) [live in] a public or private place not designed for, or ordinarily
> used as a regular sleeping accomodation [sic] for human beings.
> (WTFH 1991)

The definition captures some of the coordinator's feeling that the
homeless are just folks without homes; they are "normal" people in
bad circumstances. At the time, by this definition there were approximately fifty-two homeless families in Waimānalo.

More significantly, the definition implies there is more to having a
home than having shelter. The homeless included those in inadequate
residences; *home* had criteria of adequacy. As Peter Marcuse (1990,
138–139) writes, a home is "shelter that provides not only physical
adequacy as shelter but also privacy, personal safety, security of occupancy, comfort, space for essential residential activities. . . . It involves a set of relationships between a person and his or her housing
that supports a deeply felt personal (and socially conditioned) feeling
of identity, belonging, security." With its echo of the *'ohana* concept,
this emphasis on belonging would have suited the Waimānalo group.
The task, as they saw it, is neither to shelter nor to house, but to
"home" the homeless.

The task force had ideas about how that might work. It would *not*
work through the construction of cluster villages, isolated from the
rest of the community.[14] This negative reaction was based on good-
heartedness, a spirit of generosity, or *aloha*, and an awareness of the
problems accruing to cluster villages. Mā'ili Land, across O'ahu from
Waimānalo, was such a cluster village, a built environment whose
aspect was distinctly unappealing. A view into Mā'ili Land suggests
why the Waimānalo Task Force reacted negatively to the idea of cluster villages.

The "Exclusive" Alternative

Located on the dry Leeward Coast (see figure 9.1), Mā'ili Land was
built to house people who had been living at the beach. It was basi-
cally a cluster of concrete buildings, with small rooms for each
family. (I was never in a residence, but the square and functional
office space replicated the residential space.) Lorene, who was a
clerical case manager in the office, talked about her current living

conditions and about her move to Māʻili Land after a period of homelessness. She was appreciative of having a place to live, and had me take a picture of her in front of a bush blossoming with stunning yellow flowers as if to soften the edges of housing she acknowledged was "brutal" in its lack of physical and aesthetic amenities.

Lorene was also realistic and outlined the problems of living in a cluster village. These included crowding, lack of privacy, shame, and stigmatization. The children who lived in Māʻili Land, she reported, were teased and tormented at school: "My son was one of 'em." Lorene was preparing herself to speak at the school; "I live both lives," she said. "I can tell about being homeless." The marginalization bothered her more than the crowding. Residents of Māʻili Land had a "mark" on them, separated socially as well as physically from the community of Māʻili—probably most evident in the name given to the cluster. Appending the word "land" underlined the (figurative) boundaries around the place, as if the cluster village constituted a separate geographical and jurisdictional area. The goal, in fact, is to move people "out of" Māʻili Land and into the community (see the *Hawaii Catholic Herald,* Spring 1994).

Lorene's own story was not untypical. Married young, she and her husband moved into a small house in Waikīkī. Not too long afterward, the house was torn down to be replaced by a luxury apartment building whose rents were completely out of line for them, though at the time both Lorene and her husband were working. They had no choice but to leave Waikīkī, and, child in tow, they "went to one sister-in-law's boyfriend's family. They took us in." But that did not work out: "I couldn't live the way they did." Stays with a sister and then with her father were followed by several weeks of living in a car on the beach near Māʻili Land. At last, according to Lorene, her son went to the housing office and begged, "Please find us one place." They moved in, and over time Lorene became an advocate for the homeless, appearing before the state legislature and in protest movements. "I tell them," she told me, "People are the same. They use 'homeless' in a dirty way." If Māʻili Land was not the perfect answer, it was a base from which Lorene could work. She, too, would have preferred a home outside the cluster village and inside the community, but her husband was not working and her own income was small.[15]

In my perception, too, Māʻili Land felt isolated from the surrounding community. The marginalization that Lorene's child experienced was almost palpable, and there was little to break down the barriers between those in Māʻili Land and those who lived on the streets leading to and from the cluster. There were, in fact, no doors facing the street, as if the houses might only appropriately face each other and not the outside world. Closed off and self-contained, cluster villages, as the Waimānalo Task Force claimed, "tend to isolate and stigmatize" their tenants (WTFH 1991).

The "Inclusive" Alternative

ʻOhana values and common sense framed the alternative plan proposed by the Waimānalo Task Force. The gist of the plan was incorporation: to provide a home, not just a shelter, for people. Details of the plan constituted a definition of home that emphasized attachment, a place *in* a community as well as a place *of* social interactions. The homeless, according to the report, should belong, not simply be there. Several strategies were delineated for accomplishing social integration. They included moving the homeless in with families who already had houses in the area, into spare rooms, tents, or garages; having houses built for the homeless on land provided by those who already occupied the space and could share; and building houses for the homeless on selected sites *within,* not bounded off from, the rest of Waimānalo. (A proposal that houses be built on the school playground was voted down because people felt the children in those houses would feel "shame" and be stigmatized.) Moreover, the houses built on selected sites should be few in number and sturdy in construction.

The definition of a home, then, combined Hawaiian notions of the *ʻohana* with a practical assessment of the consequences of various housing types for individuals. There were six concrete programs, each juxtaposing the value of sociability to material considerations: programs for extended family loans; family foster care; Hawaiian Homes shelters; backyard shelters; a group shelter for singles; and a mini-cluster village. The programs all presumed a sharing of space, resources, and obligations, as well as a normalization of the population. Special, in other words, did not translate into alien needs.

The first program—by preference, I think, and not just convenience—was the extended family loan program. After asserting the "benefits" of extended families "in terms of mutual love and support, the perpetuation of social and cultural values" and the forging of bonds "of love and shared experience between the generations," the report became more pragmatic:

Under this program, the State would provide financial assistance
in the form of zero-interest loans for the construction of home
improvements designed to increase the capacity of existing living
units. Funds could be used for the construction of an additional
bathroom or bedroom, the enclosure of an existing porch, or other
home improvement project which would ease the burden on the
host family while providing temporary shelter to the homeless
members of an extended family. (WTFH 1991)

The loan program was directed to the residents of Hawaiian Home
Lands areas in order, the report went on, to help persons of Hawaiian ancestry. Such people, the report claimed, are "particularly
affected by homelessness and economic stress" (WTFH 1991). Moreover, the home improvements would be permanent and thus increase
the overall value of "housing stock" in the community.

The Home Lands shelter and the backyard shelter programs had
some of the same intentions and goals: to help people of Hawaiian
ancestry and to take advantage of the loyalty and love attributed to
family and kin ties. "The bitter irony of Hawaiians being homeless in
their native land is acutely felt by the people of Waimanalo" (WTFH
1991). The Home Lands shelter program required funds to support
the building of actual houses on Home Lands sites that had already
been granted. The backyard shelter program proposed the granting
of funds to individuals to support the construction of "supplementary housing" on existing lands—separate dwellings as opposed to
the added room or enclosed porch of the first proposal. (For many
people at the meeting, getting such funds would allow them to build
solid structures where currently tents, old trucks, and other accommodations housed their kin.) The financial details of the loans were
worked out in the report, and the necessity of following laws about
zoning and occupancy was reiterated. This was a Hawaiian housing
policy, as it were, within the context of an American state.

The significance of the 'ohana concept came out most clearly in
the second proposal, the family foster care program.[16] This stated:
"While their particular needs are diverse, all homeless families need
basic shelter. What better place to provide such shelter than with
families who are willing to reach out as individuals and offer such
shelter in their own homes?" (WTFH 1991) The proposal recommended helping the "host" families financially, and in wording and
intent it resembled the policies by which foster parents are reim-
bursed: Money would be given to families to cover general expenses,
the costs of having another person to feed, and possible medical or

other emergencies. Money was not given for expanding or improving the house; the assumption was that there would be "enough" room. At the same time, provision was made for the "screening" of families that volunteered to take in other families. For instance, no family that showed signs of "dysfunctional elements" or that was violating zoning or land use laws would be accepted for the program.

The family foster care program, then, did *not* involve a change in the physical structure of the house, but it did mean a good deal of change in who occupied the house. The choice of fellow occupants was not left totally up to the individuals, either. With the foster care program for children in mind, the report recommended criteria of "compatibility," matching, and "suitability" of one family to the other.

This kind of family fostering was not new to the community. One man, for example, stood up at the meeting and described his experience of taking in a homeless man and his children; the mother was in a rehabilitation center. People in the room, Hawaiian and *haole* alike, remarked on his generosity. Wasn't he concerned, they asked, that the man would start "using"? Yes, he answered, but it was the only thing he could do to help. The response was the more startling inasmuch as several in the audience talked about having informally fostered families. It was the one moment that a notion of "stranger" came up (Perin 1988); the man and his children remained strangers as other fostered families did not. I do not know why this was so. The reason was unlikely to be the drug and alcohol abuse, since a number of families had had some experience of this. And, in fact, the task force directly confronted the issue, adding a clause that recommended full support of health and social service agencies for foster care families. Leaning on *'ohana*-style ties of loyalty and obligation did not eliminate the need for an infrastructure, including clinics, hot lines, and accessible transportation.

Nor was the stranger status likely to be a matter of kinship or, accurately, nonkinship. Although a number of the homeless in Waimānalo were "related" to residents of the community, the concept of *'ohana* also permitted people to become kin by being incorporated into a family.[17] As in fostering, those taken in and fed were effectively kin. More likely the reaction came because the man who spoke presented his as a response to an emergency rather than as the provision of a home. He spoke of the urgency of helping someone in need, not of the ties formed with this homeless family. Providing a good or "real" home was the thrust of the task force position, and that meant making an arrangement that was solid, in a social and material sense, and permanent. Such full acceptance was not evident in the man's statement. The example underlines the task force's determination at every level of discussion to move away from "emergency" and toward incorporation.

The first four programs were addressed to homeless families—an adult and children. But the task force recognized diversity in the population of homeless and added two further programs. One was a group shelter program for singles, which was to accommodate unattached individuals; the shelter, the report stated, would be "designed to fit into the neighborhood in which it was located" (WTFH 1991). The other was a mini-cluster village plan for families that could not be handled by the other programs. Like all the programs, this too emphasized incorporation: The villages were to be small enough to be located within existing neighborhoods. Moreover, the group shelter and the mini-clusters had to provide the security, safety, and space for residential activities that defined a home. Nothing about them would suggest temporary shelter.

The task force report was approved by everyone at the meeting and certainly accomplished one of its primary goals, to show that home meant far more than a roof over one's head. Absorbing Hawaiian values, in the task force definition home meant a site of self-esteem, of community participation, and of belonging.

State Responses

The homeless problem was not resolved during that summer. Governor Waihe'e's plan for cluster villages did not work, and other programs were proposed during 1991–1992. In a letter to the editor of the *Honolulu Star Bulletin* the politician who had been at the meeting I attended wrote:

> Now, four months past deadline and over double the estimated cost, not one homeless person has been sheltered [in villages]. None, that is, except the 42 families who are being helped in Waimanalo and the 120 people, including 66 children, who are in homes rented by the Angel Network in East Honolulu. The two communities excoriated as "NIMBY's" for their opposition to the villages are the only two places where the homeless had a place to hang their stockings on Christmas Eve. (Letter from John Henry Felix, Honolulu City Council member, to the editor, *Honolulu Star Bulletin*, April 28, 1992)

By spring 1992, when the letter was written, housing policy for the homeless seemed to be in disarray. Cluster villages received some support, and so did plans for incorporation; an idea of sending the homeless back to the mainland was also floated, without much (articulated) concern for whether or when a homeless person had come from the mainland; it was simply a matter of getting rid of a problem. Scatter-shot responses suggest an uphill battle that, if complicated by competing cultural values in Hawai'i, certainly resembles struggles elsewhere in the country.[18] At the same time, given the impact of real estate interests on Hawai'i state politics, housing policy may change more rapidly there than in other states. The social construction of home will shift accordingly, varying with the personnel who make decisions and with their ability to implement a decision. By 1994, Waimānalo faced a situation for which an area on the north shore provided a model: Despite voiced objections, Waimānalo was to have a cluster village.

A cluster village had been built on O'ahu during the spring of 1992, with the help of funds from a private foundation. Near Hale'iwa, a crowded town around the northern tip of the island (see figure 9.1), the village elicited the usual mixed responses. Disagreements about providing shelter, homes, or housing surfaced instantly, and the *Honolulu Star Bulletin* greeted the completion of construction with a less-than-enthusiastic report: "It is not that the cluster of gray or beige cabins set off the ground on concrete pilings are unsightly. But the unfinished six-acre site is stark. Not a blade of greenery is to be seen" (*Honolulu Star Bulletin*, April 13, 1992). In the context, "unsightly" may be the only apt adjective.

A month later the newspaper reported another perspective:

> First time visitors will discover the mini-houses don't look at all like shacks. True, they're small—15 feet by 16 feet (240 square feet), or smaller than a two-car garage. "For what they are, I like them. They're livable units," said Rick Clary, general foreman for Oceanic Construction Inc., which coordinated construction of the village on five acres owned by Castle and Cooke Properties and Bishop Estate. (*Honolulu Star Bulletin*, May 10, 1992)

Clary, who would not himself live at the village, also planned to add greenery before people moved in. But a local resident disagreed: "It's a first-class chicken coop. If you have a family of four, no room. You gotta cook outside on the hibachi and take it in for warming up in your microwave" (*Honolulu Star Bulletin*, May 10, 1992). Home, for this man, implied space, privacy, and the opportunity to pursue "residential activities" with security and autonomy.

A few days later there were comments from people about to move into the cluster. " 'People who are criticizing this place, calling them chicken coops, are people who live in nice houses. If they were living like us in a tent, they wouldn't be saying that,' said Shirley Kaupe" (*Honolulu Star Bulletin,* May 14, 1992). For her, a solid if tiny space was better than living on the beach. The missing data, as yet, are the comments made by people who had lived in the village for some time: Would they experience the discomfort, shame, and stigma Lorene reported for the residents of Mā'ili Land?

Whether or not everyone agreed with Shirley Kaupe, the Hale'iwa village did reflect an effort to construct *homes* (see figure 9.2). The diversity of family composition was recognized, community ameni- ties (including the shared hibachis and picnic areas) were available, and people had not only a dependable roof over their heads but also access to the schools, clinics, and post office of Hale'iwa. They had an address, an aspect of having a home that is not trivial inasmuch as it announces a location—a place where a person can be found. The

9.2 When the Hale'iwa homeless cluster was first constructed in 1992, people criticized the beige or gray concrete squares set on concrete pilings as stark and unsightly. This photo was taken two years later, as a few plantings begin to soften the cluster's appearance. Bill Chismar, 1994.

significance of an address came up in another instance. On the Wai'anae Coast a center was established to provide exactly that: a mailing address for the estimated 350 homeless living on beaches. "Mostly, say project organizers, the center gives the homeless a chance to feel normal, to give out a telephone number or a permanent mailing address" (*Honolulu Star Bulletin*, March 21, 1992).

A fixed, if small, structure with privacy and the possibility of permanence for some people under some circumstances may meet the criteria for a home. One can add to this an address: a location that is linked to the surrounding system of communication and interaction. But the cluster village did not meet the criteria in the still-public aspects of residential activities, in the aesthetic, or rather, the nonaesthetic quality of a beige square mounted on concrete pilings, and, as the Waimānalo Task Force implied in its own definition of homeless, in being under the continual supervision of a "housing authority."

The cluster that was built in the spring of 1992 represented much of what the members of the Waimānalo Task Force had objected to the summer before; they refused to define such an arrangement as providing "homes" in any meaningful sense of that word. The same spring the Hale'iwa structures were completed, the city moved to banish people from the "tent city" in 'A'ala Park in downtown Honolulu. The relocation plan in this instance, too, sheds light on the values and concepts that lay behind the Waimānalo report.

In February 1992, the city had given permission to approximately one hundred people to live in tents in 'A'ala Park, presuming these would be temporary and thus not a threat to the flourishing tourist business in nearby Chinatown. The residents were families or women and children; single men were, presumably, to be sheltered a few blocks away in an abandoned pier at Honolulu Harbor. 'A'ala Park itself had characteristics of a shelter, with rules and regulations for its occupants. "Some people who have been living freestyle in the Aala Park tent city were chafing last night at their new restricted circumstances bound by a fence, an 8 P.M. curfew and a set of rules not yet clear," the *Honolulu Star Bulletin* (February 29, 1992) reported, with its usual ambivalence about the homeless.

But that the 'A'ala Park tent housing had taken on some aspects of home was evident five months later when the city decided to tear it down. " 'Who has the right to tell us to move when they don't even have a place to move us to?' demanded Lucille Kiili, one of the homeless that gathered in front of City Hall yesterday. They were petitioning for a 90-day extension to remain in the tent city at Aala Park"

(*Honolulu Star Bulletin,* June 19, 1992). The residents had created, their lawyer said, "a very stable and supportive environment." And he added: "If they have to leave the park and live in other facilities, it's going to cause a lot of hardship and damage to them" (*Honolulu Star Bulletin,* July 3, 1992).

There were no other facilities, homelike or not. (The pier experiment had been a failure: Men considered it dangerous and alienating; one whole side was open and there were no separations between sleeping spaces.) This does not mean tent housing in a central city park is the answer, no matter how forcefully 'A'ala Park residents might argue that they could make a home of it. And they did not make that argument; 'A'ala Park was shelter, temporary and expedient. That it had also become a stable and supportive environment would not justify preserving it as one solution to Honolulu's homeless problem.

The risk in accepting such temporary arrangements is clearly put by Kim Hopper, an anthropologist and advocate for the homeless in New York: "The danger, of course, is that in the absence of long-term alternatives these hastily assembled improvisations will take on an institutional life of their own. Thus does waste property come to the aid of waste people, without either altering the terms of its intrinsic value" (Hopper 1990, 168). This is the dilemma of self-help housing: If people can adjust the housing they have so it becomes homelike, governments and communities can absolve themselves of the responsibility of providing people with more than a roof over their heads. Then the significance of "home" becomes irrelevant to policies for dealing with the homeless.

The options 'A'ala Park residents had were few and can be summed up in the word *waiting:* waiting for a job that would qualify them for Section 8 federal government rent subsidies; waiting for a low-rent apartment to become available; waiting, if they were Hawaiian, to move into a family household or, perhaps, to assume a Hawaiian Home Lands plot.

> Many of the residents of Aala Park have been of Hawaiian ancestry. . . . Of those homeless, 50 percent have applied for Hawaiian Home Lands. For the 190,000 acres of Hawaiian Home Lands statewide, there is a waiting list of 14,000 unduplicated names, people waiting for a piece of land to build a home. There are those that feel if the Hawaiian Home Lands program had been properly funded and managed, the percentage of Hawaiian homeless would be far less. According to Steve Morse of the Office of Hawaiian

Affairs, 'Native Hawaiians belong on Hawaiian Home Lands, not in Aala Park.' " (*Commentary* by Joan Kenly Stebbins, *Honolulu Star Bulletin*, June 28, 1992)[19]

And so the several themes introduced at the Waimānalo Task Force meeting come up again: the irony of Hawaiians being homeless on their homelands, the violation of *'ohana* values in state housing policies, and the importance of bringing community views to bear on approaches to homelessness. Though the people at the Waimānalo town meeting would not, I think, have defined themselves as activists, their concerted response to a state policy suggests both the strengths and the weaknesses in this process of establishing housing policy.

The Waimānalo Task Force did not win against the state. It did construct a definition of home that reflected Hawaiian cultural values and that also reflected the ideas formulated by those without a home. Before drawing up the multifaceted plan, members of the task force had polled the homeless to see what kind of housing they desired. Of the fifty-two groups [families] surveyed, the report asserted, "only one expressed interest in participating in the State's homeless village"; for them, that was not a home but a provisional shelter (WTFH 1991). Whether or not the Waimānalo group set an example for other communities in Hawai'i, the actions of the task force certainly underline the multivocality of "home" when the homeless are at issue.

The "Good" Home: Hawaiian Style

Statements made at the Waimānalo meeting, by Lorene, and in the *Honolulu Star Bulletin* and *Advertiser* suggest not only the multivocality of home, but also the enormous significance of selecting a definition of home in the context of homelessness. The Waimānalo interpretation of home absorbs Hawaiian cultural values, but it is not alien to the literature on housing, policy, and the cultural and social aspects of the built environment. Just to reiterate: For those who attended the meeting in Waimānalo, having a home meant belonging to a community. More specifically, a home was a place of security, networks, and identity; home was the physical location of people bound together by ties of love and loyalty, duty and obligation.

Emphasis on social relations did not mean, however, ignoring structural features. People at the meeting had a distinct conceptualization of home in a material sense: a solid building, not a "card-board box" or "chicken coop." No shacks, was the general consen-sus. One man at the meeting mentioned Army housing;[20] this, per-haps, was an architectural reference others had as well: It would be hard to live in Hawai'i without being aware of the housing provided for American military which, while permanent, did not suggest the kind of expansive incorporativeness the people of Waimānalo intended their physical structures to allow. The lack of a human dimension was effectively conveyed by an adolescent who complained to me, "It's so *boring* there [Fort Schofield barracks]; there's *nothing* to do."

Moreover, there was Mā'ili Land, across the island, where a num-ber of people had kin and which certainly was visible in newspaper and television reports. These were buildings (rather like barracks) whose shape and form in no way reflected the needs and desires of the residents. Mā'ili Land was a shelter into which people had been placed, not homes people created out of an available space. A recent change in the physical structure, however, suggests the state had rec-ognized one of the features people claim made a structure into a "real" home: "unit kitchens have replaced communal kitchens" (*Hawaii Catholic Herald,* Spring 1994).

Barracks and Mā'ili Land were the negative examples—the "bad" homes that determined the semantics of a good home in Waimānalo. If one is to speak of aesthetics, then, it can only be in the sense of form following function: the beauty that stems from a place properly used. In Waimānalo, and doubtless other Hawaiian communities, the semantics of a good home are drawn from the concepts of kinship, family, obligation, and love. In March 1993, when I returned to Wai-mānalo, some houses had been built on the new Home Lands prop-erty. In one respect, they looked like their neighbors: mainly one-, and a few two-story buildings, with an occasional bright spot of color on the window frames or roofs. But they also looked skeletal and thin. They lacked the thick texture of human activity that com-pletes the aesthetic of domestic space in Waimānalo. They were not yet good homes, as I had come to understand the meaning of that for the people of Waimānalo. A year and a half later, in the summer of 1994, I could not distinguish those newer houses from older homes; fully occupied, they had the life marks of a good home (figure 9.3).

But the Waimānalo structures did not solve the problem of home-lessness. These would be the homes of the fortunate few, those who had reached the top of the lists of thousands waiting for Home Lands land. And, in fact, the problem of homelessness was to take on an

9.3 This older Waimānalo house—lived in, cared for, and blending well into the landscape—illustrates some of the rich texture of a "good" home. Judith Modell, 1994.

intensified significance, in the heightened political atmosphere following the January 1993 centennial commemoration of the overthrow of the last Hawaiian monarch, Queen Lili'uokalani. Subsequent months have seen yet further changes in the social construction of home in Hawai'i.

The Waimānalo Task Force had made no bones about the distinctly Hawaiian aspect of the problem and of the solution they offered. The concept of 'ohana was central, and distinguished their task force report from similar reports prepared by community groups in other parts of the nation (cf. Lang 1989). The six proposals had 'ohana at their core; a home could be constructed in various ways, as long as the guiding principle was incorporation and acceptance rather than marginalization and stigma. An extra bedroom, an accessory building or tent in the backyard, a small freestanding structure —each could be a home as long as it was embedded in social networks and a cultural milieu. The concept of 'ohana was also stretched, so that neighborhood became the incorporative unit: The newcomer was not stranger but kin by virtue of belonging (cf. Perin 1988). And though there is a danger in this emphasis on "sociability" and "ties of loyalty and obligation" rather than on the *built* environment,[21] the

formulation captures the Hawaiian values without which a roof over
one's head is never a home.

> As the Waimānalo Task Force report proclaimed, adequate hous-
> ing policy must take the real needs of the homeless into account,
> including not only the need for shelter, but their need to maintain
> a sense of dignity; the need to maintain the independence and
> integrity of their family unit; their need for independence and
> scope to exercise a degree of personal responsibility; and their
> need to contribute to the well-being of the community as a whole.
> (WTFH 1991)

While the Waimānalo plan could not solve the problems of state bud-
gets or neighborhood discrimination or competition for land, it did
lock housing policy to the notion of a good home—which is as personal and social as it is physical and structural.

The plan also suggests what is generalizable from and complicated
by the Hawaiian case, as I have summarized it: that values always fill
in the content of "home." Beginning with the social and ending with
the material conditions may well be the best basis for a humane
housing policy, in which not just a house but a "good home" is the
right of everyone. At the same time, this principle inserts housing
policy squarely into debates about cultural and political autonomy,
which are currently raging in Hawai'i. The growing (and increasingly
vociferous) preoccupation with Hawaiian sovereignty links "home"
and "homelands" inextricably, adding a political dimension to the
historical importance of land to Hawaiian interpretations of a "place
to live." The bitter irony, as the WTFH report put it, of Hawaiians
being homeless on their homeland is potential fuel in the struggle to
reclaim land and, with it, Hawaiian self-determination.[22]

The task force did not anticipate what was to happen two years
later, when home and sovereignty were merged in a direct resistance
to state policy. In the fall of 1993, the Ohana Council, a radical sovereignty group, established a village on lands they claimed were
Hawaiian. At Makapu'u Beach, a popular tourist attraction, about
150 individuals moved into various structures, including tents and
makeshift wooden bungalows (see figure 9.1).[23] They started a small
taro plot, using water provided by the state to the beach park. By
the spring of 1994, when persuasion did not work, the state turned
off the water in order to drive the residents out—creating a homeless population. This population has been moved into a non-Home
Lands area behind Waimānalo, where they are busy building the core

structures of a "new Hawaiian 'nation' " (*The Honolulu Advertiser,*
June 27, 1994). Ironically, the move achieved the essence of the
"in my own backyard" policy I had heard articulated three years
earlier.

Favoring geographical separation and an antagonistic relationship
to the state, the new residents offer a definition of "home" that does
not entirely accord with the one in the task force report. While equally
applying Hawaiian cultural values to the notion of home, the Waimānalo Task Force and the Ohana Council opposed these to state
housing policies in very different ways. The resistance shown by the
town meeting was subtle and ideological, the resistance of the Makapuʻu group, confrontative and pragmatic. Yet, from another point of
view, the Makapuʻu group had only carried to a logical extreme the
intersection of cultural values, home, and Home Lands implicit
throughout the task force report.

When I wanted to take a picture of the structures being built by
the Ohana Council, the Hawaiian elder I was with told me not to.
They want their privacy, he said; that is why they live so far off the
road. IMBY does not necessarily mean a lack of fences; a "keep out"
can be thrown up in any number of ways. Whether the physical distancing maintained by the group behind the Home Lands will entail
a social withdrawal, and thereby a blanket rejection of the Waimānalo understanding of ʻohana, remains to be seen.

Members of the task force had spoken strongly against separating
state-sponsored housing from the rest of the community. By 1994,
they saw two such "clusters" in their neighborhood: the Ohana
Council's "new nation," on land given by the state, and, despite all
their protestations, a new cluster village for the "ordinary" homeless
population originally the subject of the report. "Weinberg Village
Waimanalo, as it will likely be called [after the foundation that provided funds], will be similar to state homeless projects in Haleiwa
and Waianae" (*The Honolulu Advertiser,* September 19, 1993).
Barracks-like in appearance, the structures are adapted from modules
previously used as temporary classroom space at a local community
college.

Waimānalo seems to have inherited the Māʻili Land solution the
task force had tried valiantly to resist. On one level, then, the state
has prevailed, as thoroughly in this instance as in that of the Makapuʻu occupants. On another level, however, community resistance
has been effective in bringing forward, into the public, notions of
home that recall the social, cultural, and political dimension of

"housing" people. Adding private kitchens to the Māʻili Land structures was not a hollow victory, but a recognition that "good home"
means a place of social interaction and a source of individual dignity.
The reflection of those concepts in the built environment will shift
over time—especially in Hawaiʻi, where construction is ceaseless—
but, as the Waimānalo meeting concurred, without those concepts,
there is only shelter.

Discussions of "homing" the homeless are intensifying under the
influence of the Hawaiian sovereignty movement, itself not mono-
lithic. For these groups, beyond different particular programs, each
point to the fact that all people of Hawaiian ancestry are homeless,
displaced by two centuries of usurpation by outsiders. The real estate
patterns of today are frighteningly familiar, as non-Hawaiians
intrude into space and control construction in those spaces. The
movement to reclaim land, place, and traditional living arrangements
is also part of a pattern, one of resistance and assertion of cultural
identity (see Sahlins 1992). In that summer of 1991, the Waimānalo
Task Force was not militant, though it was definite, in its resistance
to the state plan for the homeless. In the current political context in
Hawaiʻi, such a task force may find that "homing" the homeless is
inevitably a matter of reclaiming sovereignty over homelands. In this
context, "from chicken coops to homes" inscribes a radical national-
ist gesture.

It is interesting to speculate on how distinctive the Hawaiian situation may be—in terms both of the history of dispossession and of
the importance of land to a sense of being "homed" properly. Concepts of the ʻohana and of the home constructed around social interaction are bound up with a notion of the land: a place on which
people conduct the activities necessary to cultural and physical survival. Such a profound association of social relationships, home, and
place may also come to be part of the agendas of community coalitions in other parts of the nation (see, e.g., Caton 1990), turning
these into groups whose platforms are potentially more "resistant"
than they seem at first sight.

The people at the Waimānalo meeting that July night in 1991
were not calling for sovereignty in an explicit way. In the totality of
their spoken and written texts, however, they were proclaiming that
the matter of moving from chicken coops to homes is a matter of
regaining the political, economic, spatial, and cultural independence
they are not alone in being denied by the forces of capitalism, mod-
ernization, and expansion.

Notes

First of all, of course, I must thank Gordon and Helene who brought me to the Waimānalo Task Force meeting and who have shown me all along the true meaning of *aloha*. Other people in Waimānalo also have generously invited me into their *'ohana;* among these, John Simeona deserves special mention. In Māʻili Land, Lorene honored me with the story of her move into the cluster village. In Pittsburgh, my student Steve Beaudoin did some difficult and creative library research, without always clear instruction from me. The ASAO sessions on "Housing and Social Change in the Pacific" were a wonderful context in which to think and to write. I thank all participants, members of the audience, and especially Margaret Rodman and Jan Rensel, who worked hard to get the papers together and also helped with editing, clarification of theoretical points, and provision of some valuable data.

1. My primary research focus is the relationship between Hawaiian people and the various government and private agencies that are drawn on or intervene in domestic and family crises. The project, as I explain elsewhere (Modell mss.), also touches on issues of cultural identity, autonomy in an American state, and activism in a local context.

2. There were about forty people at the meeting. I was one of five *haoles* 'whites'; the others were residents of Waimānalo, and included a local politician. The majority of people there were Hawaiian or part-Hawaiian; the issue concerned Home Lands space, the meeting was held in the Home Lands neighborhood, and, judging by the tone of discussion, the subject prompted a good deal of concern on the part of people who explicitly embraced Hawaiian values.

3. "Cluster village" describes an arrangement of separate structures gathered in one place; in some areas the arrangement has been called "campus-style" housing. "The basic justification for this style of shelter is cost. Economies of scale can be realized in larger centralized facilities" (Lang 1989, 168). One might, as some people at the meeting did, also call these "projects."

4. Not In My Back Yard—that is, objecting to a proposal's location primarily because of its proximity to one's own property interests.

5. These "character flaws" vary with time, place, and author. The hobo and tramp were replaced by the alcoholic and drug abuser; the prostitute by the woman on drugs, and so on; see Hopper 1990 for a brief summary of classic literature on the homeless population in the United States.

6. "A disproportionate 28 percent of Hawaii's homeless are Hawaiian or part Hawaiian, while Hawaiians make up only 17 percent of Hawaii's total population" (*Honolulu Sunday Star Bulletin and Advertiser,* June 28, 1992).

7. An article in the January 18, 1993, *Honolulu Star Bulletin* summarized an ongoing debate about how "Hawaiians" are to be identified and enumerated. The federal census counts anyone "who has ancestors that were natives prior to 1778" while the state of Hawaiʻi distinguishes between "Native Hawaiian"—persons with 50 percent or more Hawaiian blood quantum—

and "Hawaiian"—persons with any Hawaiian ancestry. This terribly complicates the distribution of Hawaiian Home Lands; see below.

8. The distribution of land is perhaps the most complicated aspect of Hawaiian history, worthy of a book and not just a brief summary; see Kelly 1956; Parker 1989; Sahlins 1992.

9. It is not easy to find income statistics that are broken down by ethnicity; my estimate here is based on a 1980 table in Kanahele 1982.

10. The rate of unemployment for Hawaiians in 1994 was 5.7 percent; with the exception of "other Asian/Pacific Islanders" (excluding Japanese, Chinese, Filipinos, and Korean) at 6.7 percent, this was the highest reported rate in the state (Hawai'i State Data Center 1990).

11. A report to the Legislature in 1991 suggests how persistent some form of 'ohana housing may be: "The proportion of shared rentals increased through all periods [since 1978] as the proportion of private rentals decreased" (Hawai'i State Department of Human Services 1991). Compare Perin 1988 on definitions of family (or nonstranger) in housing disputes.

12. The Waimānalo Task Force report referred to this situation. Homelessness "is even more difficult to tolerate when native Hawaiians, finally awarded homesites on Hawaiian Home Lands after decades of waiting, find that they do not have the financial means to build on the land which they have waited for so many years to receive" (WTFH 1991). By March 1993, a number of houses had been built. During the summer of 1994, new building was still going on and the 1993 houses had already blurred into the landscape.

13. The condemnation of tent, squatter, or "spontaneous" settlements (see Ward 1982) in Hawai'i undoubtedly has a great deal to do with the state's dependence on a tourist economy. Such housing does not present an appealing front to visitors, businesspeople, or prospective residents.

14. The proposed Waimānalo site was a piece of land near the ocean, separated from the most densely populated areas of the town.

15. Three years after I met her, Lorene had moved out, though she continued to be a devoted case worker in the cluster.

16. There is a model for this response to the homeless; foster family care has existed in the United States since the nineteenth century. But, and the difference is telling, it is generally a program for the mentally ill and disabled. For the people of Waimānalo, the foster care program potentially applied to any homeless person—there was no assumption of incapacity or illness in the task force report. Regarding foster family care in the United States, see Caton 1990, 118–121.

17. The creation of kin in Hawai'i is well documented, and implied by the definition of 'ohana included above; see, for instance, Sahlins 1985; Linnekin 1985.

18. Michael Lang's (1989) thorough discussion of homeless policies, and community responses, in Camden, New Jersey, suggests how common the

tug and pull between "state" and "people"—with ultimate lack of resolution —may be.

19. Others put the waiting list at 19,000 (MacKenzie 1991).

20. As a Pacific Islands population, the Hawaiians are distinct in having as a major model for housing the American-style military barracks. This provides quite a different model than, for instance, the churches and mission homes other groups look to in changing—or resisting changing—native housing style.

21. "Danger" refers to Kim Hopper's (1990) point, quoted above, that makeshift housing that seems to satisfy people's needs for community will be allowed to stand.

22. The arguments for self-determination, sovereignty, and cultural autonomy are too complex to go into in this paper; I have described them (albeit also too briefly) in another paper (Modell mss.).

23. This is the beach shown so vividly in the movie of James Jones' *From Here to Eternity*, and was a special attraction to mainland *haoles*.

10
Conclusion

MARGARET RODMAN

We shall not cease from exploration
And the end of all our exploring
Will be to arrive where we started
And know the place for the first time.

T. S. ELIOT from Four Quartets[1]

THE CONCLUSION to an edited collection seems an appropriate place to return to where we started for a moment of reflection. We began this book with an account of my encounter with changes in houses and social relationships on Ambae, an island in northern Vanuatu. Here I return to themes introduced by those "moving houses" that then are discussed in terms of the other chapters in this volume.

We hope that readers who may not previously have given much thought to changes in Pacific housing will have a sense of knowing the place for the first time. The moving houses exemplify how subtly things may change while seeming to remain the same. Many of the changes that other contributors discuss are more visible than the ones I described: giving up Samo longhouses for small, private dwellings, or moving from a Samoan *fale* to a Honolulu high-rise apartment. But the moving houses of Ambae reprise many common themes.

Like the social relations that produce them, houses change all the time. As in Vanuatu, there may be a timeless quality to domestic spaces even as they change. Houses may alter as gradually as domestic cycles of life and death, and in similar ways. Shaw, for example, touches on the reproductive quality of Samo houses, noting that old houses contributed bits of themselves to new ones while remaining more or less habitable. Or change may be sudden: a cyclone that leaves Rotumans fed up with impermanent housing. But even in the most dramatic instances of housing change, chapter authors have rejected easy, unicausal explanations and offer multifaceted analyses of the causes and consequences of housing change.

222

Meanings of Housing and Place

The most pervasive of these themes is that houses are containers not only of people but of changing cultural meanings.[2] Some of these meanings are secret. Michael Young (1993, 186), for example, sees a link between the magical paraphernalia hidden in Kalauna houses and the magical knowledge hidden in the mind. Many meanings of houses are gendered, like the *na gamal* discussed in the prologue to this chapter. Chowning points out in her chapter that the principal differences between men's and women's houses in Galilo were in what they did and did not contain.

Housing in the narrowest sense is shelter. Housing that protects people from tropical storms or the snows of New Zealand's high country or from life on the streets in Honolulu is essential. As Modell's chapter shows, there is no clearer way to define the meaning of home than in juxtaposition to homelessness.

Housing, however, is much more than shelter, and Modell's discussion also calls attention to broader definitions of home. Community may be emphasized more than privacy. Home, she observes, is a place in a community. In the introduction to an interdisciplinary book, *Housing, Culture, and Design,* Chambers and Low (both anthropologists) define housing as "those physical structures that shelter people in the pursuit of their 'private' lives" (1989, 5). They recognize the wide cross-cultural variation in meanings of privacy, but in Pacific Islands housing the importance of community, which Modell referred to above, sometimes inverts notions of public and private. As Franco and Aga show, people in Samoa live in horizontally open housing that is effectively public, albeit private in the sense of housing a domestic group. They cite Keene's (1979) finding that open houses gave Samoans "a kind of collective strategy for controlling behavior by providing an audience for it, an audience whose approval mattered a great deal to the performers" (page 179, this volume). When Samoans leave home for the vertically closed public housing of Hawai'i, ironically, the privacy becomes so much greater that children may suffer from increased domestic violence. The highrise walls block the public gaze, so that domestic behavior is less amenable to peer scrutiny. In New Zealand, as Macpherson's chapter describes, Samoans reinvent spaces that are more public by building a multipurpose garage. Not surprisingly, given the climate, much of domestic life in the Pacific Islands is lived outside the house (see Flinn, chapter 6). To varying degrees, houses become rooms off outdoor living spaces. Where houses are built without walls, the room is a semi-public shaded space. Elsewhere, walled houses become areas sheltered from the eyes of others and are especially used to store valuables and things not to be shared at the moment. Flinn shows how locked rooms and open living rooms replace this pattern as housing changes for Pollapese migrants in Chuuk. Even in the New Zealand high country, verandahs and gardens extend domestic space, and the woman's domain, outside the house (see Dominy, chapter 5).

The meaning of a house is more than what it signifies as an object: Housing is meaningful as an active process. Anthropologists have explored the symbolism of settlement design since the beginning of the discipline. Some have regarded houses and villages as metaphors about social relationships at particular points in time and space (e.g., Bourdieu 1977; Gregor 1977; Hallowell 1967; Bourdier and AlSayyad 1989, Parts 1–4). But few cross-cultural researchers have addressed housing as a process until recently (e.g., Bourdier and AlSayyad 1989, Parts 5–7; Kent 1990; Low and Chambers 1989; Waterson 1990). The chapters in this volume add to this literature. They explore the meanings that are negotiated in space as people build and dwell in places that seem always to have been home (Chowning, Dominy, Flinn, Rensel, Shaw), are homes away from home (Franco and Aga, Macpherson), or are homelands without a home (Modell).

Housing is more than a product in another sense. Phenomenologists view dwelling as identity with a place; "when we identify with a place, we dedicate ourselves to a way of being in the world" (Norberg-Schulz 1985, 12). Dwelling consists of lived relationships with places that create spatialized meaning (Heidegger 1977). Altman and Low (1992) have written about this in terms of what they call "place attachment" (see also Rosen 1979). In Vanuatu, people speak about their home place rather than house and describe themselves in Bislama as *man ples* 'local person', linking people to land (Jolly 1992, 342; Rodman 1987, 35). Rootedness is a metaphor that recurs throughout the group (see Bonnemaison 1994). People and land may be spoken of as sharing blood (Rubinstein 1978).

Several chapters in this volume suggest the importance of place attachment to identity in other Pacific societies. Chowning notes that while his father was alive, a grown man in the Lakalai area was expected not to leave his place of birth. In the past, people were almost literally rooted in place; the Lakalai dead were buried in the floors of dwelling houses with their heads sticking up above the earth until the flesh decayed. Shaw comments on the transition from a nomadic lifestyle to one more rooted in place. Yet place attachment can be strong among people who move. Shaw notes that the longhouse created a sense of belonging in two ways: first, through relationships among the people who slept there; second, as a site of subsistence and security that people would return to for food even after the longhouse had been abandoned.

Houses in the New Zealand high country are more permanent than Samo longhouses, but even there attachments may be strongest to places other than houses. Emotionally, people cannot afford to become too attached to a house that is never fully under the individual's control but rather is subject to generational and other family pressures. But, Dominy found, people are deeply attached to the properties where they grew up, and want to return "home" to be buried. A sense of attachment to all that the family stands for and to the continuity of its relationship with that property create a sense of identity and belonging that high country families share. Similarly, the *'ohana* values expressed in the task force's alternative plan described in Modell's chapter define home in a way that emphasizes attachment to place that is larger than the house. The link drawn between home and cultural identity is explicit; it is related to land rights and the situation of being homeless in one's homeland.

Domestic Groups in Domestic Space

Samoan hosts in urban New Zealand would understand all too well Robert Frost's notion that home is where they have to take you in.[3] A working woman reluctantly gives up her own bed and sleeps on the floor so that vacationing relatives may have many good nights' sleep. Clearly, this is a situation fraught with tensions, which will be considered later. For the moment, the point is to draw attention to another important theme in the chapters, namely that housing change is about changing social dynamics as well as changing built forms.

Modell notes that home in the context of native Hawaiian homelessness was defined as "the physical location of people bound together by ties of love and loyalty, duty and obligation" (page 213). The people who are bound together may be very different from the nuclear family household for whom most North American housing is designed. A broader definition of household applies to most of the situations described in this book, namely people who share a common residence (including dwelling on the same site but under multiple roofs), economic cooperation, and the socialization of children

(Wilk and Netting 1984). While Dominy's hired hands may or may not socialize children, they live on the property. Not only do they contribute economically, but they share in the consequences of an economic downturn that has turned the property owners into cooks and given the hired hands places at the family table.

As the example with which we began indicates, the mobility of people through houses, whether or not the houses themselves move, can reveal much about social life. This mobility can link rural and urban life, remote island villages and urban centers, as the chapters by Macpherson, and Franco and Aga, show. To a large extent, mobility within the local places that contributors describe is generational and due to the domestic cycle of birth, reproduction, and death. The maps discussed in the prologue contain many examples of this kind of mobility, both of people and houses.

The generational transformations of space that Dominy analyzes in the context of rural New Zealand no doubt occur in more "traditional" Pacific Islands societies, where they may also be connected to identity formation, the nuclear family, and gender roles. The impact of these spatial transformations in each generation have been less marked on the landscape where people build with natural, tropical materials: Grandmother's house becomes a place remembered by the sight of the mango tree that grew by her front door rather than evoked by her house, which soon crumbles and is gone. Of course, even where building materials are more permanent, as in the New Zealand high country, tree plantings marking the year of a marriage, for example, etch memories in the natural landscape.

Houses as History

Concrete and tin roofs have now made some grandmothers' houses almost indestructible, if not endlessly habitable. The introduction of so-called permanent materials in Pacific Islands housing has gradually transformed the landscape in new ways. Dominy quotes Adams' observation that buildings "can be usefully approached as maps to past social forms, suggesting through their spatial organization the ways in which the people who lived in them ordered their lives" (Adams 1993, 92). Increasingly, outsiders can read Pacific Islands settlements as historical maps in which the housing lasts longer than a generation.[4] Insiders, as Rensel found in Rotuma, may always have been able to do so. Her chapter emphasizes the importance of the social histories of buildings and house platforms traditionally. Nowadays, the knowledge that someone has worked hard to procure the money for, and then build, a European-style house may also be important, but the reason for that significance seems to have changed. In the past, a house expressed connection to the community; now it expresses the importance of nurturing the nuclear family and of material success. A "good provider" under these changed circumstances turns inward toward the household more than outward toward the larger social unit.

Housing has long given form to social and moral agendas. The introduction of European ideas about housing was closely linked throughout the colonial world to ideas about morality and religious salvation. This was not a one-way street. The colonies were a space in which evangelists and others negotiated the meaning of "home" back home (e.g., in England) in the course of domesticating "savages." If homelessness helps us see the meaning of home, so does the "dialectic of domesticity" highlight the meaning of domestic life as intrinsic to colonialism and to the rise of the modern bourgeoisie (Comaroff and Comaroff 1992, 293). While the Comaroffs acknowledge that colonized people may have been able to influence the way colonizers treated them, their focus is on the relationship between housing change for Tswana people on the colonial periphery and for impoverished whites in London and other urban centers. Little attention so far has been paid to the lessons that islanders' own constructions of domestic spaces taught Europeans. Indigenous housing, as both noun and verb, must have influenced many foreigners who lived in islanders' spaces, just as European housing influenced islanders who became familiar with the Westernized landscapes of mission station and plantation. Much research remains to be done on this topic. Nevertheless, Rensel's chapter suggests some of the bricolage involved in adapting European housing elements to indigenous housing, a pattern common to colonized locales. She describes, for example, how windows manufactured in Europe were incorporated into the walls of thatched houses on traditionally named foundations.

The connection between changes in ways that space (including housing), time, and bodies are constructed is especially evident in historical material. Foucauldian questions of power link all three. Religious salvation was not enough. The bodies of the saved had to be cleansed in European ways and clothed in particular clothes, which were not necessarily the same as the missionaries'. Islanders' lives had to be reorganized in time reckoned by the ringing of church bells or clocks. Married couples (and only they) were expected to sleep

under the same roof and to share that home with children; their
housing should imitate European forms. Such changes, missionaries
assumed, were cumulative. Thus a mission account in Rensel's chapter reports that once Rotumans had purchased soap, they were no
longer satisfied to live in "hovels." Failure to change native housing
was regarded as a failure of salvation by rival Europeans. Methodists
on Rotuma criticized Catholics for not elevating their people socially
and morally. The evidence was that the islanders' "houses and persons are nearly as filthy as ever they were" (page 37). The Catholics
concentrated on changing the built environment in other ways;
instead of encouraging people to build European-style houses, they
built large churches.

Technology

European-style housing is widely accepted not simply because of
technologies of power or because of what the housing signifies about
values and beliefs. Although increasingly important in Pacific Islands
cultures as the ultimate consumer good (see Philibert 1988), houses
are more than symbols of status, wealth, and power. Technology, in a
narrower, practical sense, is crucial. Modern housing is more weather
resistant and "permanent" than thatch and bamboo. Clearly, such
housing requires less routine maintenance and repair. But, as Flinn's
chapter makes clear, local occupants are less likely to be able to build
it (or build it well) themselves. They must spend money for materials
and often pay laborers to build the house rather than rely on reciprocal labor. Access to housing thus becomes more and more a matter of
access to cash, and so increasingly unequal. Both Flinn and Macpherson note that housing loans and mortgages may be difficult to obtain. For Samoans in urban New Zealand, one problem is that banks
are reluctant to include the incomes of nonowners who are coresidents when they calculate the ability to repay a loan. Pollapese women
follow a global pattern in being disadvantaged in this situation; Flinn
observes that if they work for wages at all, they tend to have lower
paying jobs than men. She wonders if women's contribution to housing is, therefore, less valued now than it was in the past.

The system of goods associated with modern homes positions
women differently as well. For Rotuman women, the production and
maintenance of furnishings is time consuming. It is one reason that
young women give for not making traditional fine mats. As in North
America (Hayden 1984), the "dream home" demands women's con-

tinual attention, and housework becomes an individual rather than a communal activity.

Like the houses in which they are used, furnishings can embody kin and land connections. This is not just a modern phenomenon. Sleeping mats, Flinn suggests, may be visible reminders of the value of women's work. But in modern houses, furniture takes on a different kind of significance as a display of social status, wealth, and taste. Chowning, Flinn, and others comment on the lack of furniture in traditional houses, and even in European-style houses, especially in rural areas. Many people want a European-style house. The financial wherewithal to furnish such a house, and the cultural preference to do so, are more limited. Comfort, Rybczynski (1986) has argued, is a European invention of the seventeenth century. Macpherson's comment that urban Samoan migrants prefer the comfort of sitting on mats on the floor to the sofas and chairs of the living room should give us pause (see also Rensel, chapter 2, note 15). Can we assume, as some contributors suggest, that comfort is increasingly associated with European-style furniture? Perhaps not. An American married to a Samoan once commented to me that they have a bed in their Australian bedroom "for show" but sleep on mats on the floor because it is so much more comfortable. A study of Pacific furniture preferences and use similar to Csikszentmihalyi and Rochberg-Halton's (1981) study of the meanings Chicago families associated with furniture and other household objects would be fascinating.

While maintenance requirements are less constant for European-style houses than for those made of local materials, when the house does need repair, the local occupants may not be able to do it themselves. In contrast, Flinn notes that despite complaints about the effort involved, repair and rebuilding of houses made with local materials can be accomplished with the help of kin and community.

While thatch and bamboo houses are easily damaged, they can be rebuilt quickly. Within a few weeks after the cyclone that hit Ambae, mentioned in the prologue, everyone had a house again. During the storm, villagers had expected the few houses made of any imported materials to be stronger than the more common thatched and bamboo structures. While buildings made of local materials suffered severe damage, so did those built from "European" materials.[5] The owner-built homes made of corrugated iron and plasterboard looked more secure than houses made of local materials, and survivors fled to these houses as their own homes threatened to blow to pieces around them. But the cyclone soon ripped apart the corrugated iron (which was generally just nailed in place) and hurled it in deadly fragments on the wind.

Community

On Ambae, the process of rebuilding after the cyclone was a collective effort that reaffirmed community identity. Several of the studies in this volume discuss the changing meanings of community that flow from changes to housing and social relationships at a domestic level. These consequences often are spatialized. Shaw's chapter provides a particularly striking example of a shift from communal long-houses to clusters of private, nuclear family dwellings. Where community houses remain symbolically important, their meaning still changes. Flinn describes a community meeting house on Pollap that occupied the spatial and symbolic center of the settlement. Responsibility for the construction and maintenance of the meeting house rested not with the community, as an aggregation of individuals, but with the municipality. This shift from collective to civic responsibility suggests a basic change in agency; villagers now organize to get the municipality to do things rather than organize to do things for the community directly.

On the other hand, Modell's chapter provides an example of people for whom a place in community was integral to the idea of home. The 'ohana strategy not only expressed these values, she notes, it outlined ways to achieve the goal of housing the homeless. The strategy emphasized inclusivity, a marked contrast with the exclusivity more often characteristic of modern urban housing. In this case, people reacted against the spatialized consequences of housing policies that had stigmatized the poor and the homeless. One of Modell's informants spoke of cluster housing for the homeless as "a first-class chicken coop" with no room for a family of four. The garages that Samoans built in Auckland were considerably larger (ten meters square) than these fifteen by sixteen foot Hawaiian homes. Instead of building more public housing, residents in Modell's study wanted to change the use of existing housing and adjacent domestic space, moving homeless people into spare rooms in host homes, using garages and tents in backyards, and encouraging family foster care.

Although the rise of the single-family home is associated with increasing isolation of households from one another and increasing individualism in the West, the Pacific examples provided here make a provocative contrast. Franco and Aga report that new homes built in Samoa from remittances invariably are large. The size of these new houses enables household heads to support and host large numbers of family members, whereas Samoans in Honolulu find the small size of both public and private housing units a constraint (Franco and Aga, chapter 8). They turn to churches to provide the spaces needed for entertaining. Samoans in Auckland also used church spaces, but found them to be both too large and too formal. Yet they needed a space that was larger than a living room and more appropriately designed for formal visits in which groups of participants were expected to sit on the floor facing each other. In Samoa, such events as weddings, title conferments, and 'ava ceremonies would have taken place in the residence of the *matai* or in large, traditional guest houses. The construction of a detached garage, Macpherson shows, provides the perfect spatial solution to this social problem. In symbolic terms the informal garage, with its emphasis on collective, social use, contrasts with the formal living room that emphasizes individual status display. The garage can be a gendered space, especially for use by young men, whereas the house is potentially always accessible to both genders. The informal space of the garage is multipurpose, as good for bingo or a rock band as for a funeral.

Boundaries and Consequences

Samoan garages in Auckland are but one example of changing definitions of domestic space. Many chapters comment on changes in what is enclosed within or separated from the house. Modern plumbing brings the toilet inside. Gas stoves can be placed in a kitchen inside the house whereas wood fuel, the danger of fire, and (in the chapters on Pacific Islands) earth ovens meant that a separate kitchen used to be essential.[6] What is cooked, and modes of food preparation, also implicate the changing spatial arrangements. Rensel notes that with the increased use of rice, noodles, and tinned meat on Rotuma, an indoor kitchen is more convenient and more private. Among Pollapese migrants in Weno the shift to indoor cooking of rice and other purchased foods is even more marked (chapter 6).

Dominy refers to Kolodny's term "a geography of enclosure," a phrase appropriate to many of the housing changes described in these chapters. Instead of occupying a single, open room, domestic spaces become compartmentalized in many of the examples. Interior walls partition space, either as curtain walls that create visual privacy (Flinn, chapter 6) or as structural walls that help strengthen the building (Rensel, chapter 2). The Auckland garages help to exclude visitors from the house while welcoming them in another domestic space. Similarly, the Pollapese migrants find that they can entertain people generously in open, front rooms of modern houses. Meanwhile they keep interior rooms, containing possessions they do not wish to share, locked against prying eyes and theft.

Such privacy gradients create boundaries that make public sharing compatible with private wealth. Nevertheless, there are often new tensions in such housing. The living room in the Auckland case is a space fraught with tensions between potential uses. In the living room, according to Macpherson, the family can best manage the impressions guests form of them. But an influx of visiting relatives could force the hosts to use the living room as extra sleeping space, which would create a bad impression.

Not only may there be competing uses for spaces, the permanence of contemporary houses can create other tensions. Rensel remarks that the common social solution of "avoidance" is much harder to practice in new housing. People who might have "moved house" following a big argument with their neighbors no longer can do so. Unlike the moving houses of Ambae, Rotuman concrete houses are firmly rooted in place and neighbors cannot turn their backs on each other.

Conclusion

Places, as Weiner observes in a chapter called "The Empty House," portray the unique historical and spatial constitution of the people who perform ordinary acts of day-to-day life there. In this sense, "places are the embodiment of human life activity—they acquire significance insofar as they are quickened by the concernful acts of people" (Weiner 1991, 203). As we have seen, houses, the most domesticated space, are especially revealing of the human life that creates them and that they, in turn, enclose. In choosing to study changes in housing and social relationships, contributors have turned their attention not just to buildings but to how lives are lived in changing times and places.

Notes

1. Reprinted in Plotz (1955, 6).
2. Clare Cooper's (1974) work on the house as a symbol of the self, and Duncan's (1982) edited book on housing and identity explore houses as containers of meaning, especially in a Western context. For a discussion of the

meaning of house, home, and identity in America, see Hummon (1989). For housing cross-culturally, see Oliver (1987) and Rapoport (1969).

3. "Home is the place where, when you have to go there,/they have to take you in." From "The Death of the Hired Man," by Robert Frost (1959, 69–75).

4. In many Pacific Islands villages, cement slab foundations remain, like the traditional stone house platforms of Rotuma, as statements about past occupation.

5. See Dupon (1984, 40) for similar findings in French Polynesia. On Ambae, the Western-style buildings at a boarding school were severely damaged. Most spectacularly, the "cyclone-proof" prefabricated local government headquarters (provided by foreign aid) was leveled; a single toilet was all that remained above the concrete slab foundation.

6. In Port Vila in 1993, I was struck by the fondness of relatively affluent urban islanders for building and using detached thatched kitchens with earthen floors. The modern kitchen inside a conventionally suburban bungalow supplemented the exterior "bush" kitchen, but could not compete with it for "comfort" as measured by a cool physical temperature and a warm social atmosphere.

References

Acland, L. G. D.
    1975 [1930] *The Early Canterbury Runs.* Fourth Edition, revised by
        W. H. Scotter. Christchurch, New Zealand: Whitcoulls Publishers.
Adams, Jane
    1993 Resistance to "modernity": Southern Illinois farm women and the
        cult of domesticity. *American Ethnologist* 20 (1): 89–113.
Allardyce, W. L.
    1885–1886 Rotooma and the Rotoomans. *Proceedings of the Queensland
        Branch of the Geographical Society of Australasia.* First sets: 130–
        144.
Allen, William
    1895 Rotuma. *Report of Australasian Association for Advancement of
        Science.* Pp. 556–579.
Altman, Irwin and Setha M. Low, eds.
    1992 *Place Attachment.* New York: Plenum Press.
Ardener, Shirley, ed.
    1993 *Women and Space: Ground Rules and Social Maps.* Revised edition.
        Cross-cultural Perspectives on Women, volume 5. Oxford: Berg.
Ashdown, Michael and Diane Lucas
    1987 *Tussock Grasslands: Landscape Values and Vulnerability.* Welling-
        ton: New Zealand Environmental Council.
Behar, Ruth
    1986 *Santa Maria del Monte: The Presence of the Past in a Spanish Vil-
        lage.* Princeton: Princeton University Press.
Bennett, George
    1831 A recent visit to several of the Polynesian Islands. *United Service
        Journal* 33:198–202, 473–482.
Bertram, G. and R. F. Watters
    1985 The MIRAB economy in South Pacific Microstates. *Pacific View-
        point* 26:497–519.
    1986 The MIRAB process: Earlier analyses in context. *Pacific Viewpoint*
        27:47–59.
Bloch, Maurice
    1992 What goes without saying: The conceptualization of Zafimaniry
        society. In *Conceptualizing Society,* edited by Adam Kuper. Pp. 127–
        146. New York: Routledge.

Boddam-Whetham, J. W.
  1876 *Pearls of the Pacific*. London: Hurst and Blackett.
Bonnemaison, Joël
  1994 *The Tree and the Canoe*. Honolulu: University of Hawai'i Press.
Bourdier, Jean-Paul and Nezar AlSayyad, eds.
  1989 *Dwellings, Settlements and Tradition: Cross-Cultural Perspectives*.
    Lanham, Md.: University Press of America.
Bourdieu, Pierre
  1977 *Outline of a Theory of Practice*. Cambridge, England: Cambridge
    University Press.
  1990 [1970] The Kabyle house or the world reversed. In *The Logic of
    Practice*. Pp. 271–283. Stanford: Stanford University Press.
Brunskill, R. W.
  1981 *Traditional Buildings of Britain: An Introduction to Vernacular
    Architecture*. London: Victor Gollancz Ltd.
Carsten, Janet and Stephen Hugh-Jones
  1995 Introduction. In *About the House: Lévi-Strauss and Beyond*. Pp. 1–
    46. Cambridge, England: Cambridge University Press.
Carter, Paul
  1987 *The Road to Botany Bay: An Essay in Spatial History*. London:
    Faber and Faber.
Caton, Carol L. M.
  1990 Crisis shelter and housing programs. In *Homeless in America*, edited
    by Carol L. M. Caton. Pp. 110–137. New York: Oxford University
    Press.
Caton, Carol L. M., ed.
  1990 *Homeless in America*. New York: Oxford University Press.
Chambers, Erve and Setha M. Low
  1989 Introduction. In *Housing, Culture and Design: A Comparative Per-
    spective*, edited by Setha M. Low and Erve Chambers. Pp. 3–9. Phil-
    adelphia: University of Pennsylvania Press.
Cheever, George N.
  1834–1835 *Log of the ship Emerald*. Pacific Manuscripts Bureau, frame
    31.
Chowning, Ann
  1965–1966 Lakalai kinship. *Anthropological Forum* 1 (3&4): 476–501.
  1989 Sex, shit and shame: Changing gender relations among the Lakalai.
    In *Culture, Kin, and Cognition: Essays in Honor of Ward H. Good-
    enough*, edited by Mac Marshall and John L. Caughey. Washington,
    D.C.: American Anthropological Association Special Publication
    25:17–32.
Chowning, Ann and Ward H. Goodenough
  1971 Lakalai political organisation. In *Politics in New Guinea*, edited by
    R. M. Berndt and P. Lawrence. Pp. 113–174. Nedlands, Australia:
    University of Western Australia Press.
Chun, Paula and David Takeuchi
  1983 *The Homeless in Hawaii: A Preliminary Study*. Honolulu: Hawai'i
    State Department of Health.

Churchward, C. Maxwell
   1940 *Rotuman Grammar and Dictionary.* Sydney: Australasian Medical
      Publishing Co.
Coiffier, Christian
   1988 *Traditional Architecture in Vanuatu.* Translated by Veronica Arjun
      and Pat Hereniko. Suva, Fiji: Institute of Pacific Studies and Van-
      uatu Extension Centre of the University of the South Pacific.
Comaroff, Jean and John Comaroff
   1992 Homemade Hegemony. In *Ethnography and the Historical Imagina-
      tion.* Pp. 265–294. Boulder, Colo.: Westview.
Cook, Edwin A.
   1970 On the conversion of non-agnates into agnates among the Manga,
      Jimi River, Western Highlands District, New Guinea. *Southwestern
      Journal of Anthropology* 26:190–196.
Cooper, Clare
   1974 The house as symbol of the self. In *Designing for Human Behavior,*
      edited by Jon Lang et al. Pp. 130–146. Stroudsburg, Pa.: Dowden,
      Hutchinson and Ross.
Csikszentmihalyi, Mihaly and Eugene Rochberg-Halton
   1981 *The Meaning of Things: Domestic Symbols and the Self.* Cambridge,
      England: Cambridge University Press.
Del Rosario, Dave
   1989 "Hawai'i's Youth Gangs." In-service training presentation, Victim-
      Witness Assistance Division. Honolulu.
Dick, Betty
   1964 *High Country Family.* Wellington, New Zealand: A. H. and
      A. W. Reed.
Dominy, Michèle D.
   1993 "Lives were always here": The inhabited landscape of the New
      Zealand High Country. *Anthropological Forum* VI (4): 567–586.
   1995a Toponymy: Positionality and containment on New Zealand High
      Country stations. *Landscape Review: Journal of Landscape Archi-
      tecture–South Pacific* 2:16–29.
   1995b White settler assertions of native status. *American Ethnologist* 22
      (2):358–374.
Douglas, I. M.
   1963 Report of Survey and Building of Rest Houses in the [Samo] Area,
      July–August 1963. Government Patrol Report.
Duly, Colin
   1979 *The Houses of Mankind.* London: Thames and Hudson.
Duncan, James
   1982 *Housing and Identity.* New York: Holmes and Meier.
Dupon, J-F
   1984 Where the exception confirms the rule: The cyclones of 1982–1983
      in French Polynesia. *Disasters* 8 (1): 34–47.
Durkheim, Emile and Marcel Mauss
   1963 [1903] *Primitive Classification.* Chicago: University of Chicago
      Press.

Eagleston, John Henry
    1832 *Log of the ship Emerald, volume 3.* Archived in the Peabody
        Museum, Salem, Massachusetts.
Ensor, Peter
    1990 Many Good Years, Some Not So Good: A History of Double Hill
        Station. Unpublished manuscript.
Erikson, Jon and Charles Wilhelm
    1986 *Housing the Homeless.* New Brunswick, N.J.: Rutgers University
        Press.
Evans, H. S.
    1951 Notes on Rotuma. Typescript.
Fatiaki, Anselmo et al.
    1991 *Rotuma: Hanua Pumue (Precious Land).* Suva, Fiji: Institute for
        Pacific Studies, University of the South Pacific.
Fischer, John L.
    1949 Western Field Trip Notes. Manuscript, Archives of the Bernice P.
        Bishop Museum, Honolulu.
Forbes, Litton
    1875 *Two Years in Fiji.* London: Longmans, Green, and Co.
Fox, James J.
    1993 *Inside Austronesian Houses: Perspectives on Domestic Designs for
        Living.* Canberra: Department of Anthropology in association with
        the Comparative Austronesian Project, Research School of Pacific
        Studies, The Australian National University.
Franco, Robert
    1987 *Samoans in Hawai'i: A Demographic Profile.* Honolulu: East-West
        Center Population Institute.
    1991 *Samoan Perceptions of Work: Moving Up and Moving Around.*
        New York: AMS Press.
    1992 Western schooling and transformations in Samoan social status in
        Hawai'i. In *Social Change in the Pacific,* edited by Albert B. Robil-
        lard. Pp. 308–321. London: Kegan Paul.
Frost, Robert
    1959 *You Come Too: Favorite Poems for Young Readers.* New York:
        Holt, Rinehart and Winston.
Gans, Herbert J.
    1991 From the bulldozer to homelessness. In *People, Plans and Policies:
        Essays on Poverty, Racism, and Other National Urban Problems.*
        Pp. 212–224. New York: Columbia University and Russell Sage
        Foundation.
Gardiner, J. Stanley
    1898 Natives of Rotuma. *Journal of the Royal Anthropological Institute*
        27:396–435, 457–524.
Gerber, Eleanor
    1975 Cultural Patterning of Emotion in Samoa. Ph.D. Dissertation, Uni-
        versity of California, San Diego.
Goodenough, Ward H.
    1962 Kindred and hamlet in Lakalai, New Britain. *Ethnology* 1:5–12.

Gregor, T.
   1977 *Mehinaku.* Chicago: University of Chicago Press.
Haley, Nelson Cole
   1948 *Whale Hunt, the Narrative of a Voyage . . . 1849–1853.* New York: Ives Washburn, Inc.
Hallowell, I.
   1967 *Culture and Experience.* New York: Schocken Books.
Harper, Barbara
   1967 *Kettle on the Fuchsia: The Story of Orari Gorge.* Wellington, New Zealand: A. H. and A. W. Reed.
Hatch, Elvin
   1992 *Respectable Lives: Social Standing in Rural New Zealand.* Berkeley: University of California Press.
Hawai'i State Data Center
   1990 Comparative Civilian Labor Force Information by Race and Sex. (Source: U.S. Bureau of the Census, 1990 Census.)
Hawai'i State Department of Human Services
   1991 Report to the Sixteenth Legislature: Adequacy of Welfare Allowances. Honolulu.
Hayden, Dolores
   1984 *Redesigning the American Dream.* New York: Norton.
Hees, F.
   1915–1916 Ein beitrag aus den sagen und erzaehlungen der Nakanai. *Anthropos* 10–11, 34–64, 562–585, 861–887.
Heidegger, Martin
   1977 Building dwelling thinking. In *Martin Heidegger: Basic Writings,* edited by D. Krell. Pp. 319–339. New York: Harper and Row.
Hocart, A. M.
   1913 Field notes. Archived in Turnbull Library, Wellington, New Zealand.
Hoch, Charles and Robert A. Slayton
   1989 *New Homeless and Old: Community and the Skid Row Hotel.* Philadelphia: Temple University Press.
Hockings, John
   1989 *Traditional Architecture in the Gilbert Islands: A Cultural Perspective.* St. Lucia, Australia: University of Queensland Press.
Honolulu Star Bulletin, The Honolulu Advertiser, and *The Sunday Star Bulletin and Advertiser*
   1991–1994 Miscellaneous articles.
Hooper, Antony and Judith Huntsman
   1973 A demographic history of the Tokelau Islands. *Journal of the Polynesian Society* 82:366–411.
Hopper, Kim
   1990 Advocacy for the homeless in the 1980s. In *Homeless in America,* edited by Carol L. M. Caton. Pp. 160–173. New York: Oxford University Press.
Howard, Alan
   1960 Unpublished field notes.

1970 *Learning to Be Rotuman.* New York: Columbia Teachers College Press.

Hummon, David
1989 House, home, and identity in contemporary American culture. In *Housing, Culture and Design: A Comparative Perspective,* edited by Setha M. Low and Erve Chambers. Pp. 207–228. Philadelphia: University of Pennsylvania Press.

IHS Newsletter
1994 Homelessness in Hawaii and the Role of IHS. Honolulu: Institute for Human Services, Spring 1994.

Japan, Nanyō-chō
1931 Nanyō Gunto Tōsei Chōsa-sho, Showa 5 nen (A summary of conditions in the Japanese Mandated Territories, 1930). Four volumes. Palau: Nanyō-chō.
1937 Nanyō Gunto Tōsei Chōsa-sho, Showa 10 nen (A summary of conditions in the Japanese Mandated Territories, 1930). Two volumes. Tokyo: Nanyō-chō.

Jolly, Margaret
1992 Custom and the way of the land: Past and present in Vanuatu and Fiji. *Oceania* 62:330–354.

Kaberry, Phyllis M.
1967 The plasticity of New Guinea kinship. In *Social Organization: Essays Presented to Raymond Firth,* edited by M. Freedman. Pp. 105–123. London: Frank Cass & Co.

Kanahele, George S.
1982 *Current Facts and Figures about Hawaiians.* Honolulu: Project WAIAHA.

Kea, Jody Lynn
1991 Honolulu's ohana zoning law. *University of Hawai'i Law Review* 13 (2): 505–535.

Keene, D. Thomas
1979 Houses without Walls: Samoan Social Control. Ph.D. Dissertation, University of Hawai'i, Mānoa.

Kelly, Marion
1956 Changes in Land Tenure in Hawaii, 1778–1850. Unpublished M.A. Thesis. Hamilton Library, University of Hawai'i.

Kembol, L., N. Koleala, J. Kutal, P. Kutapae, T. Pyakalya, A. Ruhan, and F. Yakopya Pakene
1976 *Enga Housing and Enga Tradition.* Occasional Paper No. 4. Boroko, Papua New Guinea: Institute of Papua New Guinea Studies.

Kent, Susan, ed.
1990 *Domestic Architecture and the Use of Space: An Interdisciplinary Cross-cultural Study.* New Directions in Archaeology series. Cambridge, England: Cambridge University Press.

King, Anthony
1976 *Colonial Urban Development: Culture, Social Power and Environment.* London: Routledge and Kegan Paul Ltd.

Kolodny, Annette
    1972 The unchanging landscape: The pastoral impulse in Simm's Revolutionary War romances. *Southern Literary Journal* 5 (1): 46–67.
Koopman-Boyden, P., ed.
    1978 *The Social Structure of the New Zealand Family.* Wellington, New Zealand: Methuen Press.
Krämer, Augustin
    1935 *Inseln um Truk.* Ergebnisse der Südsee Expedition 1908-1910, ser. 2, subser. B, band 6, part 1, edited by G. Thilenius. Hamburg: Friederichsen, de Gruyter & Co.
Lang, Michael
    1989 *Homelessness Amid Affluence.* New York: Praeger.
Lawrence, Denise L. and Setha M. Low
    1990 The built environment and spatial form. *Annual Review of Anthropology* 19:453–505.
Lawrence, Roderick J.
    1987 *Housing, Dwellings and Homes: Design Theory, Research and Practice.* New York: John Wiley & Sons.
Lesson, René
    1838–1839 *Voyage Autour du Monde . . . sur . . . "La Coquille."* Paris: Pourrat Fréres.
Linnekin, Jocelyn
    1985 *Children of the Land.* New Brunswick, N.J.: Rutgers University Press.
Low, Setha M. and Erve Chambers, eds.
    1989 *Housing, Culture, and Design: A Comparative Perspective.* Philadelphia: University of Pennsylvania Press.
Lucatt, Edward
    1851 *Rovings in the Pacific, 1837–49 . . . by a Merchant Long Resident in Tahiti.* London: Longman, Brown, Green, and Longman.
MacKenzie, Melody Kapilialoha, ed.
    1991 *Native Hawaiian Rights Handbook.* Honolulu: Native Hawaiian Legal Corporation.
Macpherson, Cluny
    1974 Extended Kinship Among Urban Samoan Migrants: Toward an Explanation. Ph.D. Dissertation, Department of Sociology, University of Waikato.
    1992 Economic and political restructuring and the sustainability of migrant remittances: The case of Western Samoa. *The Contemporary Pacific* 4 (1): 109–135.
    1994 Changing patterns of commitment to island homelands: A case study of Western Samoa. *Pacific Studies* 17 (3): 83–116.
Marcuse, Peter
    1990 Homelessness and housing policy. In *Homeless in America,* edited by Carol L. M. Caton. Pp. 138–159. New York: Oxford University Press.
Marsh, Ngaio
    1973 [1945] *Died in the Wool.* New York: A Jove Book.

Mayo, Larry
    1987 Urbanization in the Pacific and Guam. *City and Society* 1 (2): 99–
    121.
McDonald, J.
    n.d. *Racism in the Rental Accommodation Market.* Auckland: The
    Office of the Race Relations Conciliator.
McElhanon, Kenneth A. and C. L. Voorhoeve
    1970 *The Trans-New Guinea Phylum: Explorations in Deep Level
    Genetic Relationships.* Pacific Linguistics B-16. Canberra: Austra-
    lian National University.
McLeod, David
    1974 *Kingdom in the Hills: The Story of A Struggle.* Christchurch, New
    Zealand: Whitcombe and Tombs.
    1980 *Down from the Tussock Ranges.* Christchurch, New Zealand: Whit-
    coulls Publishers.
Methodist Church of Australasia, Department of Overseas Missions
    1855–1879 Letters Received, Fiji-Rewa, Rotuma, Ovalau, Bau & miscel-
    laneous. Unpublished documents, file 98. Archived in Mitchell
    Library, Sydney.
    1873–1876 Diaries and other personal papers of Rev. William Fletcher,
    Noatau. Unpublished documents, file 329. Archived in Mitchell
    Library, Sydney.
Modell, Judith
    mss. *Aloha ʻĀina:* Narratives of Place, Claims to Land.
Momeni, Jamshid A., ed.
    1990 *Homelessness in the United States.* New York: Greenwood Press.
Morgan, Lewis Henry
    1965 (1881) *Houses and House-Life of the American Aborigines.* Chi-
    cago: University of Chicago Press.
Netting, Robert McC., Richard R. Wilk, and Eric J. Arnould
    1984 Introduction. In *Households: Comparative and Historical Studies of
    the Domestic Group.* Pp. xiii–xxxviii. Berkeley: University of Cali-
    fornia Press.
New Zealand Department of Statistics
    n.d. *New Zealand Official Yearbook.* Wellington, New Zealand: The
    Government Printer. [Annual Series]
    1986 *New Zealand Census of Population and Dwellings.* Wellington: The
    Government Printer.
    1991 *New Zealand Census of Population and Dwellings.* Wellington: The
    Government Printer.
    1992 *1991 Census: Pacific Islands Population and Dwellings.* Wellington:
    The Department of Statistics.
Norberg-Schulz, Christian
    1985 *The Concept of Dwelling: On the Way to Figurative Architecture.*
    New York: Rizzoli.
O'Meara, Timothy
    1986 Why is Village Agriculture Stagnating? A Test of Social and Eco-
    nomic Explanations in Western Samoa. Ph.D. Dissertation, Univer-
    sity of California–Santa Barbara.

Oliver, Paul
1987 *Dwellings: The House Across the World.* Oxford: Phaidon Press Ltd.
Osborn, Joseph W.
1834–1835 *Log of the ship Emerald of Salem,* Capt. John H. Eagleston. Pacific Manuscripts Bureau microfilm 223, frame 151.
Parker, Linda S.
1989 *Native American Estate.* Honolulu: University of Hawai'i Press.
Parliamentary Debates: Senate
1974–1984 *Fiji Legislative Papers.* Suva, Fiji: Government Printing Office.
Perin, Constance
1988 *Belonging in America.* Madison: University of Wisconsin Press.
Philibert, Jean-Marc
1984 Affluence, commodity consumption, and self-image in Vanuatu. In *Affluence and Cultural Survival,* edited by Richard F. Salisbury and Elisabeth Tooker. Proceedings of the American Ethnological Society, 1981. Pp. 87–94. Washington, D.C.: American Ethnological Society.
1989 Consuming culture: A study of simple commodity consumption. In *The Social Economy of Consumption,* edited by Henry J. Rutz and Benjamin S. Orlove. Monographs in Economic Anthropology, no. 6. Pp. 59-84. Lanham, Md.: University Press of America.
Pitt, D. C., and C. Macpherson.
1974 *Emerging Pluralism: The Samoan Community in Urban New Zealand.* Auckland: Longman Paul.
Plant, Chris
1991 The development dilemma. In *Rotuma: Hanua Pumue (Precious Land),* Fatiaki, Anselmo et al. Pp. 204–226. Suva, Fiji: Institute for Pacific Studies, University of the South Pacific.
Plocki, Z.
1975 *Towards a Melanesian Style in Architecture.* Occasional Paper No. 3. Boroko, Papua New Guinea: Institute of Papua New Guinea Studies.
Plotz, Helen, compiler
1955 *Imagination's Other Place: Poems of Science and Mathematics.* New York: Thomas Crowell Co.
Pukui, Mary Kawena, E. W. Haertig, and Catherine A. Lee
1972 *Nānā I Ke Kumu (Look to the Source).* Honolulu: Queen Lili'uokalani's Children's Center.
Pynoos, J., R. Schafer, and C. W. Hartman, eds.
1980 *Housing Urban America.* New York: Aldine.
Rabinow, Paul
1989 *French Modern: Norms and Forms of the Social Environment.* Cambridge, Mass.: The MIT Press.
Rapoport, Amos
1969 *House Form and Culture.* Englewood Cliffs, N.J.: Prentice-Hall.
Reafsnyder, Charles B.
1984 Emergent Ethnic Identity in a Migrant Atoll Population in Truk State, Federated States of Micronesia. Ph.D. Dissertation, Indiana University.

Redburn, F. Stevens and Terry F. Buss
   1986 *Responding to America's Homeless*. New York: Praeger.
Rensel, Jan
   1993 The Fiji connection: Migrant involvement in the economy of
       Rotuma. *Pacific Viewpoint* 34 (2): 215–240.
   1995 Review of *Inside Austronesian Houses: Perspectives on Domestic
       Designs for Living*, edited by James J. Fox. *Asian Perspectives* 34
       (1): 137–139.
Riwas, Dilcris
   1985 *The Traditional Architecture of Drundrai Village in the Manus
       Province*. Lae, Papua New Guinea: Papua New Guinea University of
       Technology, Department of Architecture and Building.
Robben, Antonius C. G. M.
   1989 Habits of the home: Spatial hegemony and the structuration of
       house and society in Brazil. *American Anthropologist* 91 (30): 570–
       588.
Rodman, Margaret
   1985 Moving houses: Residential mobility and the mobility of residences
       in Longana, Vanuatu. *American Anthropologist* 87:56–73.
   1987 *Masters of Tradition: Consequences of Customary Land Tenure in
       Longana, Vanuatu*. Vancouver: University of British Columbia
       Press.
Rodman, Margaret and William L. Rodman
   1992 The eye of the storm: Cyclones and the social construction of place
       in Vanuatu. Prepared for *Spatializing Narratives: An Anthropology
       of Place*, edited by Terri Cundy Aihoshi and Margaret Rodman. In
       preparation. First presented at the American Anthropological Asso-
       ciation annual meeting, San Francisco.
Rosen, Larry
   1979 Social identity and points of attachment: Approaches to social
       organization. In *Meaning and Order in Moroccan Society:
       Three Essays in Cultural Analysis*, C. Geertz, H. Geertz, and
       L. Rosen. Pp.19–122. New York: Cambridge University
       Press.
Rossi, Peter H.
   1989 *Down and Out in America: The Origins of Homelessness*. Chicago:
       University of Chicago Press.
Rotuma District Office
   n.d. Outward Letters. Archived in the Central Archives, Suva, Fiji.
Rubinstein, Robert
   1978 Placing the Self on Malo: An Account of the Culture of Malo Island,
       New Hebrides. Ph.D. Dissertation, Department of Anthropology,
       Bryn Mawr.
Rutz, Henry J.
   1984 Material affluence and social time in village Fiji. In *Affluence and
       Cultural Survival*, edited by Richard F. Salisbury and Elizabeth
       Tooker. Proceedings of the American Ethnological Society, 1981. Pp.
       105–118. Washington, D.C.: American Ethnological Society.

Rybczynski, Witold
1986 *Home: A Short History of an Idea.* New York: Viking Penguin.
Saegert, Susan
1985 The role of housing in the experience of dwelling. In *Home Environments,* edited by Irwin Altman and Carol M. Werner. Pp. 287–309. New York: Plenum Press.
Sahlins, Marshall
1985 *Islands of History.* Chicago: University of Chicago Press.
1992 *Anahulu: The Anthropology of History in the Kingdom of Hawaii.* Volume 1: *Historical Ethnography.* Chicago: University of Chicago Press.
Salmond, Jeremy
1986 *Old New Zealand Houses, 1800–1940.* Auckland: Reed Methuen.
Samoan Service Providers Association
1990 Samoan Community 2000. Conference Report. Honolulu.
Severance, Craig
1976 Land, Food and Fish: Strategy and Transaction on a Micronesian Atoll. Ph.D. Dissertation, Department of Anthropology, University of Oregon.
Shankman, Paul
1976 *Migration and Underdevelopment: The Case of Western Samoa.* Boulder, Colo.: Westview Press.
1992 The Samoan exodus. In *Contemporary Pacific Societies: Studies in Development and Change,* edited by Victoria S. Lockwood, Thomas G. Harding, and Ben J. Wallace. Pp. 156–170. Englewood Cliffs, N.J.: Prentice Hall.
Shaw, R. Daniel
1974a Samo sibling terminology. *Oceania* 44:233–239.
1974b The geographical distribution of Samo relationship terms: Where have all the women gone? In *Kinship Studies in Papua New Guinea,* edited by R. D. Shaw. Pp. 223–246. Ukarumpa, Papua New Guinea: Silprint.
1976 Samo Social Structure: A Socio-Linguistic Approach to Understanding Interpersonal Relationships. Ph.D. Dissertation, Department of Anthropology and Sociology, University of Papua New Guinea.
1986 The Bosavi language family. *Pacific Linguistics* Series A-70:45–76. Canberra.
1990 *Kandila: Samo Ceremonialism and Interpersonal Relationships.* Ann Arbor: University of Michigan Press.
1996 *From Longhouse to Village: Samo Social Change.* Case Studies in Cultural Anthropology Series, edited by George and Louise Spindler. Fort Worth, Tex.: Harcourt Brace College Publishers.
Shaw, R. Daniel and Karen A. Shaw
1977 Samo phonemes: Distribution, interpretation and resulting orthography. *Workpapers in Papua New Guinea Languages* 19:97–135.

Shiroma, Marlene
  1992 Youth Gangs and the Sons of Samoa. Paper submitted for Interna-
       tional Student Conference, Kapi'olani Community College. Hono-
       lulu.
Shore, Bradd
  1977 A Samoan Theory of Action. Ph.D. Dissertation, University of Chi-
       cago.
  1982 *Sala'ilua: A Samoan Mystery*. New York: Columbia University
       Press.
Strongman, Thelma
  1984 *The Gardens of Canterbury: A History*. Wellington, New Zealand:
       A. H. and A. W. Reed.
Sutter, Frederick K.
  1977 Communal Versus Individual Socialization at Home and in School
       in Rural and Urban Samoa. Ph.D. Dissertation, University of
       Hawai'i, Mānoa.
Sykes, J. W.
  1948 Confidential Report on Rotuma. The Secretariat, Suva, Fiji.
Taito, F.
  1940 *My Own Story*. Sydney: Methodist Overseas Missions of Australa-
       sia, Literature Department.
Thomas, Nicholas
  1994 *Colonialism's Culture: Anthropology, Travel and Government*.
       Princeton, N.J.: Princeton University Press
Thornton, Geoffrey G.
  1986 *The New Zealand Heritage of Farm Buildings*. Auckland: Reed
       Methuen.
Tiffany, Sharon
  1974 The land and titles court and the regulation of customary
       title successions and removals in Western Samoa. *Oceania*
       1:35-57.
United States Department of State
  1954–1980 *Annual Report to the United Nations on the Administration
       of the Trust Territory of the Pacific Islands*. Department of State,
       Bureau of International Organization Affairs, Office of United
       Nations Political Affairs.
United States Navy Department
  1948 *Handbook of the Trust Territory of the Pacific Islands*. Office
       of the Chief of Naval Operations. Prepared at the School
       of Naval Administration, Hoover Institute, Stanford University.
Upton, Dell and John Michael Vlach
  1986 *Common Places: Readings in American Vernacular Architecture*.
       Athens, Ga.: University of Georgia Press.
Valentine, C. A.
  1961 *Masks and Men in a Melanesian Society: The* Valuku *or* Tubuan
       of the Lakalai of New Britain. Lawrence, Kans.: University of
       Kansas.

1965 The Lakalai. In *Gods Ghosts and Men in Melanesia: Some Religions of Australian New Guinea and the New Hebrides,* edited by P. Lawrence and M. J. Meggitt. Pp. 162–197. Melbourne: Oxford University Press.

Vea, Isileli
1985 *Changing Shape of Traditional House Forms in Tonga: A Case Study.* Lae, Papua New Guinea: Papua New Guinea University of Technology, Department of Architecture and Building.

Waimānalo Task Force on the Homeless
1991 Shelter for Waimanalo's Homeless: A Community-Based, Multi-Faceted Plan. Typescript.

Ward, Peter
1982 Introduction and purpose. In *Self-Help Housing: A Critique,* edited by P. M. Ward. Pp. 1–14. London: Mansell Publishing Ltd.

Waterson, Roxana
1990 *The Living House: An Anthropology of Architecture in South-East Asia.* Singapore: Oxford University Press.

Watson, James B.
1970 Society as organized flow: The Tairora case. *Southwestern Journal of Anthropology* 26:107–124.

Weiner, James
1991 *The Empty Place: Poetry, Space, and Being among the Foi of Papua New Guinea.* Bloomington, Ind.: Indiana University Press.

Wilk, Richard R. and R. M. Netting
1984 Households: Changing forms and functions. In *Households: Comparative and Historical Studies of the Domestic Group,* edited by R. M. Netting, R. R. Wilk, and E. J. Arnould. Pp. 1–28. Berkeley: University of California Press.

Wright, Gwendolyn
1991 Colonial opportunities. In *The Politics of Design in French Colonial Urbanism.* Pp. 53–84. Chicago: University of Chicago Press.

Young, Michael
1993 The Kalauna house of secrets. In *Inside Austronesian Houses,* edited by James J. Fox. Pp. 180–193. Canberra: Department of Anthropology in association with the Comparative Austronesian Project, Research School of Pacific Studies, Australian National University.

Contributors

Simeamativa Mageo Aga, a Samoan community advocate for many years, is tenant relations advisor with Hawai'i Housing Authority's Kūhiō Homes/Kūhiō Park Terrace Housing Projects. Some of her contributions to the Samoans and tenants of public housing include paralegal services, translations, and coordination of community activities. Aga served as the American Samoa government representative in Hawai'i from 1989–1992. Additionally, she is the director of Fetu Ao Organization's health and cultural programs and is the vice chair of the O'ahu Private Industry Council.

Ann Chowning recently retired as professor of anthropology at Victoria University of Wellington, New Zealand. She has carried out long-term fieldwork in four Papua New Guinea societies and has published extensively on Melanesian cultures and languages, including *An Introduction to the Peoples and Cultures of Melanesia* (second edition, 1977).

Michèle D. Dominy is professor of anthropology at Bard College. She received her AB (Honors) degree from Bryn Mawr College and her Ph.D. from Cornell University, where she focused on social anthropology and women's studies. Her work on settler descendent identity and place attachment in Aotearoa (New Zealand) high country has appeared in *Anthropology Today, Anthropology Forum, Cultural Anthropology, American Ethnologist,* and *Landscape Review.*

Juliana Flinn is professor of anthropology in the Department of Sociology and Anthropology at the University of Arkansas at Little Rock. Her research in Micronesia has focused on issues of kinship, cultural identity, and change among Pollapese and among Saipan Carolinians, and she has published *Diplomas and Thatch Houses: Asserting Tradition in a Changing Micronesia* (1992).

Robert Franco is associate professor of anthropology at Kapiʻolani Community College, Honolulu, Hawaiʻi. He has worked with Samoan urban communities since 1974, conducted fieldwork in American and Western Samoa, and taught at American Samoa Community College. He is a National Endowment for the Humanities (NEH) mentor for the NEH community college project, "Exploring America's Communities: Quest for Common Ground."

Cluny Macpherson is professor of sociology at the University of Auckland, where he was also chair of the Department of Sociology (1993–1996), and has been convener of the graduate program since 1991. With coresearcher Laʻavasa Macpherson, he has published on suicide, health knowledge and practice, and economic development in the Pacific, including *Samoan Medical Belief and Practice* (1991). His present research focuses on relations between metropolitan and small island states within the Pacific.

Judith Modell is associate professor of anthropology, history, and art at Carnegie Mellon University. In collaboration with a photographer, she has recently completed *Envisioning Homestead,* a book about the famous steel town outside Pittsburgh, Pennsylvania. Her other publications include *Kinship with Strangers: Adoption and American Cultural Interpretations of Kinship* (1994) and *Ruth Benedict: Patterns of a Life* (1983). Currently, she is undertaking a second study of adoption and writing a life history of a Hawaiian man.

Jan Rensel is an adjunct faculty member of the Department of Anthropology at the University of Hawaiʻi–Mānoa. She received a Ph.D. in 1994 from the University of Hawaiʻi for her dissertation, For Love or Money: Interhousehold Exchange and the Economy of Rotuma. Her ongoing research in Rotuma and Rotuman migrant communities has led to a number of articles about Rotuman culture, history, economy, and migration, including several with her husband and coresearcher, Alan Howard.

Margaret Rodman is professor of anthropology at York University, where she was also director of the graduate program in social anthropology for six years, until 1997. Her other books include *Deep Water: Development and Change in Pacific Village Fisheries* (1989) and *Masters of Tradition: Consequences of Customary Land Tenure in Longana, Vanuatu* (1987), as well as two books with Matthew Cooper: *New Neighbours: A Case Study in Cooperative Housing in Toronto* (1992) and *The Pacification of Melanesia* (1979), an edited volume.

R. Daniel Shaw is professor of anthropology and translation at Fuller Seminary in Pasadena, California. His publications, based on twelve years of living among the Samo, include *Kandila: Samo Ceremonialism and Interpersonal Relationships* (1990) and *From Longhouse to Village: Samo Social Change* (1996).

Index

Schafer, R., 197
schools: buildings, 37, 38, 88, 91, 144,
    147; rooms, 123, 129
screens, 96
seating: 82, 97; chiefly, 166; floor, 54n,
    139, 157, 159, 165, 229, 231. *See
    also* furniture: chairs
security: in Galilo 85, 99; in Hawai'i, 23,
    176, 183, 185, 190, 191, 203, 208,
    210, 213; in Port Moresby, 26n;
    Samo, 225. *See also* protection
self-determination, Hawaiian, 216, 217,
    218, 221n
self-sufficiency, 12, 21, 28, 132, 136
sennit, 134, 137
settlement patterns, 11, 14, 18, 224,
    226; Galilo, 87, 99; Gilbert Islands,
    13; Pollapese, 132, 134, 135, 141,
    142, 145, 147; Samoan village, 173n,
    177–178, 181
Severance, Craig, 27
sewing rooms, 123, 129
sexual intimacy, 60, 70, 76, 78n, 83
Shankman, Paul, 27
sharing: food, 27, 33, 44, 82, 91, 93,
    137, 138, 148–149, 150, 179, 201;
    public, 22, 131, 133, 148–149, 150,
    232; space, 62, 67, 70, 86, 95, 150,
    179, 205, 210, 225
Shaw, Karen A., 78n
Shaw, R. Daniel, 14, 18, 19, 26n, 58,
    63, 67, 72, 73, 77n, 78n, 222, 224,
    230
shelter. *See* protection
shelters: fishermen's, 81; garden, 19, 60,
    66, 74, 81; homeless, 198, 203, 205,
    208, 209, 211, 213, 214 (*see also*
    emergency housing; tent housing);
    pig, 81, 88. *See also* temporary hous-
    ing
shipping, 46, 133
Shiroma, Marlene, 189
Shore, Bradd, 173n, 175, 177, 178, 179,
    181
sitting rooms, 115, 117, 120, 165, 169.
    See also living rooms; lounges
Slayton, Robert A., 198
sleeping spaces, 19, 53n, 62, 70, 77,
    78n, 82, 86, 97, 123, 137, 212, 232;
    children's, 87, 98, 145, 164; guest,
    156, 157 (*see also* guest houses);
    men's, 33, 43, 53n, 60, 70, 98,
    138, 145, 164 (*see also* canoe

houses; men's houses); women's, 60,
    70, 83, 98, 145, 164, 177. *See also*
    bedrooms
social control, 175, 178, 179, 180, 192
socialization, 23, 25n, 175, 178, 181,
    192, 225, 226. *See also* parenting;
    youth supervision
social maps, 104, 121, 226
social order, 9, 178, 199; colonial para-
    digm of, 14
sod construction, 112, 117, 131n
solar orientation, 108, 109, 110, 111
spatial organization, 24, 26n, 226; in
    Galilo, 79, 100; and hegemony, 13,
    14; in New Zealand homestead, 104,
    115, 121, 122; in Rotuma, 231; in
    Samoan village, 175, 177, 181
spatial redesignation: of garages, 152,
    161, 166–167, 168, 170–171, 173n;
    of homestead rooms, 123, 129; of
    lounges, 157, 159
squatter housing, 26n, 202, 216, 212,
    220n
status symbols, buildings as, 7, 228; in
    Chuuk, 141, 144; in New Zealand,
    157, 161, 162, 164; in Rotuma, 49–
    50, 51. *See also* symbolism
stone, 37, 39, 40, 43, 117, 123, 131n.
    See also walls: stone
storage: in Galilo, 81, 82–83, 88, 97; in
    New Zealand homestead, 113, 118,
    122; in Pollap, 137; in Rotuma, 34;
    in urban New Zealand, 159, 165
stoves, 144; gas, 17, 231; kerosene, 139,
    141, 148; wood, 111. *See also* ovens
Strongman, Thelma, 110, 126
subsistence gardening: Pollap, 139, 141;
    Rotuma, 28, 30; Samo, 18, 58, 59,
    63, 66, 70, 74, 225. *See also* gardens
sunrooms, 115, 118, 123, 127. *See also*
    solar orientation
Sutter, Frederick K., 175, 178, 179, 180
swimming pools, 107, 122, 130n, 181
Sykes, J. W., 39, 45
symbolism, 9, 13, 24, 197, 224, 232–
    233n; in Chuuk, 132, 138, 140, 147,
    229, 230; in Galilo, 90, 101; of New
    Zealand homestead, 103, 104, 112,
    121, 127, 130; in Rotuma, 16, 17,
    18, 24, 27, 33, 36, 39, 48; in Samoa,
    173n, 177; in urban New Zealand,
    164, 231. *See also* status symbols,
    buildings as

DATE DUE

			Printed in USA

HIGHSMITH #45230